Contents

Published by CGP

Editors: Katherine Craig, Adam Moorhouse

Contributors: Catherine Baird, John Deane, Elena Delaney, Matthew Delaney, Rob Hall, Peter Hooper, Bryony Jones, David Jones, Angela E Major, Peter Maries, Mel McIntyre, Sam Norman, Maria Roberts, Faye Stringer.

With thanks to Nikki Ball and Caley Simpson for the proofreading.
With thanks to Laura Jakubowski for the copyright research.

Audio CD edited and mastered by Neil Hastings.

ISBN: 978 1 84146 378 0

Groovy website: www.cgpbooks.co.uk
Jolly bits of clipart from CorelDRAW®

Printed by Elanders Ltd, Newcastle up

Based on the classic CGP style created

The Basics

These two pages give the <u>essential basics</u> you'll need to get through Music GCSE.
Make sure you know everything here before you go on into the rest of the book.

③ TWO LINES OF MUSIC

The top line of music has got a tune — it's the <u>melody</u>. The bottom line is the <u>accompaniment</u>.

① CLEF

These symbols at the start of a line tell you how <u>high</u> or <u>low</u> to play the notes. All the different clefs are covered on <u>page 4</u>.

② NOTE

Each note is shown by a separate <u>oval</u>. The symbol also tells you how <u>long</u> or <u>short</u> the note is. The symbols are shown on <u>page 10</u>.

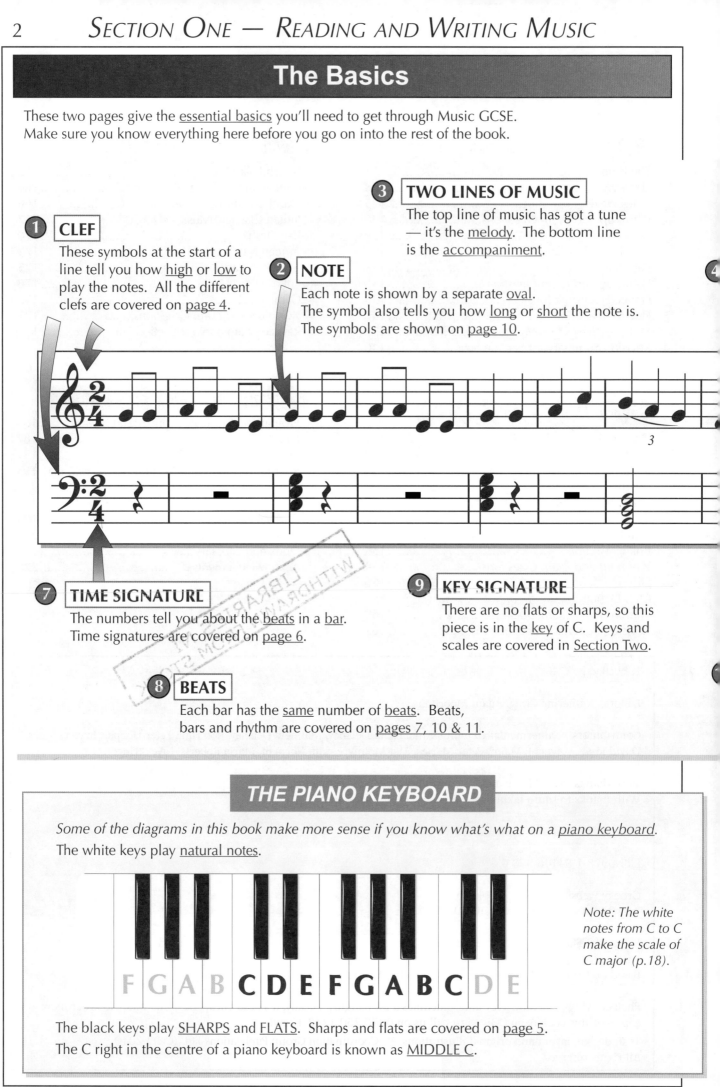

⑦ TIME SIGNATURE

The numbers tell you about the <u>beats</u> in a <u>bar</u>. Time signatures are covered on <u>page 6</u>.

⑨ KEY SIGNATURE

There are no flats or sharps, so this piece is in the <u>key</u> of C. Keys and scales are covered in <u>Section Two</u>.

⑧ BEATS

Each bar has the <u>same</u> number of <u>beats</u>. Beats, bars and rhythm are covered on <u>pages 7, 10 & 11</u>.

THE PIANO KEYBOARD

Some of the diagrams in this book make more sense if you know what's what on a <u>piano keyboard</u>. The white keys play <u>natural notes</u>.

F G A B **C D E F G A B C** D E

Note: The white notes from C to C make the scale of C major (p.18).

The black keys play <u>SHARPS</u> and <u>FLATS</u>. Sharps and flats are covered on <u>page 5</u>.
The C right in the centre of a piano keyboard is known as <u>MIDDLE C</u>.

The Basics

BAR

The vertical bar lines split the music into <u>bars</u>.

bar line

⑤ STAVE

The five lines are called a <u>stave</u>. Notes can go <u>on</u> or <u>between</u> the lines, or on separate short lines above or below.

⑥ TRIPLETS

The '3' and the curved line show these notes are <u>triplets</u>. They're explained on <u>page 11</u>.

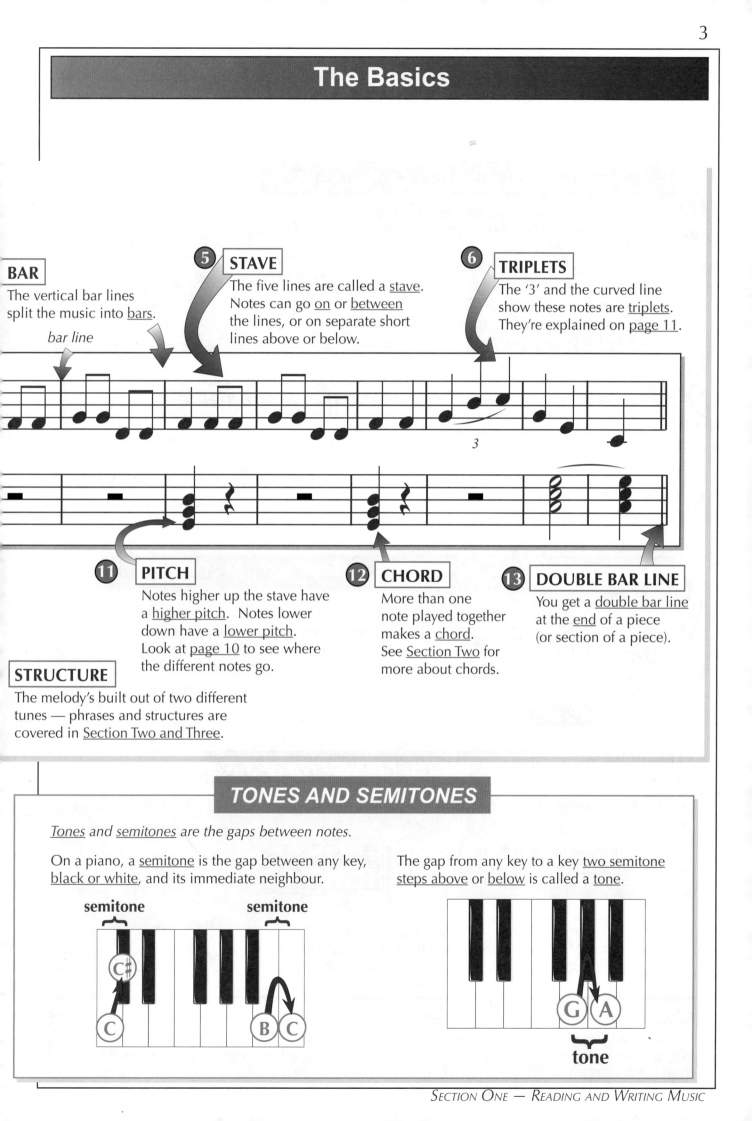

3

⑪ PITCH

Notes higher up the stave have a <u>higher pitch</u>. Notes lower down have a <u>lower pitch</u>. Look at <u>page 10</u> to see where the different notes go.

STRUCTURE

The melody's built out of two different tunes — phrases and structures are covered in <u>Section Two and Three</u>.

⑫ CHORD

More than one note played together makes a <u>chord</u>. See <u>Section Two</u> for more about chords.

⑬ DOUBLE BAR LINE

You get a <u>double bar line</u> at the <u>end</u> of a piece (or section of a piece).

TONES AND SEMITONES

<u>Tones</u> and <u>semitones</u> are the gaps between notes.

On a piano, a <u>semitone</u> is the gap between any key, <u>black or white</u>, and its immediate neighbour.

The gap from any key to a key <u>two semitone steps above</u> or <u>below</u> is called a <u>tone</u>.

semitone   **semitone**

C#

C   B   C

G   A

tone

Clefs

Clefs are the curly symbols that you find right at the start of most written music. The treble clef is used for high-pitched music. The bass and alto clefs are used for lower-pitched music.

The Treble Clef is the Most Common Clef

1) The treble clef is used for higher-pitched melody instruments, e.g. flute, oboe, clarinet, violin, trumpet and horn.
2) Music for soprano and alto voices is written on the treble clef, too.
3) The sign always goes in the same place on the stave, with the curly bit wrapped around the line for the G above middle C.

MIDDLE C

The Bass Clef is used for Low-pitched Instruments

1) The bass clef is used for lower-pitched instruments like the tuba, trombone, bassoon, cello and double bass.
2) It's also used for bass voices.
3) The big blob always goes on the line for the F below middle C, and the two little dots go either side of the line.

MIDDLE C

The Vocal Tenor Clef is for Tenor Voices and Lead Guitar

MIDDLE C

Here's the 8.

1) Each line and gap in the vocal tenor clef stands for exactly the same note as it does in the treble clef, BUT, that tiny little '8' underneath means that the notes are played one octave lower.
2) It's used by tenor voices and lead guitar parts.

The C Clef can Move Up and Down on the Stave

The C clef always has its middle point on middle C. It can be used as two different clefs, depending on its position on the stave.

1) When its middle point is on the middle line, it's the alto clef and is used for viola parts.

MIDDLE C

2) When the middle point is on the fourth line up, it's called the tenor clef, which is used for the higher notes in bass instruments like trombones, bassoons and cellos.

MIDDLE C

Make sure you know your clefs...

You don't see the vocal tenor or C clefs very often, but you've got to know what they are when they do turn up. The treble and bass clefs are used all the time — aim to get so good at reading and writing them that it's easier than English. The only way is to practise. The notes are written in full on page 10.

Sharps, Flats and Naturals

On a piano, <u>natural</u> notes are the <u>white</u> ones. <u>Sharps</u> are the <u>black</u> notes to the <u>right</u> of the white notes. <u>Flats</u> are the blacks to the <u>left</u> of the whites. So each black is both sharp <u>and</u> flat.

♯ A **Sharp** Makes a Note One Step **Higher**

1) A sharp sign next to a note tells you to play it <u>one semitone higher</u>.

When you're writing on the stave, put sharps, flats and naturals before the note they affect. If you're writing text, put them afterwards — F#.

2) A <u>double sharp</u> —✘— makes a note <u>two semitones higher</u>. If you see <u>C✘</u> you play <u>D</u> — it's the <u>same note</u> going by a different name. The fancy name for notes that sound the same but have different names is <u>enharmonic equivalents</u>.

♭ A **Flat** Makes a Note One Step **Lower**

1) A flat symbol next to a note means you have to play it <u>one semitone lower</u>.

2) A <u>double flat</u> — ♭♭ — makes a note two semitones (a tone) lower.

The **Key Signature** is Shown with Sharps or Flats

KEY SIGNATURE

1) Sharps or flats written at the <u>start</u> of a piece, straight after the clef, tell you the <u>key signature</u>.
2) The key signature makes notes sharp or flat <u>all the way through</u> a piece of music.
3) Sharps and flats that you see by individual notes — but not in the key signature — are called <u>accidentals</u>. Once an accidental has appeared in a bar, it applies to all notes of the same pitch for the rest of the bar, unless it's cancelled out by a <u>natural sign</u>...

More about key signatures on p.18.

This key signature's got one sharp — on the F line. You have to play every F in the piece as an F#.

♮ A **Natural** Sign **Cancels** a Sharp or Flat

A <u>natural</u> sign before a note <u>cancels</u> the <u>effect of a sharp or flat</u> sign from earlier in the bar or from a key signature. You <u>never</u> see natural signs in the key signature, only in the music, as accidentals.

This stuff should all come naturally in no time...

Double sharps and flats are very <u>rare</u> and quite peculiar — it doesn't seem that <u>logical</u> to write C✘ when you could write D, but sometimes you just have to, I'm afraid. It all depends what key you're in.

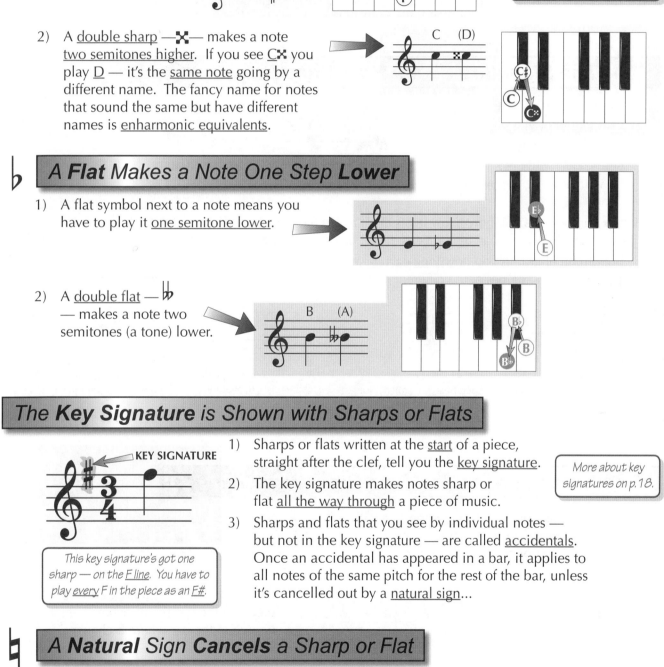

Time Signatures

Those <u>two numbers</u> at the beginning of a piece of music tell you <u>how many beats</u> there are in a bar and <u>how long</u> they are. Whatever you're playing, don't ignore them.

Music has a **Regular Beat**

1) You can tap your foot along to the <u>beat</u> of any piece of music, as long as it hasn't got a horribly complicated rhythm. The beat is also called the <u>pulse</u>.

2) If you listen a bit harder, you can hear that some beats are <u>stronger</u> than others.

3) The strong beats come at <u>regular intervals</u> — usually every <u>2</u>, <u>3</u> or <u>4</u> beats.

4) The strong beat is the <u>first</u> beat of each <u>bar</u>. If the strong beat comes every 3 beats, then the piece of music you're listening to has <u>three beats</u> in a bar.

The **Time Signature** Shows **How Many** Beats are in a Bar

1) There's always a <u>time signature</u> at the beginning of a piece of music.

2) It goes to the <u>right</u> of the clef and the key signature.

3) It's written using <u>two numbers</u>.

TOP NUMBER goes between the middle line and the top line

BOTTOM NUMBER goes between the middle line and the bottom line

The <u>top number</u> tells you <u>how many beats</u> there are in each bar, e.g. a '2' means two beats in a bar, a '3' means three beats in a bar and so on.

The <u>bottom number</u> tells you <u>how long</u> each beat is (see <u>page 10</u> for the names of the different notes).

> *If you see a big 'C' in place of the time signature, it stands for 'common time', which means it's in 4/4. If it's ₵, then it's 'cut common time' — 2/2.*

A <u>2</u> at the bottom means each beat is <u>1 minim</u> long.

2 = 𝅗𝅥

A <u>4</u> at the bottom means each beat is <u>1 crotchet</u> long.

4 = 𝅘𝅥

An <u>8</u> at the bottom means each beat is <u>1 quaver</u> long.

8 = 𝅘𝅥𝅮

A <u>16</u> at the bottom means each beat is <u>1 semiquaver</u> long.

16 = 𝅘𝅥𝅯

If the **Beat Changes**, the **Time Signature Changes**

1) The time signature usually <u>stays the same</u> all the way through a piece of music. If it does, it's written just <u>once</u>, at the beginning.

2) Sometimes the beat <u>changes</u> during a piece. If it does, the new time signature's written in the bar where it <u>changes</u>.

3) Not all pieces start on the first beat of the bar — some start on an <u>unaccented beat</u> called an <u>anacrusis</u> (or <u>upbeat</u>).

You can practise listening for the beat any time...

Whatever music you're listening to — practise <u>listening for the beat</u> and work out the time signature.

Counting the Beat

Counting the beat's fairly easy, but it's a crucial skill. It can help you work out how to <u>play</u> a new piece and how to <u>write a tune down</u> when you've only heard it on a CD or in your head.

In *Simple Time* You Count *All the Beats*

1) <u>Simple</u> time signatures have <u>2</u>, <u>3</u> or <u>4</u> as their <u>top</u> number.

2) In simple time, if you're counting to the music, you count <u>every beat</u>.
For $\frac{4}{4}$ you'd count, "<u>One, two, three, four.</u>" For $\frac{3}{2}$, you'd count, "<u>One, two, three.</u>"

3) If you want to count out the rhythm of <u>smaller notes</u> as well as the beats, try using "<u>and</u>", "<u>eye</u>" and "<u>a</u>" — it seems to make the rhythm come out just right.

> Count "<u>One and two and</u>" for quavers, and "<u>One eye and a</u>" for semiquavers.

4) Any shorter notes are usually a <u>half</u>, a <u>quarter</u>, an <u>eighth</u> or a <u>sixteenth</u> of the main beat.

In *Compound Time* Only Count the *Big Beats*

1) Compound time signatures have <u>6</u>, <u>9</u> or <u>12</u> as their <u>top</u> number — you can always divide the top number by <u>three</u>.

2) If the music is fairly fast, it's too <u>awkward</u> to count to nine or twelve for every bar. You end up with so many little beats that the rhythm sounds <u>mushy</u>.

3) To make the rhythm <u>clear</u>, you can just count the <u>main beats</u>:

4) If you were counting out the main beats in $\frac{6}{8}$, you'd count, "One, two. One, two." $\frac{9}{8}$ would go, "One, two, three. One, two, three."

5) To count the <u>in-between notes</u>, use "<u>&</u>" and "<u>a</u>".

6) Shorter notes are made by dividing by three — so they're <u>thirds</u>, <u>sixths</u>, <u>twelfths</u>, etc. of the main beat.

7) Music in compound time <u>sounds different</u> from music in simple time because the beat is divided into threes — <u>practise</u> spotting the difference.

The *Patterns* the Beats Make are Called the *Metre*

Depending on the time signature, the beats make different <u>patterns</u>.
The pattern is known as the <u>metre</u>. Metre can be:

Regular
The strong beats make the <u>same pattern</u> all the way through.
<u>two</u> beats per bar = <u>duple</u> metre
<u>three</u> beats per bar = <u>triple</u> metre
<u>four</u> beats per bar = <u>quadruple</u> metre

Irregular
There could be <u>five</u> beats in a bar grouped in twos and threes, or <u>seven</u> beats in a bar grouped in threes and twos or fours.

Free
Music with <u>no particular metre</u>. This one's fairly unusual.

> You can describe a time signature based on its beat and metre — e.g. a piece in $\frac{4}{4}$ is in simple quadruple time, and a piece in $\frac{6}{8}$ is in compound duple time.

One and a, two and a, three and a, four and a...

Counting the beat's not really that hard. The tricky bit on this page is the stuff about <u>metre</u>. You could get asked about the metre of a piece in your listening exam, so learn <u>all three sorts</u>.

Rhythms and Metres

When <u>different rhythms</u> are played at the <u>same time</u>, some of them <u>fit together</u> well, but some of them <u>don't</u>. Rhythms that <u>don't fit</u> can create interesting and crazy <u>effects</u>.

Different Rhythms Can be Played at the Same Time

Polyrhythms

1) When <u>two or more</u> rhythms are played at the <u>same time</u>, the music is <u>polyrhythmic</u>.
2) The rhythms will often have <u>accents</u> in different places, but still feel as though they <u>fit together</u>.
3) Lots of <u>African</u> music is polyrhythmic.

Bi-rhythms

1) Time signatures can be <u>split up</u> into <u>different patterns</u> of <u>beats</u>. For example, $\frac{3}{4}$ can be divided into 3 groups of two quavers or 2 groups of three quavers.
2) In a similar way, $\frac{4}{4}$ can be divided into 4 groups of two quavers or 2 groups of three quavers and one of two quavers.

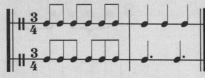

3) These are known as <u>bi-rhythms</u>.

Cross-rhythms

1) <u>Cross-rhythms</u> are when <u>two or more</u> rhythms that <u>don't</u> fit together are played at the same time, e.g. when <u>triplets</u> are played in one part and normal <u>quavers</u> in another.
2) Cross-rhythms create <u>tension</u> in music.
3) Most <u>percussive</u> music will use some cross-rhythms, and they're used a lot in <u>African</u> music.

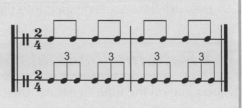

Drum Fills are Little Drum Solos

> There's a little drum fill between the <u>first</u> and <u>second</u> verses in *'She Loves You'* by the <u>Beatles</u>.

1) <u>Drum fills</u> are fairly <u>short</u> — they often only last for a <u>few beats</u>.
2) Fills are normally used to <u>build</u> the music up, or to <u>change</u> between <u>sections</u>.
3) They give the drummer a (very short) chance to <u>show off</u>.
4) Most <u>rock</u>, <u>pop</u> and <u>jazz</u> pieces will have drum fills in them.

Rhythms make me very cross...

Learn the <u>differences</u> between <u>polyrhythms</u>, <u>bi-rhythms</u> and <u>cross-rhythms</u>, and don't get them confused. Listen out for them in African music — you could even include some in your own compositions.

Warm-up and Exam Questions

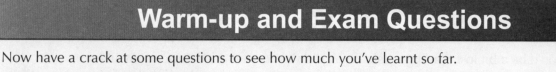

Now have a crack at some questions to see how much you've learnt so far.

Warm-up Questions

1) Draw the symbols for a treble clef, bass clef, vocal tenor clef and C alto clef.
2) Explain what a sharp sign, a flat sign and a natural sign do.
3) Draw a time signature describing three minim beats per bar.
4) How many beats are there per bar if the time signature is 9/8?
5) What's the difference between simple and compound time?
6) Name the three main types of metre.

Exam Question

This is the type of question you could get in your listening test. You'll need a track from the CD for this question. Use it to test your understanding of the last few pages and as practice for the real thing.

Play the following extract **four** times. Leave a short pause between each playing of the extract.

It's a good idea to read the whole question through before you listen to the track.

Track 1

a) Fill in the **8 missing notes** from the vocal part, using the rhythm supplied.

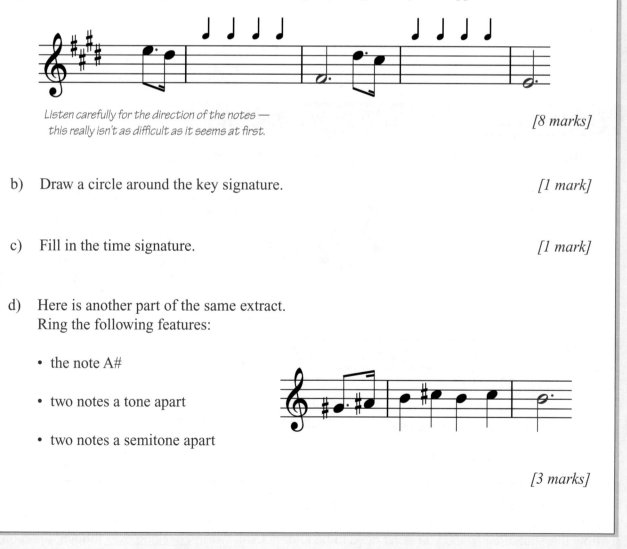

Listen carefully for the direction of the notes — this really isn't as difficult as it seems at first.

[8 marks]

b) Draw a circle around the key signature.

[1 mark]

c) Fill in the time signature.

[1 mark]

d) Here is another part of the same extract.
Ring the following features:

• the note A#

• two notes a tone apart

• two notes a semitone apart

[3 marks]

Notes and Rests

Let's face it, you'd be a bit lost reading music if you didn't know what all those funny little dots and squiggles meant. Make sure you know all this stuff <u>better than the alphabet</u>.

The **Symbols** Tell You **How Long** Notes and Rests Are

1) <u>Notes</u> tell you how many beats to hold a <u>sound</u> for.

2) <u>Rests</u> tell you how many beats to hold a <u>silence</u> for.

3) Notes and rests have <u>names</u>, depending on how long they are.
   Two beats is a <u>minim</u> note or rest. A half-beat is a <u>quaver</u> note or rest.

Learn this table now — you need to know exactly how to <u>write</u> these out, and how to <u>play</u> them.

NAME OF NOTE	NUMBER OF CROTCHET BEATS	NOTE SYMBOL	REST SYMBOL
semibreve	**4**	o	▬
minim	**2**	♩	▬
crotchet	**1**	♩	𝄽
quaver	½	♪ or ♫ *if there are 2 or more*	𝄾
semiquaver	¼	♬ or ♬ *if there are 2 or more*	𝄿

The **Position** of the Note Tells You the **Pitch**

<u>Just in case</u> you don't know, this is where the notes go in the <u>bass</u> and <u>treble</u> clefs:

In the <u>bottom</u> half of the stave, the tails on the notes go <u>upwards</u>.

There is some overlap — e.g. these are the same note written in different clefs.

In the <u>top</u> half of the stave, the tails on the notes go <u>downwards</u>.

The tail of the note on the <u>middle line</u> can go <u>up</u> or <u>down</u>.

These lines are called <u>ledger lines.</u> You use them to work out how <u>high</u> or <u>low</u> notes <u>above</u> and <u>below</u> the stave are.

There's no excuse for not knowing this stuff...

Those of you who were playing the church organ before you could crawl might be feeling a bit like you know this stuff already and you don't need to be told. It's still worth <u>checking over</u> though, I reckon.

Dots, Ties and Triplets

You can only get so far with the note lengths from page 10. If you use <u>dot</u>, <u>tie</u> and <u>triplet</u> symbols you can create more complicated, interesting and sophisticated rhythms.

A **Dot** After a Note or Rest Makes It **Longer**

1) A dot just <u>to the right</u> of a note or rest makes it <u>half as long again</u>.

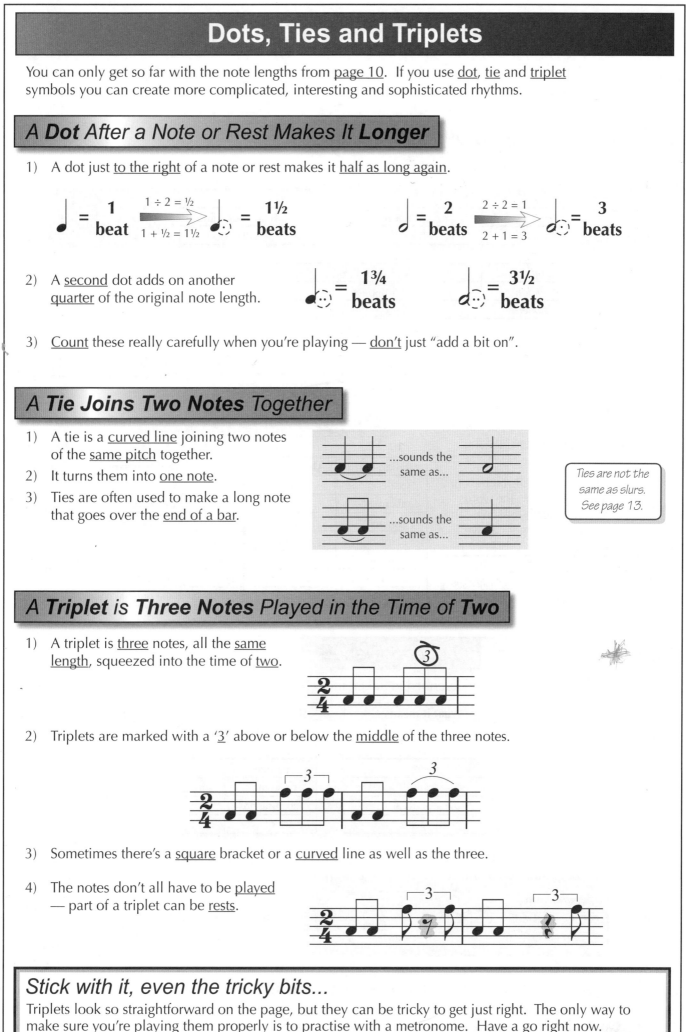

2) A <u>second</u> dot adds on another <u>quarter</u> of the original note length.

3) <u>Count</u> these really carefully when you're playing — <u>don't</u> just "add a bit on".

A **Tie** Joins Two Notes Together

1) A tie is a <u>curved line</u> joining two notes of the <u>same pitch</u> together.
2) It turns them into <u>one note</u>.
3) Ties are often used to make a long note that goes over the <u>end of a bar</u>.

...sounds the same as...

...sounds the same as...

Ties are not the same as slurs. See page 13.

A **Triplet** is **Three Notes** Played in the Time of **Two**

1) A triplet is <u>three</u> notes, all the <u>same length</u>, squeezed into the time of <u>two</u>.

2) Triplets are marked with a '<u>3</u>' above or below the <u>middle</u> of the three notes.

3) Sometimes there's a <u>square</u> bracket or a <u>curved</u> line as well as the three.

4) The notes don't all have to be <u>played</u> — part of a triplet can be <u>rests</u>.

Stick with it, even the tricky bits...

Triplets look so straightforward on the page, but they can be tricky to get just right. The only way to make sure you're playing them properly is to practise with a metronome. Have a go right now.

Tempo and Mood

Composers don't just tell you the notes — they tell you <u>how fast</u> to play them, and what the <u>atmosphere</u> of the piece should be too. You need to understand all the different <u>terms</u> they use.

The *Tempo* is the *Speed* of the Music

Tempo is Italian for "<u>time</u>". In a lot of music the instructions for how fast to play are written in Italian too. Here are the words you're <u>most</u> likely to come across:

Italian word	What it means	Beats per minute
largo	broad and slow	40 - 60
larghetto	still broad, not so slow	60 - 66
adagio	bit faster than largo	66 - 76
andante	walking pace	76 - 108
moderato	moderate speed	108 - 120
allegro	quick and lively	120 - 168
vivace	very lively — quicker than allegro	168 - 180
presto	really fast	180 - 200

<u>60</u> beats a minute means each crotchet lasts <u>one</u> second. <u>120</u> beats a minute means each crotchet lasts <u>half a second</u>. And so on...

This is where you put the <u>tempo</u> and <u>beats per minute</u> on the stave. ♩= 110 means there are 110 crotchet beats per minute. This is called a <u>metronome marking</u>.

These words tell you how to <u>vary</u> the speed. The <u>words</u> go <u>underneath</u> the stave. The <u>pause</u> symbol goes <u>above</u>.

Rubato means '<u>robbed time</u>' — you can <u>slow</u> some bits down and <u>speed</u> others up.

Italian word	Abbreviation	What it means
accelerando	accel.	speeding up
rallentando	rall.	slowing down
ritenuto	rit.	holding back the pace
allargando	allarg.	slowing down, getting a bit broader
rubato	rub.	can be flexible with pace of music
⌢		pause — longer than a whole beat
a tempo		back to the original pace

Mood is the *Overall* Feel of a Piece

The <u>mood</u> of a piece is usually described in Italian too.

Italian word	What it means
agitato	agitated
alla marcia	in a march style
amoroso	loving
calmato	calm
dolce	soft and sweet
energico	energetic

Italian word	What it means
giocoso	playful, humorous
grandioso	grandly
pesante	heavy
risoluto	strong, confident, bold
sospirando	sighing
trionfale	triumphant

To describe the <u>overall mood</u> put the word at the beginning of the piece.

Andante Grandioso (♩=100)

ff

To describe a <u>change of mood</u> write the word under the stave.

p   giocoso

Sometimes parts are marked <u>obbligato</u>, which means they are <u>really important</u> and can't be missed out (obbligato means '<u>obligatory</u>').

Yes, you do have to learn it all — even the Italian bits...
When you're learning this page, start with words that sound a bit like English — they're easy. Once you've learnt them, cross them off and you'll find you have a <u>much shorter</u> list to learn.

Dynamics and Articulation

More ways for composers to tell players <u>exactly</u> how they want their music to sound...

Dynamic Markings Tell You How **Loud** or **Quietly** to Play

Music that was all played at the <u>same volume</u> would be pretty dull.

To get a <u>variety</u> of different volumes you can use these symbols:

symbol	...stands for...	...what it means...
pp	pianissimo	very quiet
p	piano	quiet
mp	mezzopiano	fairly quiet
mf	mezzoforte	fairly loud
f	forte	loud
ff	fortissimo	very loud
<	crescendo	getting louder
>	diminuendo	getting quieter

*You might also see dynamics combined together in other ways. E.g. **fp** means you play a sudden loud bit followed by a sudden quiet bit.*

The markings go <u>underneath</u> the stave.

Crescendos and diminuendos are sometimes called <u>hairpins</u> when they're written like this.

Articulation Tells You How Much to **Separate** the **Notes**

In theory all the notes of a bar should add up to one <u>continuous</u> sound — but actually there are <u>tiny gaps</u> between them. If you <u>exaggerate</u> the gaps you get a <u>staccato</u> effect. If you smooth the gaps out, the notes sound <u>slurred</u>.

STACCATO All the dotted notes are played slightly short.

SLUR All the notes below or above the slur are played smoothly, with no breaks between.

<u>Tenuto</u> marks (<u>lines</u> above or below a note) tell you that a note should be held for its <u>full length</u>, or even played slightly <u>longer</u>.

If the articulation goes <u>all the way through</u> a piece, there's an overall instruction at the <u>beginning</u>.

If this piece was marked <u>legato</u> you would have to play smoothly all the way through.

Staccato

Nothing to do with articulated lorries then...

Don't just learn the symbols, learn what they're <u>called</u> too — it'll sound far more impressive if you write about the "dynamics" and "articulation" in your listening exam rather than "loudness and quietness".

More Instructions

Once a composer has told you how <u>fast</u> and how <u>loud</u> to play and how to <u>articulate</u> it, they sometimes put in <u>extra instructions</u>. Things like <u>accents</u>, <u>sforzandos</u> and <u>bends</u> make the music more <u>interesting</u>.

An *Accent Emphasises* a Note

1) An <u>accent</u> is a type of articulation that tells you to <u>emphasise</u> (or <u>stress</u>) a note.

2) On a <u>wind</u> instrument, this is often done by <u>tonguing</u> a note <u>harder</u> than normal.

3) Accents are usually written like this **>** or like this **Λ**.

4) If a whole <u>section</u> should be accented, it can be marked '*marcato*' (which means 'marked').

5) A <u>sforzando</u> is a <u>strongly accented</u> note. It's shown by writing *sfz* or *sf* underneath the note.

6) A sforzando is often a <u>sudden</u> accent — e.g. a <u>very loud</u> note in a <u>quiet</u> <u>section</u> of a piece. This makes the music more <u>dramatic</u>.

A *Glissando* is a *Slide* Between Notes

1) A <u>glissando</u> is a <u>slide</u> from one note to another. Usually you're <u>told</u> which notes to <u>start</u> and <u>finish</u> on.

2) A glissando can be played <u>effectively</u> on a <u>violin</u> (or other <u>string</u> instrument), <u>piano</u>, <u>harp</u>, <u>xylophone</u> (or similar instrument), <u>timpani</u> and <u>trombone</u>. Other instruments can play them too, but they often <u>won't</u> sound as <u>good</u>.

3) On some instruments (e.g. piano, harp and xylophone), <u>every note</u> is played in the glissando. Think about it — if you were to play a glissando on a xylophone, you'd run your beater over every note, so they'd all be played.

4) On other instruments, like the trombone and strings, the notes you hear <u>aren't fixed notes</u> — the glissando covers all the <u>tiny differences</u> in pitch between the two notes. For example, you <u>can't</u> pick out <u>individual notes</u> in a glissando on the trombone.

5) A glissando can be shown by writing *gliss.* underneath the stave, or by putting a <u>line</u> between <u>two notes</u>.

Notes can be *Bent*

1) A <u>bend</u> (or <u>bent note</u>) changes the <u>pitch</u> of the note slightly — it sounds a bit like a <u>wobble</u>.

2) They're often played by starting just <u>above</u> or <u>below</u> the note then <u>bending</u> to it.

3) Bends are often used in <u>jazz music</u>.

4) Bent notes can be played on <u>most</u> instruments — including <u>guitars</u>, <u>trumpets</u>, <u>trombones</u> and <u>harmonicas</u>. <u>Singers</u> can bend notes too.

Roundabouts, swings, climbing frames, glissandi...

All the things on this page are little <u>extras</u> composers can add to their music to make it more <u>interesting</u>. Accented notes and sforzando notes are quite <u>similar</u>, but sforzando notes are usually more <u>unexpected</u>.

Warm-up and Exam Questions

Get your brain going with these warm-up questions before tackling the exam question below.

Warm-up Questions

1) Draw a 4-beat note, and write down its full name.

2) Draw a 4-beat rest.

3) Name the following notes and give the time value of each of them.

♩. ♪ 𝅗𝅥.

dotted crotchet, quaver, minim (dotted)
1½   1

4) Explain the difference between a tie and a slur.

5) Look at the tempo words below. Write them out in order, fastest first.

Andante   Largo   Presto   Moderato   Allegro

Exam Question

Here's another exam-style question for you to try.

Play the following extract **three** times. Leave a short pause between each playing of the extract.

Track 2

a) Listen to the rhythm of the opening melody.
Tick one feature that matches what you hear.

Staccato notes   ☐

Triplets   ☐

Dotted notes   ☐

[1 mark]

Turn over

Exam Question

b)   Which word best describes the tempo of this piece of music? Underline your answer.

largo   **adagio**   **andante**   **allegro**   *[1 mark]*

c)   Which word describes the dynamic at the opening? Underline your answer.

pianissimo   **piano**   **forte**   **fortissimo**   *[1 mark]*

d)   Which of the following describes the mood of this extract? Tick the box.

agitato   ☐

dolce   ☐

energico   ☐

pesante   ☐   *[1 mark]*

Revision Summary for Section One

You'll find a page of questions like this at the end of every section. They're <u>not</u> here just to fill up space — they're here to <u>help you</u> test yourself. The basic idea is, if you can answer all the Revision Summary questions without looking back through the section, you can be pretty sure you've understood and remembered all the important stuff. Look back through the section the first and second time you try the questions (if you must), but by the third time you do the questions, you should be aiming to have all the answers <u>off by heart</u>.

1) Does a clef tell you:
   a) how wide the stave is, b) what instrument it's for, or c) how high or low the notes on it are?
2) Draw a stave with a treble clef at the beginning.
3) Draw a stave with a bass clef at the beginning.
4) Which voices read music from the treble clef?
5) Name two instruments that read music from the bass clef.
6) What's the difference between the symbol for a treble clef and the symbol for the vocal tenor clef?
7) Where does middle C go on a vocal tenor clef?
8) Draw staves showing the C clef in both positions and write the correct name by each one.
9) Draw a sharp sign, a flat sign and a natural sign.
10) What does a sharp do to a note?
11) What does a flat do to a note?
12) Draw each of these signs and explain what you do if you see them by a note:
    a) a double sharp   b) a double flat
13) Draw a treble clef stave and add a key signature with one sharp.
14) What do you call a sharp, flat or natural sign when it's in the music but not in the key signature?
15) One beat in the bar usually feels stronger than the others. Which one?
16) What do you call the two numbers at the start of a piece of music?
17) What does the top number tell you about the beats?
18) What does the bottom number tell you about the beats?
19) When a time signature changes in a piece of music, where's the new one written?
20) What's the difference between simple and compound time?
21) What's the difference between regular and irregular metre?
22) What is meant by a cross rhythm?
23) Draw the symbol for each of the following notes and write down how many crotchet beats it lasts:
    a) semibreve   b) minim   c) crotchet   d) quaver   e) semiquaver
24) What does a dot immediately after a note or rest do?
25) What's the time value of:
    a) a dotted crotchet   b) a dotted minim   c) a dotted semibreve   d) a double dotted minim?
26) What does a 'tie' do?
27) How much time, in crotchet beats, does a crotchet triplet take up?
28) Where do you put the tempo marking on a stave?
29) Which is slower, *allegro* or *moderato*?
30) Where would you write the word *agitato* on the stave?
31) How does a composer show on the written music that he wants the notes to be played smoothly?
32) How are accents usually indicated in a piece of music?
33) What's a glissando?

Major Scales

There are two main types of scales — <u>major</u> and <u>minor</u>. Once you've got the hang of how scales are put together, you should find keys and chords start to make a lot more sense.

Ordinary Scales have *Eight Notes*

> *The gap between the bottom and top notes of a scale is called an octave. See p.22.*

1) An ordinary major (or minor) scale has <u>8 notes</u>, starting and ending on notes of the <u>same name</u>, e.g. C major goes C, D, E, F, G, A, B, C.

2) Each of the eight notes has a <u>name</u>.

1st note	2nd note	3rd note	4th note	5th note	6th note	7th note	8th note
tonic	supertonic	mediant	subdominant	dominant	submediant	leading note	tonic
I	II	III	IV	V	VI	VII	VIII

3) You can just use the <u>numbers</u> or the <u>Roman numerals</u> to name the notes too.

Major Scales Sound *Bright* and *Cheery*

Whatever note they start on, all major scales sound <u>similar</u>, because they all follow the same <u>pattern</u>. This pattern is a set order of <u>tone</u> and <u>semitone</u> gaps between the notes:

I tone II tone III semitone IV tone V tone VI tone VII semitone VIII

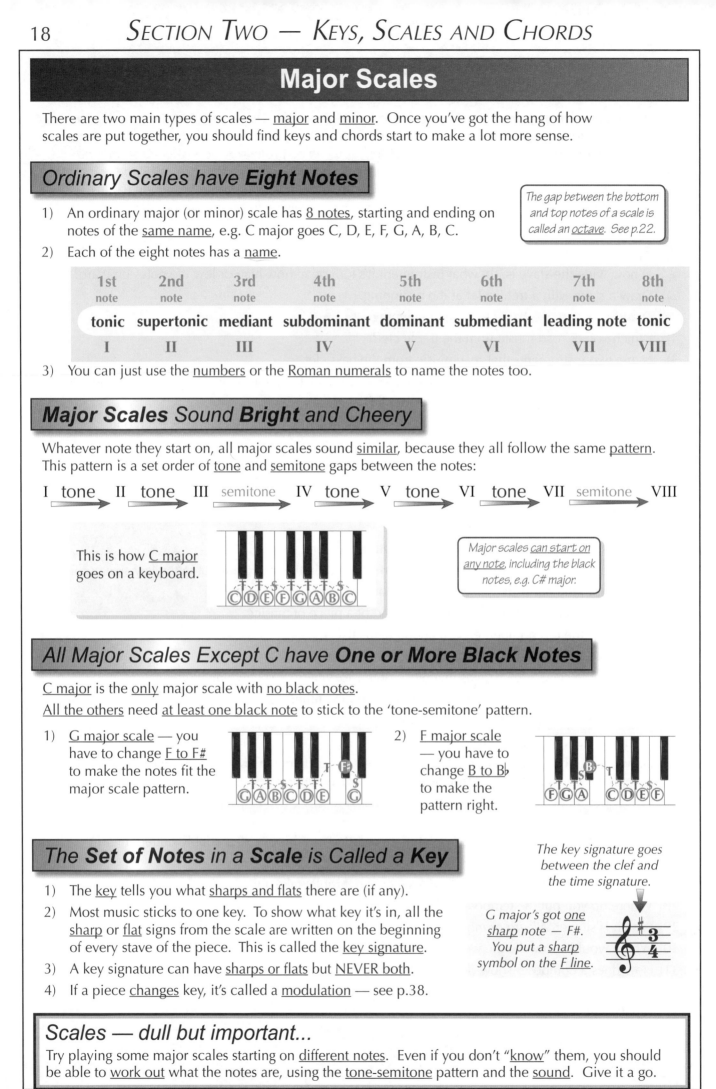

This is how <u>C major</u> goes on a keyboard.

> *Major scales can start on any note, including the black notes, e.g. C# major.*

All Major Scales Except C have *One or More Black Notes*

<u>C major</u> is the <u>only</u> major scale with <u>no black notes</u>.

<u>All the others</u> need <u>at least one black note</u> to stick to the 'tone-semitone' pattern.

1) <u>G major scale</u> — you have to change <u>F to F#</u> to make the notes fit the major scale pattern.

2) <u>F major scale</u> — you have to change <u>B to B♭</u> to make the pattern right.

The *Set of Notes* in a *Scale* is Called a *Key*

> *The key signature goes between the clef and the time signature.*

1) The <u>key</u> tells you what <u>sharps and flats</u> there are (if any).

2) Most music sticks to one key. To show what key it's in, all the <u>sharp</u> or <u>flat</u> signs from the scale are written on the beginning of every stave of the piece. This is called the <u>key signature</u>.

3) A key signature can have <u>sharps or flats</u> but NEVER both.

4) If a piece <u>changes</u> key, it's called a <u>modulation</u> — see p.38.

> *G major's got <u>one</u> sharp note — F#. You put a <u>sharp</u> symbol on the <u>F line</u>.*

Scales — dull but important...

Try playing some major scales starting on <u>different notes</u>. Even if you don't "<u>know</u>" them, you should be able to <u>work out</u> what the notes are, using the <u>tone-semitone</u> pattern and the <u>sound</u>. Give it a go.

Minor Scales

Minor scales have fixed patterns too. There are <u>three</u> different kinds you need to know.

Minor Scales *All Sound a Bit* **Mournful**

Minor scales sound <u>completely different</u> from major scales, because they've got a different tone-semitone pattern. There are <u>three</u> types of minor scale, and all of them sound a bit <u>mournful</u>.

1) The **Natural Minor** Uses All the **Same Notes** as the **Relative Major**

These are easy. Start from the <u>sixth</u> note of any major scale. Carry on up to the same note an octave higher. You're playing a <u>natural minor scale</u>.

The sixth note of <u>C major</u> is <u>A</u>. If you play from <u>A to A</u> using the notes of C major, you're playing <u>A natural minor</u> (usually just called '<u>A minor</u>').

Pairs of keys like <u>A minor and C major</u> are called "<u>relative</u>" keys.
A minor is the <u>relative minor</u> of C major.
C major is the <u>relative major</u> of A minor.

<u>All the notes</u> in a natural minor are <u>exactly the same</u> as the ones in the <u>relative major</u>. The <u>key signature's</u> exactly the same too.

2) The **Harmonic Minor** has **One Accidental**

1) The <u>harmonic minor</u> has the same notes as the relative major, except for the <u>seventh note</u>.

2) The <u>seventh</u> note is always raised by <u>one semitone</u>.

3) You use the harmonic minor when you're writing <u>harmonies</u>. That <u>sharpened seventh note</u> makes the harmonies work much better than they would with notes from a natural minor. It's probably because it feels like it wants to move up to the <u>tonic</u>.

3) The **Melodic Minor** has **Two Accidentals** to Make It **More Tuneful**

1) The <u>melodic minor</u> is just like a natural minor, using the notes from the relative major scale, <u>except for notes 6 and 7</u>.

2) On the way <u>up</u>, notes <u>6</u> and <u>7</u> are each <u>raised</u> by <u>one semitone</u>.

3) On the way <u>down</u>, the melodic minor goes just like the natural minor.

4) The melodic minor is used for writing <u>melodies</u>. The accidental on note 6 makes tunes sound <u>smoother</u> by avoiding the big jump between notes 6 and 7 in the harmonic minor.

And not forgetting the Morris Minor...

All these scales have a <u>minor third</u> between the first and third notes in the scale — that's why they sound melancholy. You need to learn <u>all three</u> — names, notes and what they're used for.

The Circle of Fifths

The circle of fifths looks complicated but it's very <u>useful</u> once you understand how it works — it tells you <u>all the keys</u>, all the <u>relative keys</u> and their <u>key signatures</u>.

The *Circle of Fifths* Shows *All the Keys*

1) Altogether there are <u>12 major keys</u>. They're all shown on the <u>circle of fifths</u>.

2) Don't expect to fully get it if this is the first time you've seen it. Just <u>have a look</u>, then read on.

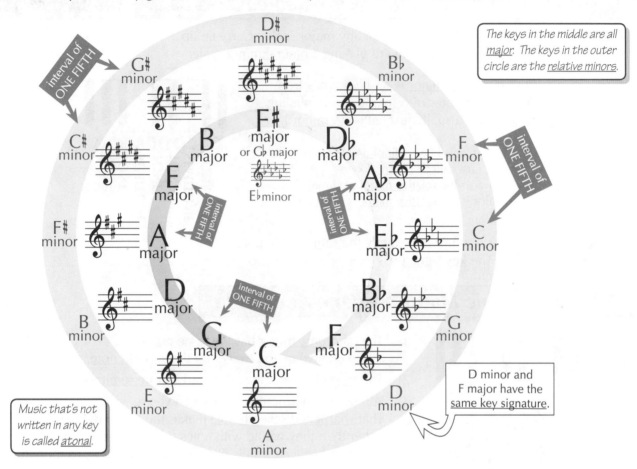

The keys in the middle are all <u>major</u>. The keys in the outer circle are the <u>relative minors</u>.

D minor and F major have the <u>same key signature</u>.

Music that's not written in any key is called <u>atonal</u>.

Each Key *Links* to the Next One

1) The circle <u>starts</u> with <u>C major</u> at the bottom. The next key round is <u>G</u>. G's the <u>fifth note</u> of C major.

2) The fifth note of G major is D, the <u>next</u> key on the circle. This pattern repeats <u>all the way round</u>. That's why the chart's called the circle of fifths.

3) As you go round the circle the number of <u>sharps</u> in the <u>key signature</u> goes up <u>one</u> for each key.

4) When you get to <u>F# major</u> at the top there are <u>six sharps</u>. From here, you start writing the key signature in <u>flats</u> — you don't need as many so it's clearer to read.

5) The number of <u>flats</u> keeps going <u>down</u> until you get back to C major, with no sharps and no flats.

The <u>relative minors</u> in the outer circle work just the same way as the major keys — the <u>fifth note</u> of <u>A minor</u> is <u>E</u> and the next minor key's <u>E minor</u>... and so on. Don't forget you can always work out the relative minor by counting up or down to the <u>sixth note</u> of a major scale, (see p.19) or the relative major by counting up to the <u>third note</u> of the minor scale.

Don't worry if it's making your head spin...

In one way the circle of fifths is very <u>simple</u>, but if you think about it too much it starts melting your brain. Memorise it if you want, but it's more useful to <u>learn and remember</u> how it works.

Modes and Other Types of Scales

Most music uses notes from a <u>major</u> or a <u>minor scale</u> — and they're the <u>most important</u> ones to learn, but there are a few <u>more unusual scales</u> and <u>modes</u> that you need to know about too.

Modes *Follow* Different Patterns *of* Tones *and* Semitones

Just like scales, you can start a <u>mode</u> on any note.

1) The most common mode is the one you get by playing a <u>major scale</u> (e.g. C major — just play the white notes on a keyboard from C to C). The pattern is <u>tone-tone-semitone-tone-tone-tone-semitone</u>.

2) Another mode can be formed by playing the notes of the same major scale, starting from the <u>second note</u>, e.g. D to D:

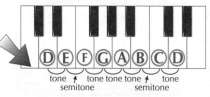

3) Starting on E gives you another mode...

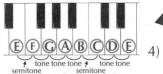

This one sounds a bit Spanish — it's used a lot in flamenco music.

4) ...<u>and so on</u>. Each forms its own semitone / tone pattern and they all have different names. You don't need to know them all though — it's more important that you <u>know what they sound like</u>. (E.g. it's handy to know that playing the white notes starting from G forms a mode that sounds quite bluesy.)

5) Different modes are used in the solos on the Miles Davis album "Kinda Blue". Worth a listen, whether or not you normally like jazz. Guitarists like Joe Satriani use modes too.

Pentatonic *Scales are Used a Lot in* Folk *and* Rock Music

Pentatonic scales use <u>five</u> notes. They're really easy to compose with, because there are <u>no semitone steps</u> — <u>most combinations</u> of notes sound fine. There are <u>two types</u> of pentatonic scale.

1) The <u>major pentatonic</u> uses notes 1, 2, 3, 5 and 6 of a <u>major</u> scale.

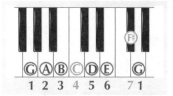

2) The <u>minor pentatonic</u> uses notes 1, 3, 4, 5 and 7 of the <u>natural minor</u> scale.

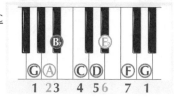

Whole Tone *and* Chromatic Scales *Sound* Spooky

Whole tone scales

Whole tone scales are pretty simple to remember — <u>every step is a tone</u>. From bottom to top there are only <u>seven notes</u> in a whole tone scale.

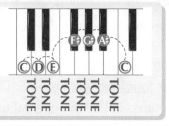

Major and minor scales are known as <u>diatonic scales</u>.

Chromatic scales

Chromatic scales are fairly easy too. On a keyboard you play <u>every white and black note</u> until you get up to an octave above the note you started with. From bottom to top there are <u>13 notes</u>. Basically <u>every step</u> of a chromatic scale is <u>a semitone</u>.

You know the score...

You <u>could</u> get a piece of music in your <u>listening</u> that's written in a <u>mode</u> or one of the other <u>scales</u>. And you could get <u>asked</u> what kind of scale it's written with. So you'd better learn this page.

Intervals

Not the break halfway through a concert, but the <u>distance</u> between two notes.

An **Interval** is the **Gap** Between **Two Notes**

An interval is the <u>musical word</u> for the <u>gap</u> or <u>distance</u> between <u>two notes</u>.
Notes <u>close together</u> make <u>small</u> intervals. Notes <u>further apart</u> make <u>larger</u> intervals.
There are <u>two ways</u> of playing an interval.

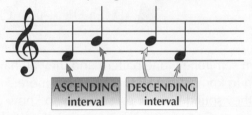

Melodic interval
When one note <u>jumps</u> up or down to another note, you get a <u>melodic interval</u>.

ASCENDING interval   DESCENDING interval

Harmonic interval
When <u>two notes</u> are played at the <u>same time</u>, they make a <u>harmonic interval</u>.

1) You can use the <u>melodic intervals</u> to describe the <u>pattern</u> of a <u>melody</u>.

2) In some melodies, there are only <u>small</u> intervals between the notes — no bigger than a <u>tone</u>.

3) When the notes are <u>close together</u> like this, the melody can be called <u>stepwise</u>, <u>conjunct</u> or <u>scalic</u> (because it moves up and down the notes of a <u>scale</u>).

4) Tunes with <u>big</u> melodic intervals (larger than a tone) are called <u>disjunct</u>.

An **Interval** has **Two Parts** to its Name...

1) A <u>number</u>

an augmented fifth

2) A <u>description</u>

The **Number** Tells You **How Many Notes** the Interval Covers

1) You get the number by counting up the stave from the bottom note to the top note. You <u>include</u> the bottom and top notes in your counting.

2) C to E is a <u>third</u> because it covers <u>three letter names</u> — C, D and E.

3) C to F is a <u>fourth</u> because it covers <u>four letter names</u> — C, D, E and F.

4) The number of an interval is sometimes called the <u>interval quantity</u>.

The "description" bit is covered at the top of the next page...

The interval between G and D is a <u>fifth</u>.

G	A	B	C	D
1	2	3	4	5

An interval covering <u>eight letters</u> — say, A to A — is called an <u>octave</u>. It's just got one name — it doesn't follow the two-part name rule.

The interval between D and F sharp is a <u>third</u> (you can just <u>ignore</u> the accidentals when counting).

D	E	F♯
1	2	3

Intervals

The *Description* Tells You How the Interval *Sounds*

There are <u>five names</u> for the five main sounds:

> perfect   major   minor   diminished   augmented

1) To work out the <u>description part</u> of an interval's name, think of the <u>lower note</u> of the interval as the <u>first</u> note of a <u>major scale</u>.

2) If the top note of the interval is part of that major scale it's either <u>perfect</u> or <u>major</u>:

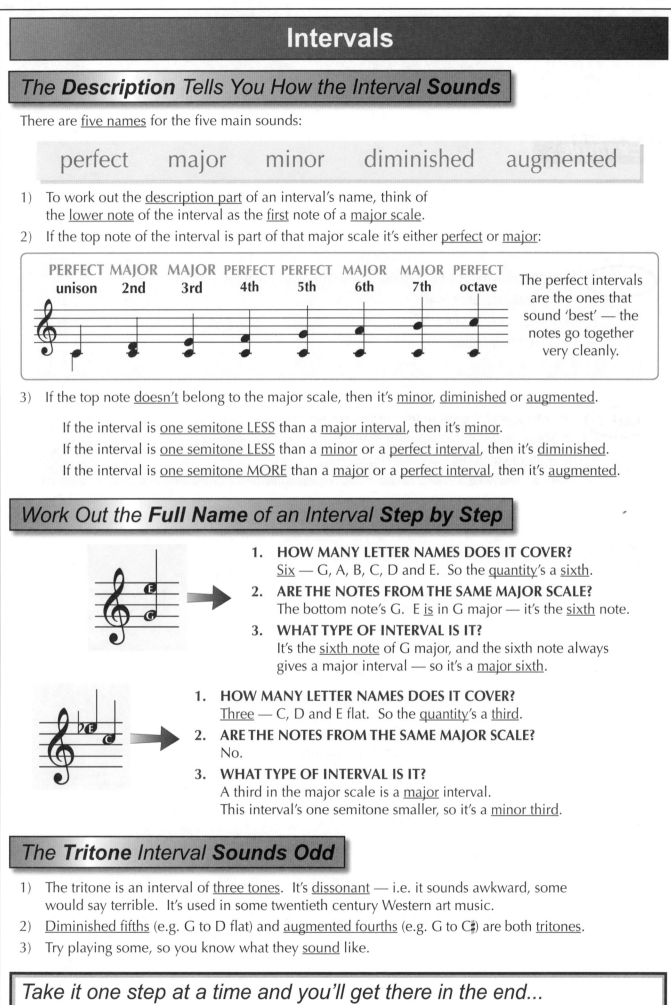

| PERFECT | MAJOR | MAJOR | PERFECT | PERFECT | MAJOR | MAJOR | PERFECT |
| unison | 2nd | 3rd | 4th | 5th | 6th | 7th | octave |

The perfect intervals are the ones that sound 'best' — the notes go together very cleanly.

3) If the top note <u>doesn't</u> belong to the major scale, then it's <u>minor</u>, <u>diminished</u> or <u>augmented</u>.

If the interval is <u>one semitone LESS</u> than a <u>major interval</u>, then it's <u>minor</u>.

If the interval is <u>one semitone LESS</u> than a <u>minor</u> or a <u>perfect interval</u>, then it's <u>diminished</u>.

If the interval is <u>one semitone MORE</u> than a <u>major</u> or a <u>perfect interval</u>, then it's <u>augmented</u>.

Work Out the *Full Name* of an Interval *Step by Step*

1. **HOW MANY LETTER NAMES DOES IT COVER?**
   <u>Six</u> — G, A, B, C, D and E. So the <u>quantity</u>'s a <u>sixth</u>.

2. **ARE THE NOTES FROM THE SAME MAJOR SCALE?**
   The bottom note's G. E <u>is</u> in G major — it's the <u>sixth</u> note.

3. **WHAT TYPE OF INTERVAL IS IT?**
   It's the <u>sixth note</u> of G major, and the sixth note always gives a major interval — so it's a <u>major sixth</u>.

1. **HOW MANY LETTER NAMES DOES IT COVER?**
   <u>Three</u> — C, D and E flat. So the <u>quantity</u>'s a <u>third</u>.

2. **ARE THE NOTES FROM THE SAME MAJOR SCALE?**
   No.

3. **WHAT TYPE OF INTERVAL IS IT?**
   A third in the major scale is a <u>major</u> interval.
   This interval's one semitone smaller, so it's a <u>minor third</u>.

The *Tritone* Interval *Sounds Odd*

1) The tritone is an interval of <u>three tones</u>. It's <u>dissonant</u> — i.e. it sounds awkward, some would say terrible. It's used in some twentieth century Western art music.

2) <u>Diminished fifths</u> (e.g. G to D flat) and <u>augmented fourths</u> (e.g. G to C♯) are both <u>tritones</u>.

3) Try playing some, so you know what they <u>sound</u> like.

Take it one step at a time and you'll get there in the end...

The tritone interval used to be called '<u>the Devil's interval</u>' — because it has such an awkward, clashing sound. It's supposed to be unlucky, so use it in your composition at your own risk...

Examples and Practice

You need to <u>hear</u> the difference between different types of scales and chords. Tracks 3-9 are practical examples of the theory on pages 18-23. Listen to the tracks as you read the info below.

Examples

Track 3 — A <u>major scale</u>, with <u>F#</u> as the tonic, played over two octaves. *(see p.18)*
Try writing out the notes of the scale on a stave. Remember — TTSTTTS.

Track 4 — The <u>three</u> different types of <u>minor scale</u> with <u>D</u> as the tonic. *(see p.19)*
a) The <u>natural minor</u> scale
b) The <u>harmonic minor</u>
c) The <u>melodic minor</u>

Track 5 — The two different types of pentatonic scale. *(see p.21)*
a) <u>Major pentatonic</u> scale starting on <u>C</u>
b) <u>Minor pentatonic</u> scale starting on <u>A</u>
These are relative scales, and because they're pentatonic all the notes are the same.

Track 6 — A <u>whole tone</u> scale. *(see p.21)*
It starts off like the major scale, but the 4th and 5th notes are further apart (<u>harmonically distant</u>) than in a major scale, so it sounds odd.

Track 7 — A <u>chromatic</u> scale. *(see p.21)*
This one starts on <u>G</u>, but all <u>chromatic</u> scales use all the notes, so they sound nearly the same.

Track 8 — The <u>major</u> and <u>perfect</u> intervals. *(see p.23)*
They're played at the same time so they're <u>harmonic</u>.

Track 9 — The <u>minor</u> and <u>diminished intervals</u>. *(see p.23)*
a) Minor 2nd
b) Augmented 2nd / minor 3rd
c) Augmented 4th / diminished 5th
d) Augmented 5th / minor 6th
e) Augmented 6th / minor 7th

Examples and Practice

Now check you've got the hang of it all with these practice questions.

Practice Questions

Track 10   Listen to the four different types of scale. What are they?

a) ....

b) ....

c) ....

d) ....

You can play these tracks more than once — some of them are quite tricky.

Track 11   What type of scale does this tune use?

....

Track 12   Listen to these harmonic intervals. Write down what each of them is called.

a) ....   b) ....

c) ....   d) ....

e) ....   f) ....

g) ....   h) ....

Track 13   Now name these melodic intervals.

a) ....   b) ....

c) ....   d) ....

e) ....   f) ....

g) ....   h) ....

Warm-up and Exam Questions

Time for another round of questions...

Warm-up Questions

1) How many notes would you find in a normal scale?
2) What does a key or key signature tell you about the music?
3) What do the scales of C major and A minor have in common?
4) Name the **three** types of minor scales.
5) Which scale uses only notes 1, 2, 3, 5 and 6 from the major scale?
6) Why is a chromatic scale unusual?
7) What do you call the type of interval formed when two notes are played together at the same time?
8) Which is smaller, a minor 7th or a diminished 7th?

Exam Question

This exam-style question will help you test how well you know your intervals.

Track 14

Play the extract **three** times. Leave a short pause between each playing.

a) Here are the first two bars.

Exam Question

i)   How many beats are there in a bar?

.... *[1 mark]*

ii) What is the interval between the two notes bracketed at letter **a**?

.... *[1 mark]*

iii) What is the interval between the lowest and highest notes in the right-hand chord indicated at letter **b**?

.... *[1 mark]*

b)   What key is this extract in?

.... *[1 mark]*

c)   What does the mark *fp* tell the performer to do?

.... *[1 mark]*

Chords — The Basics

A <u>chord</u> is two or more notes played together. Chords are great for writing <u>accompaniments</u>.

Only **Some** Instruments **Play Chords**

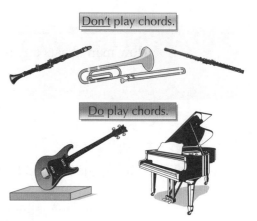

Don't play chords.

Do play chords.

1) A lot of instruments only play <u>one note at a time</u> — flutes, recorders, trumpets, clarinets, trombones... You can't play a chord with one note, so these instruments <u>don't</u> play chords.

2) You can <u>only</u> play chords on <u>instruments</u> that play <u>more than one</u> note at a time. <u>Keyboards</u> and guitars are both great for playing chords — you can easily play several notes together.

3) Other <u>stringed instruments</u> like violins and cellos can play chords, but not very easily, so chords are only played from time to time.

Some Chords Sound **Great**, Others Sound **Awful**

1) The notes of some chords <u>go together</u> really well — like apple pie and ice-cream.

> When you have nice-sounding chords it's called <u>CONCORDANCE</u> or <u>CONSONANCE</u>.

2) Other chords have <u>clashing notes which disagree</u> — more like apple pie and pickled eggs.

> When you have horrible-sounding chords it's called <u>DISCORDANCE</u> or <u>DISSONANCE</u>.

The **Best-Sounding** Chords are Called **Triads**

1) You can play <u>any</u> set of notes and make a chord — but most of them sound <u>harsh</u>.

2) An <u>easy, reliable</u> way of getting nice-sounding chords is to play <u>triads</u>.

3) Triads are chords made up of three notes, with <u>set intervals</u> between them.

4) Once you know the intervals, you can easily play <u>dozens</u> of decent chords.

How to make a triad...

1) On a piano, start with any white note — this is called the <u>root note</u>. You <u>build</u> the triad <u>from the root</u>.

2) Count the root as 'first' and the next white note to the <u>right</u>, as 'second'. The <u>third</u> note you reach is the <u>third</u> — the middle note of the triad.

3) Keep counting up and you get to the <u>fifth</u> — the final note of the triad.

4) The intervals between the notes are <u>thirds</u>.

5) If the root note's a <u>B</u>, then you end up with a <u>B triad</u>. If the root note's a <u>C</u>, you end up with a <u>C triad</u>.

6) You can build triads on black notes too, so long as the intervals between notes are <u>thirds</u>.

ROOT   THIRD   FIFTH

C   E   G

Good things come in threes...

This might look like one of those pages where you think you know it all already. It won't hurt to read through again and <u>check</u> you <u>really do</u> know it all. From here on this section gets a bit tricky.

Triads

There's more than one type of triad...

Triads Use Major and Minor Thirds

1) All triads have an interval of a <u>third</u> between each pair of notes.

2) The intervals can be <u>major</u> or minor <u>thirds</u>.

A <u>major third</u> is <u>four</u> semitones.

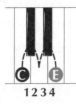

A <u>minor third</u> is <u>three</u> semitones.

3) Different <u>combinations</u> of major and minor thirds give different types of triad:

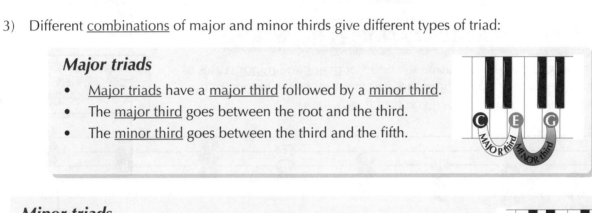

Major triads
- <u>Major triads</u> have a <u>major third</u> followed by a <u>minor third</u>.
- The <u>major third</u> goes between the root and the third.
- The <u>minor third</u> goes between the third and the fifth.

Minor triads
- <u>Minor triads</u> use a <u>major</u> and a <u>minor third</u> too, but in the opposite order.
- The <u>minor third</u> goes between the root and the third.
- The <u>major third</u> goes between the third and the fifth.

DIMINISHED TRIADS use <u>two minor thirds</u>.
AUGMENTED TRIADS use <u>two major thirds</u>.

These two kinds aren't nearly as common as major and minor triads.

You Can Add a Note to a Triad to Get a 7th Chord

1) <u>7th chords</u> are triads with a fourth note added — the <u>seventh</u> note above the root.

2) The interval between the root and the 7th can be a <u>major seventh</u> or a <u>minor seventh</u> — see p.23.

These Symbols Stand for Chords

C = C major **Cm** = C minor

Caug or **C+** = augmented C chord **Cdim** or **C-** or **Co** = diminished C chord

C7 = C major with added minor 7th **Cm7** = C minor with added minor 7th

Cmaj7 = C major with added major 7th **Cm maj7** = C minor with added major 7th

For chords other than C, just change the <u>first letter</u> to show the <u>root note</u>.

It's not as hard as it looks and it's VERY useful...

If you play the guitar or play in a band you need to learn these symbols <u>right now</u>. Even if you only ever play classical music they're still worth learning — they're really useful as shorthand.

Fitting Chords to a Melody

There are some basic rules about fitting chords to a melody:
No.1: All the notes in the chords have got to be in the same key as the notes in the melody.

The *Melody* and *Chords* Must be in the *Same Key*

1) A melody that's composed in a certain key sticks to that key.

2) The chords used to harmonise with the melody have got to be in the same key or it'll clash.

3) As a general rule each chord in a harmony should include the note it's accompanying, e.g. a C could be accompanied by a C chord (C, E, G), an F chord (F, A, C) or an A minor chord (A, C, E).

There's a Chord for *Every Note* in the *Scale*

You can make dozens of triads using the notes of major and minor scales as the roots. Every note of every chord, not just the root, has to belong to the scale. This is how C major looks if you turn it into chords:

> *The odd accidental or ornament in a different key is OK — see p.35.*

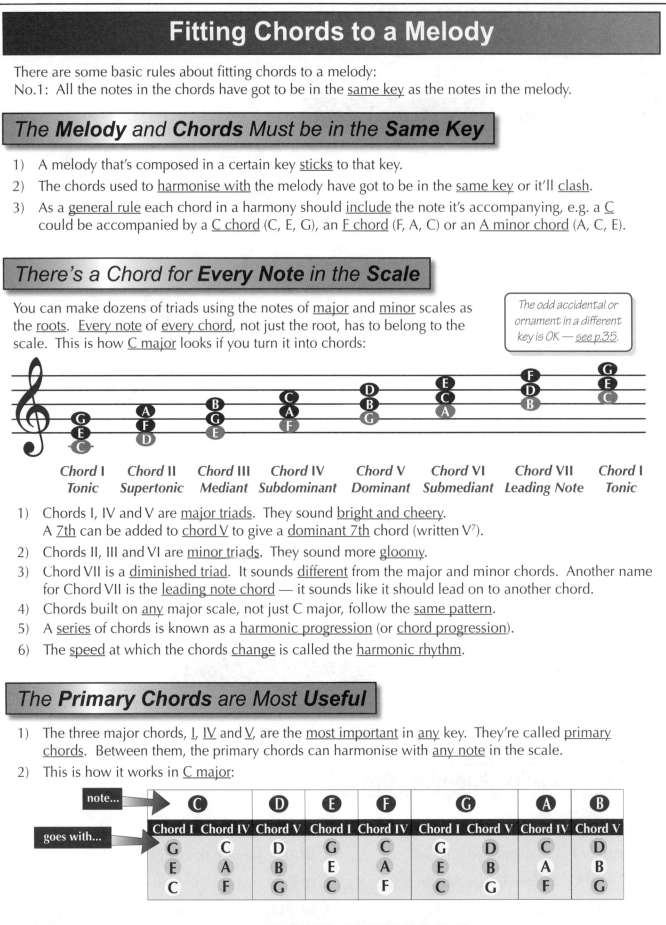

Chord I	Chord II	Chord III	Chord IV	Chord V	Chord VI	Chord VII	Chord I
Tonic	Supertonic	Mediant	Subdominant	Dominant	Submediant	Leading Note	Tonic

1) Chords I, IV and V are major triads. They sound bright and cheery.
A 7th can be added to chord V to give a dominant 7th chord (written V^7).

2) Chords II, III and VI are minor triads. They sound more gloomy.

3) Chord VII is a diminished triad. It sounds different from the major and minor chords. Another name for Chord VII is the leading note chord — it sounds like it should lead on to another chord.

4) Chords built on any major scale, not just C major, follow the same pattern.

5) A series of chords is known as a harmonic progression (or chord progression).

6) The speed at which the chords change is called the harmonic rhythm.

The *Primary Chords* are Most *Useful*

1) The three major chords, I, IV and V, are the most important in any key. They're called primary chords. Between them, the primary chords can harmonise with any note in the scale.

2) This is how it works in C major:

note...	C		D	E	F		G		A	B
goes with...	Chord I	Chord IV	Chord V	Chord I	Chord IV	Chord I	Chord V	Chord IV	Chord V
	G	C	D	G	C	G	D	C	D
	E	A	B	E	A	E	B	A	B
	C	F	G	C	F	C	G	F	G

Minor Chords Make Harmony *More Interesting*

1) Primary chords can get a bit boring to listen to after a while — the harmonies are fairly simple.

2) Composers often mix in a few of the other chords — II, III, VI or VII — for a change.

3) Instead of just having endless major chords, you get a mixture of minor and diminished chords too.

Inversions

Inverting triads means changing the order of the notes. It make accompaniments more varied.

Triads with the **Root at the Bottom** are in **Root Position**

These triads are all in root position — the root note's at the bottom.

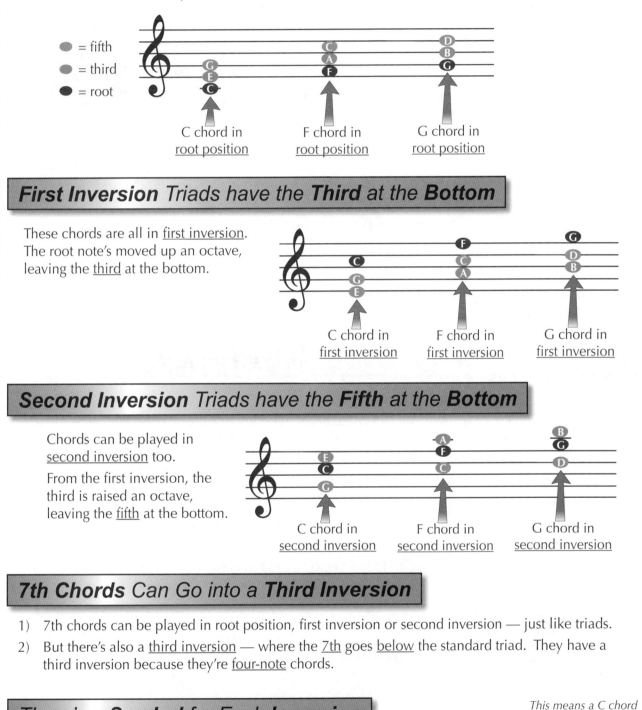

● = fifth
● = third
● = root

C chord in
root position

F chord in
root position

G chord in
root position

First Inversion Triads have the **Third** at the **Bottom**

These chords are all in first inversion. The root note's moved up an octave, leaving the third at the bottom.

C chord in
first inversion

F chord in
first inversion

G chord in
first inversion

Second Inversion Triads have the **Fifth** at the **Bottom**

Chords can be played in second inversion too.

From the first inversion, the third is raised an octave, leaving the fifth at the bottom.

C chord in
second inversion

F chord in
second inversion

G chord in
second inversion

7th Chords Can Go into a **Third Inversion**

1) 7th chords can be played in root position, first inversion or second inversion — just like triads.

2) But there's also a third inversion — where the 7th goes below the standard triad. They have a third inversion because they're four-note chords.

There's a **Symbol** for Each **Inversion**

This means a C chord with E at the bottom.

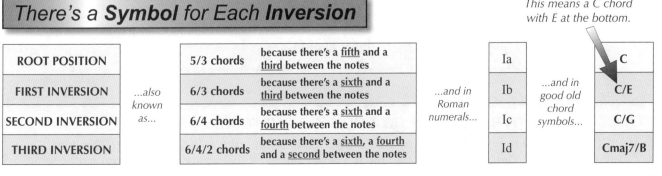

ROOT POSITION	...also known as...	5/3 chords	because there's a fifth and a third between the notes	...and in Roman numerals...	Ia	...and in good old chord symbols...	C
FIRST INVERSION		6/3 chords	because there's a sixth and a third between the notes		Ib		C/E
SECOND INVERSION		6/4 chords	because there's a sixth and a fourth between the notes		Ic		C/G
THIRD INVERSION		6/4/2 chords	because there's a sixth, a fourth and a second between the notes		Id		Cmaj7/B

Inversions

So now you know what inversions <u>are</u>. Now get to grips with what to <u>do</u> with them too...

Inversions are Handy for Moving Between Chords

When you play chords one after another, it sounds <u>nicer</u> if the notes move <u>smoothly</u> from one chord to the next. Inversions help to smooth out any rough patches...

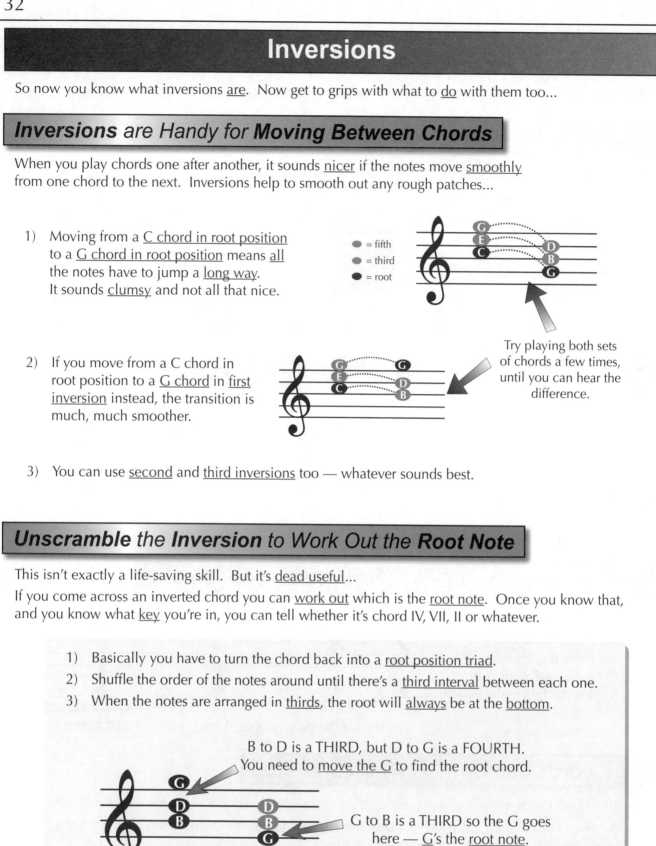

1) Moving from a <u>C chord in root position</u> to a <u>G chord in root position</u> means <u>all</u> the notes have to jump a <u>long way</u>. It sounds <u>clumsy</u> and not all that nice.

● = fifth
● = third
● = root

2) If you move from a C chord in root position to a <u>G chord</u> in <u>first inversion</u> instead, the transition is much, much smoother.

Try playing both sets of chords a few times, until you can hear the difference.

3) You can use <u>second</u> and <u>third inversions</u> too — whatever sounds best.

Unscramble the Inversion to Work Out the Root Note

This isn't exactly a life-saving skill. But it's <u>dead useful</u>...

If you come across an inverted chord you can <u>work out</u> which is the <u>root note</u>. Once you know that, and you know what <u>key</u> you're in, you can tell whether it's chord IV, VII, II or whatever.

1) Basically you have to turn the chord back into a <u>root position triad</u>.
2) Shuffle the order of the notes around until there's a <u>third interval</u> between each one.
3) When the notes are arranged in <u>thirds</u>, the root will <u>always</u> be at the <u>bottom</u>.

B to D is a THIRD, but D to G is a FOURTH.
You need to <u>move the G</u> to find the root chord.

G to B is a THIRD so the G goes here — <u>G</u>'s the <u>root note</u>.

4) There are no sharps or flats in the key signature, so the piece is in C major.
G's the fifth note of C major, so this is <u>chord V</u>.

Unscramble inversions — go back to your roots...

There's a lot to take in when it comes to inversions. It can seem quite confusing at first. Don't go racing through this page — go over it one bit at a time, letting all the facts sink in, till you <u>really</u> get it.

Different Ways of Playing Chords

So far, the chords in this section have all been written as three notes. It sounds dull if you do it all the time. To liven things up there are <u>chord figurations</u> — different ways of playing the chords.

Block Chords are the Most Basic

This is probably the <u>easiest</u> way to play chords.
The notes of each chord are played <u>all together</u>
and then <u>held</u> until the next chord.

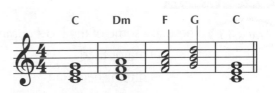

Rhythmic Chords Give You Harmony and Rhythm

1) Rhythmic chords are <u>chords</u> played to a <u>funky rhythm</u>.
2) You play all the notes of each chord at the same time, like you do for block chords.
3) You don't <u>hold</u> the notes though — you play them to a <u>rhythm</u> that <u>repeats</u> in each bar.
4) <u>Rhythm guitar</u> and <u>keyboards</u> often play rhythmic chords.

In Broken and Arpeggiated Chords the Notes are Separate

An accompaniment doesn't <u>have</u> to have chords with all the notes played at once.
You can play the notes <u>separately</u> too.

1) Here's one way of doing it —
   it goes <u>root</u>, <u>fifth</u>, <u>third</u>, <u>root</u>.

2) This pattern was really popular around
   the time <u>Mozart</u> was alive (last half of the
   1700s). It's called <u>Alberti bass</u> after the
   composer Domenico Alberti — it usually
   goes <u>root</u>, <u>fifth</u>, <u>third</u>, <u>fifth</u>.

3) The <u>notes of a chord</u> are sometimes <u>played in
   order</u> (e.g. root, third, fifth, root) <u>going up</u> or
   <u>coming down</u>. This is called an <u>arpeggio</u>
   (are-pedge-ee-o).

4) A <u>walking bass</u> usually moves in <u>crotchets</u>, often either in <u>steps</u> (see p.22) or <u>arpeggios</u>.
5) A <u>drone</u> is a <u>long, held-on note</u>, usually in the <u>bass</u>, that adds harmonic interest.
6) <u>Pedal notes</u> are a bit different — they're <u>repeated</u> notes, again usually in the <u>bass part</u>. However, the <u>harmony</u> on top of a pedal note <u>changes</u> (whereas a drone sets up the harmony for the whole piece).

Think about using an Alberti bass in your composition...
When you get chord symbols over the music you can play the chords <u>any way you like</u>. Try all these ways of playing chords and think about <u>using them</u> in your compositions. They'll get you marks.

Examples and Practice

Read on for some more examples of the different kinds of chords.

Examples

Track 15 These are some of the most <u>common</u> chords — learn to recognise them.

- a) <u>major</u> triad
- b) <u>minor</u> triad
- c) <u>diminished</u> triad
- d) <u>augmented</u> triad
- e) <u>major</u> triad with a <u>major</u> 7th
- f) <u>major</u> triad with a <u>minor</u> 7th
- g) <u>minor</u> triad with a <u>major</u> 7th
- h) <u>minor</u> triad with a <u>minor</u> 7th

Track 16 A <u>sequence</u> of chords, showing different <u>inversions</u>:

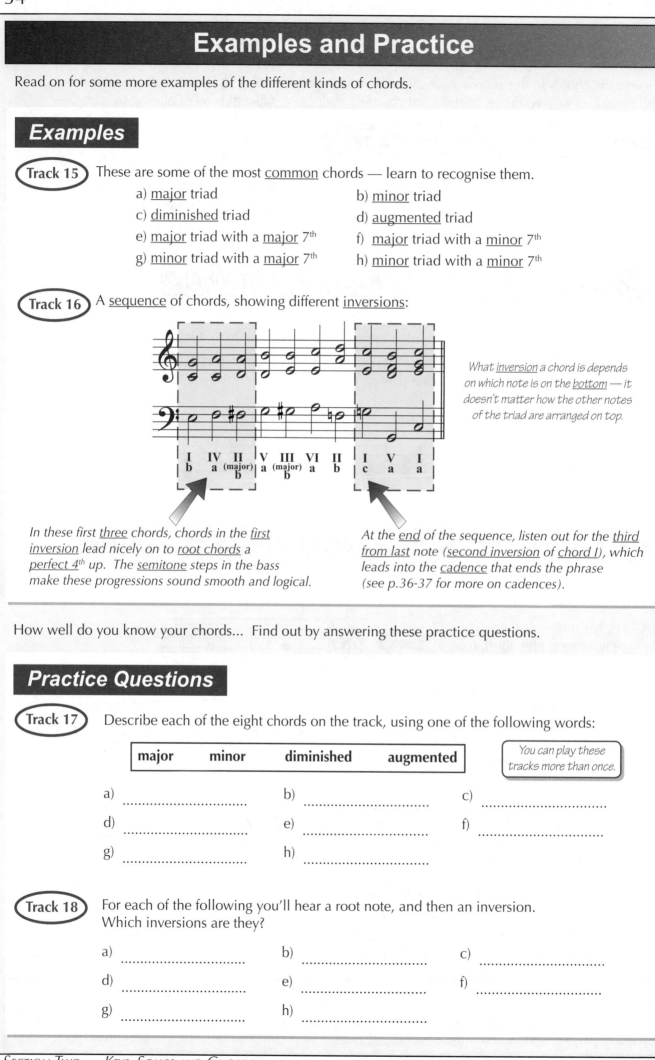

What <u>inversion</u> a chord is depends on which note is on the <u>bottom</u> — it doesn't matter how the other notes of the triad are arranged on top.

In these first <u>three</u> chords, chords in the <u>first inversion</u> lead nicely on to <u>root chords</u> a <u>perfect 4th</u> up. The <u>semitone</u> steps in the bass make these progressions sound smooth and logical.

At the <u>end</u> of the sequence, listen out for the <u>third from last</u> note (<u>second inversion</u> of <u>chord I</u>), which leads into the <u>cadence</u> that ends the phrase (see p.36-37 for more on cadences).

How well do you know your chords... Find out by answering these practice questions.

Practice Questions

Track 17 Describe each of the eight chords on the track, using one of the following words:

major	minor	diminished	augmented

You can play these tracks more than once.

a) ....

b) ....

c) ....

d) ....

e) ....

f) ....

g) ....

h) ....

Track 18 For each of the following you'll hear a root note, and then an inversion. Which inversions are they?

a) ....

b) ....

c) ....

d) ....

e) ....

f) ....

g) ....

h) ....

Using Decoration to Vary the Harmony

If you want to <u>liven things up</u> in a harmony you can add a sprinkle of <u>melodic decoration</u>.

Melodic Decoration **Adds Notes** to the Tune

1) <u>Decorative notes</u> are <u>short notes</u> that move between notes or create <u>fleeting clashes</u> (<u>dissonance</u>) with the accompanying chord. They make things sound <u>less bland</u>.
2) Decoration that belongs to the key of the melody (e.g. B in C major) is called <u>diatonic</u>.
3) Decoration that <u>doesn't</u> belong to the key (e.g. F# in C major) is called <u>chromatic</u>.
4) There are <u>four</u> main ways of adding melodic decoration.

1) **Auxiliary** Notes are **Higher** or **Lower** than the Notes Either **Side**

1) An auxiliary note is either a <u>semitone</u> or <u>tone above</u> or <u>below</u> the notes either side.
2) The two notes before and after the auxiliary are always the <u>same pitch</u>, and always belong to the accompanying chord.

2) **Passing** Notes **Link** the Notes **Before** and **After**

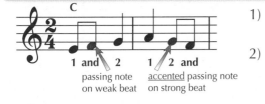

1) A passing note <u>links</u> the notes before and after. They either belong to the same chord or link one chord with another.
2) They're usually put on <u>weak beats</u>. When they <u>are</u> on the strong beat they're called 'accented passing notes'.

3) **Appoggiaturas Clash** with the Chord

1) An appoggiatura <u>clashes</u> with the accompanying chord.
2) The note <u>before</u> it is usually quite a <u>leap</u> away (jumps between notes of more than a <u>2nd</u> are called <u>leaps</u>).
3) The note after the appoggiatura is always <u>just above</u> or <u>below</u>. It's called the <u>resolution</u>. The <u>resolution</u> has to be from the <u>accompanying chord</u>.
4) Appoggiaturas usually fall on a <u>strong beat</u>, so the resolution note falls on a <u>weaker beat</u>.

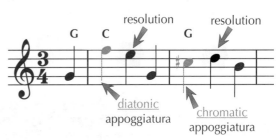

4) **Suspensions Clash** then Go Back to Harmonising

A suspension is a series of three notes called the <u>preparation</u>, <u>suspension</u> and <u>resolution</u>.

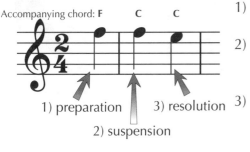

1) The <u>preparation</u> note belongs to the accompanying chord. It's usually on a weak beat.
2) The <u>suspension</u> is the <u>same pitch</u> as the preparation note. It's played at the same time as a <u>chord change</u>. It <u>doesn't go</u> with the new chord, so you get <u>dissonance</u>.
3) The <u>resolution</u> note moves up or down (usually down) from the suspension to a note in the accompanying chord. This <u>resolves</u> the dissonance — everything sounds lovely again.

Phrases and Cadences

Notes in a melody fall into 'phrases' just like the words in a story are made up of sentences.
A cadence is the movement from the second-to-last to the last chord of a phrase — it finishes it off.

A *Phrase* is Like a Musical *'Sentence'*

There should be clear phrases in any melody. A tune without phrases would
sound odd — just like a story with no sentences wouldn't make much sense.

1) Phrases are usually two or four bars long.

2) Phrases are sometimes marked with a curved
line called a phrase mark, that goes above
the stave. Not all music has phrase marks but
the phrases are always there. Don't confuse
phrase marks and slurs. A phrase mark
doesn't change how you play the notes.

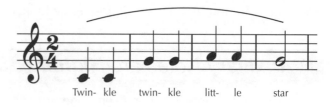

Cadences *Emphasise* the *End of a Phrase*

1) A cadence is the shift between the second-to-last chord and the last chord in a phrase.

2) The effect you get from shifting between the two chords works like a comma or a full stop.
It underlines the end of the phrase and gets you ready for the next one.

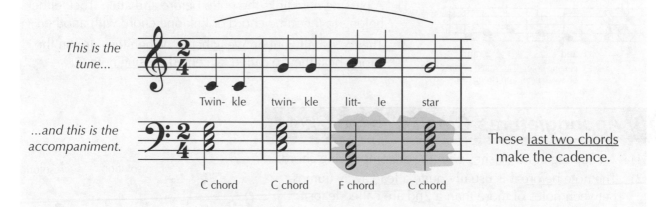

This is the tune...

Twin- kle   twin- kle   litt- le   star

...and this is the accompaniment.

These last two chords make the cadence.

C chord   C chord   F chord   C chord

There are *Four Main Types* of Cadence

These pairs of chords are only cadences when they come at the end of a phrase.
Anywhere else in a phrase, they're just chords.

Second Last Chord	Last Chord	Cadence
Chord V	Chord I	PERFECT
Chord IV	Chord I	PLAGAL
Chord I, II or IV	Chord V	IMPERFECT
Chord V	any except Chord I, (usually Chord VI)	INTERRUPTED

More on these over the page...

Cadences

Learning the <u>names</u> of the different cadences is no use unless you also learn what they're <u>for</u>.

Perfect and Plagal Cadences Work Like Full Stops

1) A <u>perfect cadence</u> makes a piece of music feel <u>finished or complete</u>.

2) It goes from <u>Chord V</u> to <u>Chord I</u> — in C major that's a <u>G chord</u> to a <u>C chord</u>.

3) This is how a perfect cadence goes at the <u>end</u> of 'Twinkle, Twinkle, Little Star':

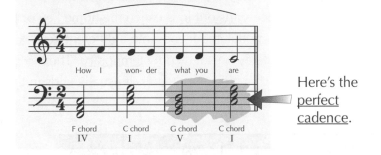

Here's the <u>perfect cadence</u>.

4) A <u>plagal cadence</u> sounds really different from a perfect cadence but it has a <u>similar effect</u> — it makes a piece of music sound finished.

5) A plagal cadence in C major is an <u>F chord</u> (IV) to a <u>C chord</u> (I). Play it and see what it sounds like. The plagal cadence gets used at the <u>end</u> of lots of <u>hymns</u> — it's sometimes called the '<u>Amen</u>' cadence.

Imperfect and Interrupted Cadences are Like Commas

<u>Imperfect</u> and <u>interrupted</u> cadences are used to end <u>phrases</u> but <u>not</u> at the end of a piece. They work like <u>commas</u> — they feel like a <u>resting point</u> but not an ending.

An <u>imperfect cadence</u> most commonly goes from chord <u>I</u>, <u>II</u> or <u>IV</u> to <u>V</u>. Here's one going from <u>chord I</u> to <u>chord V</u> at the end of the <u>third line</u> of 'Twinkle, Twinkle':

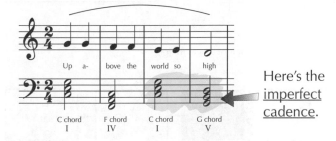

Here's the <u>imperfect cadence</u>.

In an <u>interrupted cadence</u> chord V can go to any chord except I, but it usually goes to chord VI. You expect it to go to chord I — so it sounds "interrupted". In C major an interrupted cadence may go from a <u>G chord</u> (V) to an <u>Am chord</u> (VI).

Some Minor pieces Finish with a Tierce de Picardie

1) If a piece of music is in a <u>minor key</u>, you'd expect it to <u>finish</u> with a <u>minor chord</u>.

2) However, some composers (especially <u>Baroque</u> composers) choose to finish a <u>minor piece</u> with a <u>major chord</u>, by using a <u>major third</u> in the last chord. This is known as a <u>Tierce de Picardie</u>.

This extract is from <u>Scarlatti's Piano Sonata in G Minor</u> (<u>Cat's Fugue</u>). Even though the piece is in <u>G minor</u>, it finishes with a <u>G major chord</u>.

You need to listen to cadences to understand them...

This is another of those topics that isn't going to make much sense unless you sit down and try playing them. <u>Play</u> the cadences lots of times until you can <u>hear</u> the differences between them.

Modulation

Most of the notes in a piece of music come from one key — but to vary the tune or harmony you can <u>modulate</u> (change key). It can happen just once, or a few times. It's up to the composer.

The *Starting Key* is Called *'Home'*

1) The key a piece <u>starts out in</u> is called the <u>home key</u> or <u>tonic key</u>.

2) If the music's modulated it goes into a <u>different key</u>.

3) The change of key is usually only <u>temporary</u>. The key <u>goes back</u> to the home key after a while.

4) However much a piece modulates, it usually <u>ends</u> in the home key.

There are **Two** Ways to Modulate

1) Modulation by *Pivot Chord*

1) A pivot chord is a chord that's in the home key <u>and</u> the key the music modulates to.

2) <u>Chord V</u> (G, B, D) in <u>C major</u> is exactly the same as <u>chord I</u> in <u>G major</u> — so it can be used to <u>pivot</u> between C major and G major.

3) Sometimes, the <u>key signature</u> changes to show the new key.
   More often, <u>accidentals</u> are written in the music where they're needed.

The home key here is <u>C</u>.
At the end of the <u>first bar</u> the accompaniment uses the chord <u>G, B, D</u> to pivot into G major:

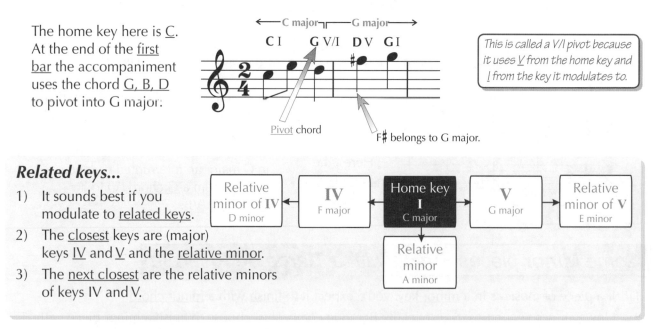

This is called a V/I pivot because it uses <u>V</u> from the home key and <u>I</u> from the key it modulates to.

Pivot chord

F♯ belongs to G major.

Related keys...

1) It sounds best if you modulate to <u>related keys</u>.

2) The <u>closest</u> keys are (major) keys <u>IV</u> and <u>V</u> and the <u>relative minor</u>.

3) The <u>next closest</u> are the relative minors of keys IV and V.

2) *Abrupt* Modulation

1) In abrupt modulation there's <u>no pivot chord</u>, and no other preparation either. It just happens.

2) Often the modulation is between two keys just <u>one semitone apart</u>, e.g. from <u>C major</u> to <u>C♯ major</u>.

3) <u>Pop songs</u> often modulate <u>up</u> one semitone. It creates a <u>sudden</u>, <u>dramatic effect</u> — it's meant to give the music an <u>excited</u>, <u>uplifting</u> feeling.

You can choose related keys but you can't choose your family...

If you see <u>accidentals</u> it often means the music's modulated, but <u>not always</u>. The accidental could also be there because: 1) the music's written in a <u>minor key</u> — harmonic or melodic (see p.19); or 2) the composer fancied a spot of <u>chromatic</u> decoration (see p.35). That's composers for you...

Texture

Here's one last way composers vary the harmony — by changing the <u>texture</u>. Texture's an odd word to use about music — what it means is how the chords and melody are <u>woven together</u>.

Texture is How the parts Fit Together

1) An important part of music is how the <u>different parts</u> are <u>woven together</u>.
   This is known as <u>texture</u> — it describes how the <u>melody</u> and <u>accompaniment</u> parts <u>fit together</u>.
2) <u>Monophonic</u>, <u>homophonic</u> and <u>polyphonic</u> are all different types of texture.
3) Some textures are made up of the <u>same</u> melodic line that's passed round <u>different parts</u>.
   <u>Imitation</u> and <u>canons</u> are good examples of this.

Monophonic Music is the Simplest

In <u>monophonic</u> music there's <u>no harmony</u> — just one line of tune. Monophonic music has a <u>thin texture</u>.

Polyphonic Music Weaves Tunes Together

1) <u>Polyphonic</u> music gives quite a complex effect because there's <u>more than one tune</u> being played at once.

2) It's sometimes called <u>contrapuntal</u> music.
3) Parts that move in <u>contrary motion</u> (one part goes <u>up</u> and another goes <u>down</u>) are polyphonic.

In Homophonic Music, the Parts Move Together

1) If the lines of music move at more or less the <u>same time</u>, it's <u>homophonic</u> music.
2) Melody and chords (chordal music) is a good example.
3) <u>Parallel motion</u> (when parts move with the <u>same interval</u> between them, e.g. parallel 5ths) is also homophonic.

Melody

Accompaniment

In Heterophonic Music the Instruments Share the Tune

Flute

Oboe

In heterophonic music there's <u>one tune</u>. <u>All</u> the instruments play it, but with <u>variations</u>, and often at <u>different times</u>.

Polyphonic, homophonic and heterophonic music all have quite a thick texture.

You might have to write about texture in the exam...

It's hard talking about texture — a bit like trying to describe a smell... If you need to write about <u>texture</u> in your listening test, these are handy words to use: smooth, rough, dense, light...

Texture

When there's one part, the music's pure and simple, but put more parts in and it's much more complex.

Imitation — Repeat a Phrase With Slight Changes

1) In imitation a phrase is repeated with slight changes each time.
2) It works particularly well if one instrument or voice imitates another and then overlaps.

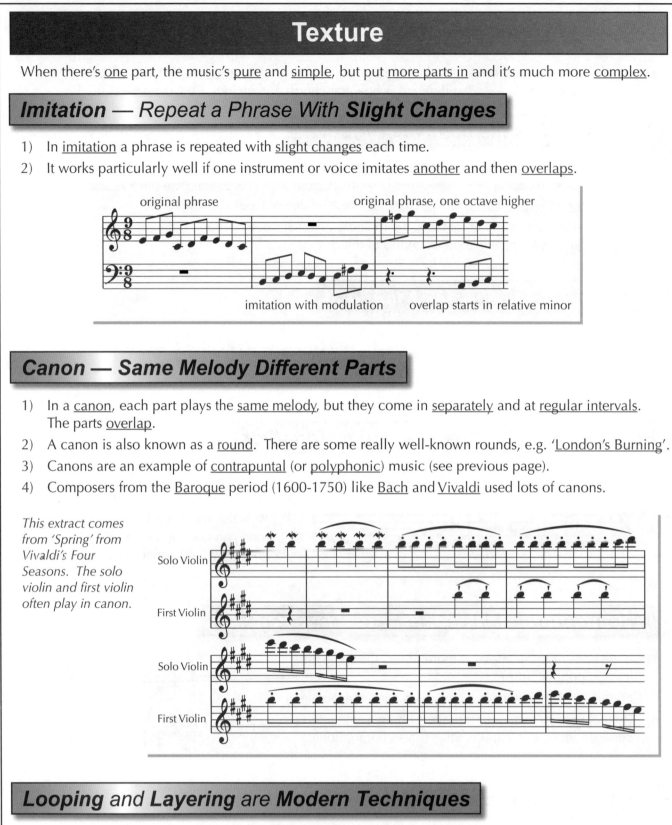

Canon — Same Melody Different Parts

1) In a canon, each part plays the same melody, but they come in separately and at regular intervals. The parts overlap.
2) A canon is also known as a round. There are some really well-known rounds, e.g. 'London's Burning'.
3) Canons are an example of contrapuntal (or polyphonic) music (see previous page).
4) Composers from the Baroque period (1600-1750) like Bach and Vivaldi used lots of canons.

This extract comes from 'Spring' from Vivaldi's Four Seasons. The solo violin and first violin often play in canon.

Looping and Layering are Modern Techniques

1) In the 1960s and 70s, composers like Steve Reich started developing new techniques in their music.
2) They took recordings of sections of music, words, rhythms and other sounds and repeated them over and over again. These are called loops.
3) The loops were often created by cutting pieces of tape and sticking the ends together so they could be played over and over again — this is looping.
4) If there are lots of different loops being played at the same time it's called layering.

A layer of fruit, a layer of sponge, a layer of custard...

There are a few more words on this page that'll be useful if you need to write about musical texture in the listening exam — imitation, canon, looped and layered. Make sure you know what they mean.

Texture

Composers use <u>different textures</u> to <u>vary</u> their music. They can change the <u>number</u> of instruments and whether they play the <u>same notes</u> or in <u>harmony</u>. They can also <u>split</u> tunes between <u>different instruments</u>.

More Than One Part Can Play the Same Melody

1) If there's just <u>one part</u> playing with <u>no accompaniment</u>, there's just a <u>single melody line</u>.

2) If there's <u>more than one</u> instrument playing the <u>same melody</u> at the <u>same pitch</u>, they're playing in <u>unison</u>.

3) If there's <u>more than one</u> instrument playing the <u>same notes</u> but in <u>different ranges</u>, they're playing in <u>octaves</u>.

The examples on this page use the melody from Handel's 'Water Music'.

Some Instruments Play Accompanying Parts

1) The instruments that <u>aren't</u> playing the tune play the <u>accompaniment</u>. Different <u>types</u> of accompaniment give different <u>textures</u>.

2) If the accompaniment is playing <u>chords</u> underneath the melody (or the <u>same rhythm</u> of the melody but <u>different notes</u>), the texture is <u>homophonic</u>. It sounds <u>richer</u> than a single melody line, unison or octaves.

3) If there are <u>two choirs</u> singing at <u>different times</u>, the music is <u>antiphonal</u>. The two choirs will often sing <u>alternate phrases</u> — like <u>question and answer</u> or <u>call and response</u>. A lot of <u>early religious vocal music</u> was antiphonal. You can also get the same effect with two groups of <u>instruments</u>.

4) If there's <u>more than one</u> part playing <u>different melodies</u> at the <u>same time</u>, the music is <u>contrapuntal</u> (or <u>polyphonic</u>). Contrapuntal parts <u>fit together</u> harmonically.

Would you care to accompany me to the cinema...

Quite a few tricky <u>textures</u> to learn on this page — and it's important that you don't get them <u>muddled up</u>. Listen to the different types, and try and <u>recognise</u> what they sound like in case they come up in the <u>exam</u>.

Examples

Track 19 should help you get a better idea about cadences, and Track 20 gives you some different examples of modulation. Listen to them lots of times until you can recognise them straight away.

Examples

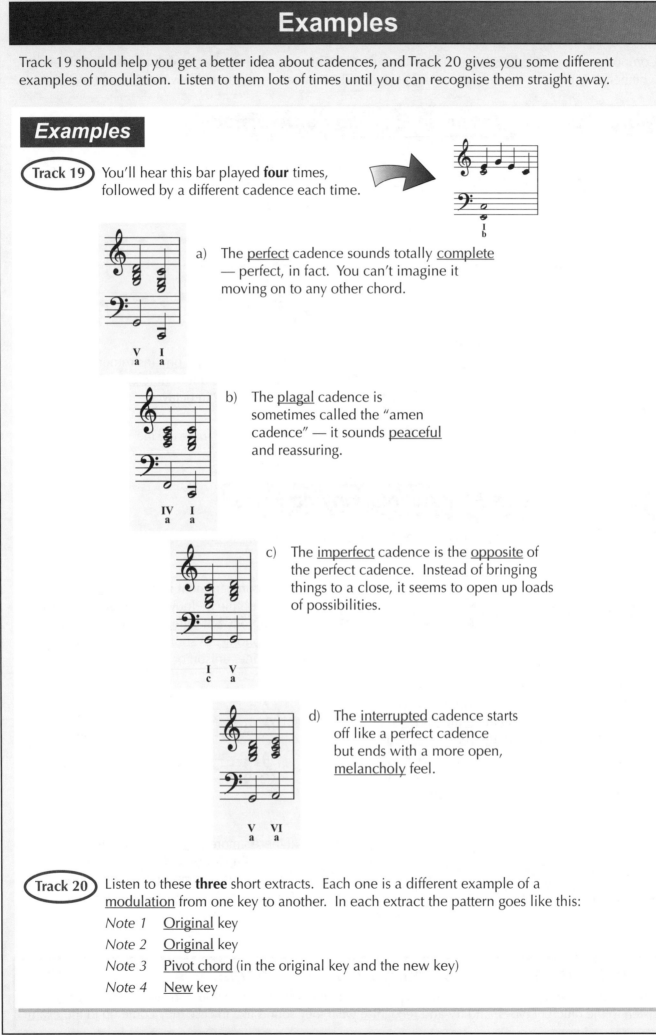

Track 19 You'll hear this bar played **four** times, followed by a different cadence each time.

a) The perfect cadence sounds totally complete — perfect, in fact. You can't imagine it moving on to any other chord.

b) The plagal cadence is sometimes called the "amen cadence" — it sounds peaceful and reassuring.

c) The imperfect cadence is the opposite of the perfect cadence. Instead of bringing things to a close, it seems to open up loads of possibilities.

d) The interrupted cadence starts off like a perfect cadence but ends with a more open, melancholy feel.

Track 20 Listen to these **three** short extracts. Each one is a different example of a modulation from one key to another. In each extract the pattern goes like this:

Note 1 Original key
Note 2 Original key
Note 3 Pivot chord (in the original key and the new key)
Note 4 New key

Practice

Practise your hard-won knowledge of chords, modulation and texture with the questions on this page and the next. Listen to each track a few times to make sure you've heard it properly.

Practice Questions

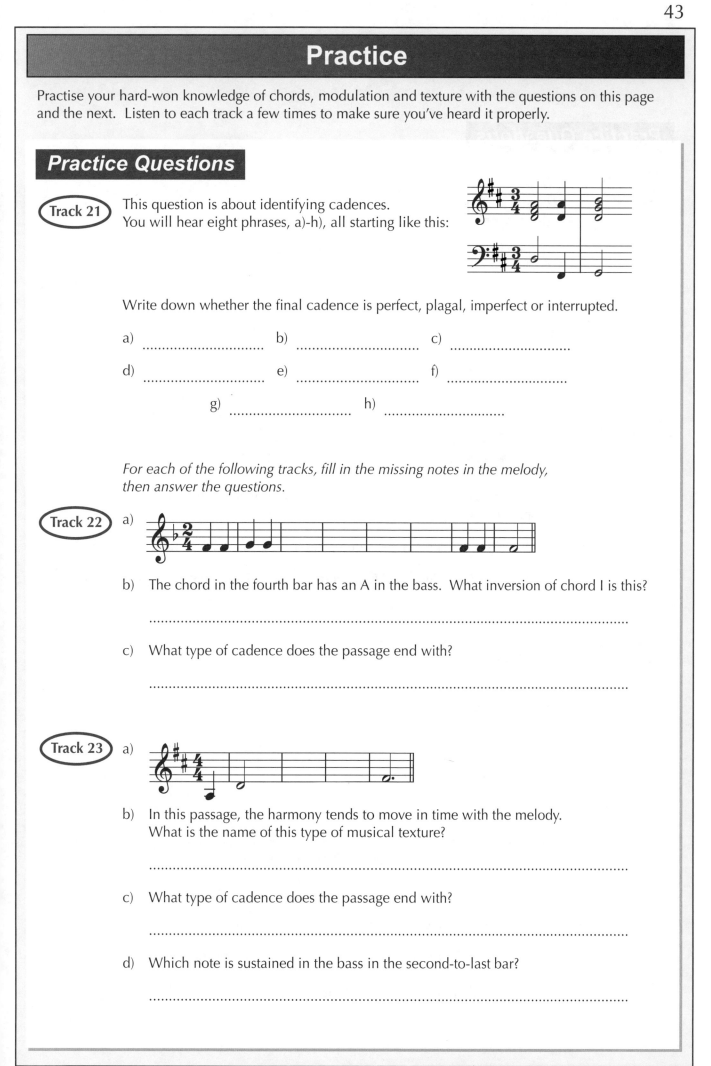

Track 21 This question is about identifying cadences.
You will hear eight phrases, a)-h), all starting like this:

Write down whether the final cadence is perfect, plagal, imperfect or interrupted.

a) .... b) .... c) ....

d) .... e) .... f) ....

g) .... h) ....

*For each of the following tracks, fill in the missing notes in the melody,
then answer the questions.*

Track 22 a)

b) The chord in the fourth bar has an A in the bass. What inversion of chord I is this?

....

c) What type of cadence does the passage end with?

....

Track 23 a)

b) In this passage, the harmony tends to move in time with the melody.
What is the name of this type of musical texture?

....

c) What type of cadence does the passage end with?

....

d) Which note is sustained in the bass in the second-to-last bar?

....

Practice

Practice Questions

Track 24 a)

b) The first chord in bar 2 is the major of chord II.
Which note in this chord is not in the scale of the home key?

....

c) What type of cadence does the passage end with?

....

Track 25 a)

b) Circle each auxiliary note in the passage, and say whether each is
diatonic or chromatic.

c) Which one of the following best describes the chord in bar 4? Ring your answer.

1st inversion   **harmonic**   **relative minor**   **suspension**

Track 26 a)

b) What key does this passage start in?

....

c) What key does it finish in?

....

d) The B-flat chord at the start of bar 3 comes before the dominant chord of the new key.
Give the name of a chord in this position in a modulation.

....

e) Fill in the blanks in the following sentence with the appropriate Roman numerals:

The B-flat chord is chord .... in the home key

and chord .... in the final key.

Warm-up and Exam Questions

Warm-up Questions

1) Name **two** instruments that are frequently used to play chords.

2) Which **three** chords in a major key produce major triads?

3) If the *root* of a chord is on the top, and the *third* of the chord is on the bottom, which inversion is the chord in?

4) Name **three** different ways of playing chords.

5) What do you call a melodic decoration that belongs to the same key as the main melody?

6) List **three** ways melodies can be decorated to help vary the harmony within a piece of music.

7) At what point in a piece of music would you expect to find an imperfect or interrupted cadence?

8) What's another name for the texture known as polyphonic?

Exam Question

Now practise your exam technique with the question below and over the page.

Track 27

Play the extract **four times** then answer the questions on the next page.
Leave a short pause for writing time before each playing.
Here is the complete score for the extract:

Exam Question

a)   What instrument is playing this piece?

    ....   *[1 mark]*

b)   How would you describe the way the left hand is playing at **1**?

    ....   *[1 mark]*

c)   Which of the following best describes the cadence at **2**?
     Circle your choice from the options below.

    perfect   **plagal**   **imperfect**   *[1 mark]*

d)   Which key is this extract in?

    ....   *[1 mark]*

e)   Look at the key of the piece. How would you explain the sharpened note at **3**?

    ....   *[1 mark]*

f)   What term is used to describe the dots above the notes at **4**?

    ....   *[1 mark]*

g)   Which of these options best describes the texture of this music?
     Circle your choice.

    monophonic   **homophonic**   **heterophonic**   *[1 mark]*

Revision Summary for Section Two

There's a lot to remember here: four types of triad, four types of triad inversion, cadences, different ways of using decoration with chords, modulation, the something-phonic words... It's too much to tackle all in one go. Test yourself a page at a time and make sure you really know it. You'll know you've done it properly when you can answer all these questions <u>without</u> looking back.

1) How many notes are there in a major scale? How many notes are there in a minor scale?
2) Write out the names of the notes of a scale in words, numbers and Roman numerals.
3) Write down the tone-semitone pattern for a major scale.
4) Which major scale only uses the white notes on the keyboard?
5) What does a key signature tell you?
6) How do you find the 'relative minor' of a major scale?
7) D major has two sharps — F and C. What's the key signature of the relative minor?
8) Write out A minor in each of the three types of minor scale and label the tone and semitone gaps.
9) How many major scales are there altogether?
10) How many minor scales are there altogether?
11) The circle of fifths starts with C major. Write down all the major scales in order around the circle, starting with C.
12) Write out two common modes.
13) What's a pentatonic scale? What types of music often use pentatonic scales?
14) What are the notes in a G major pentatonic scale?
15) What's a chromatic scale? How many notes are there in a chromatic scale?
16) What's a whole tone scale?
17) What's the difference between a melodic and a harmonic interval?
18) Give the name and number of each of these intervals: a) A to C   b) B to F   c) C to B   d) D to A
19) What's a tritone?
20) What do you call chords with: a) clashing notes   b) notes that sound good together?
21) What are the two most common types of triad? Describe how you make each one.
22) What makes a 7th chord different from a triad?
23) Write down the letter symbols for these chords:
    a) G major   b) A minor   c) A minor with a major 7th   d) D diminished triad
24) Draw the scale of G major on a stave, then build a triad on each note. *(Don't forget the F sharps.)*
25) Which three chords of any major or minor scale are known as the 'primary' chords?
26) Write out the notes of the three primary chords in C major, G major and D major.
27) Where do the root, third and fifth go in: a) a first inversion chord   b) a second inversion chord?
28) Are these chords in root position, first inversion, second inversion or third inversion?
    a) 6/4   b) C/E   c) IVa   d) 6/4/2
29) Name and describe four different chord figurations.
30) What's the difference between a 'diatonic' decoration and a 'chromatic' decoration?
31) Explain the following terms: a) auxiliary note   b) passing note   c) appoggiatura
32) Write a one-sentence definition of a musical phrase.
33) What job does a cadence do in a phrase?
34) How many chords make up a cadence?
35) Write down the four different types of cadence and which chords you can use to make each one.
36) What do you call it when a piece in a minor key ends on a major chord?
37) What do people mean when they talk about the 'texture' of music?
38) Explain the difference between monophonic music, homophonic music and polyphonic music.

Common Melody Structures

You need a few good <u>technical</u> words to describe <u>melodies</u> — like <u>conjunct</u>, <u>disjunct</u>, <u>triadic</u> or <u>scalic</u>.

Melodies can be Conjunct or Disjunct

1) <u>Conjunct</u> melodies move mainly by <u>step</u> — notes that are a <u>major 2nd</u> (a <u>tone</u>) apart.

2) The melody <u>doesn't</u> jump around, so it sounds quite <u>smooth</u>.
   This example shows a conjunct melody:

Soprano 1

The sil - ver swan, who liv - ing had no note,

This extract's from 'The Silver Swan' by Orlando Gibbons.

3) <u>Disjunct</u> melodies move using a lot of <u>jumps</u> — notes that are more than a <u>major 2nd</u> (a <u>tone</u>) apart.

4) The melody sounds quite <u>spiky</u> as it jumps around a lot.

5) Disjunct melodies are <u>harder</u> to sing or play than conjunct ones.
   This example shows a disjunct melody:

Vin - cer - ò! Vin - cer - ò!

This one's from 'Nessun Dorma' by Puccini.

Triadic Melodies Use the Notes of a Triad

1) Triads are chords made up of <u>two intervals</u> of a third on top of each other — so triadic melodies usually move between the notes of a triad. (There's more on triads on page 29.)

2) For example, a <u>C major</u> triad is made up of the notes <u>C</u>, <u>E</u> and <u>G</u>. There's a <u>major third</u> between C and E, a <u>minor third</u> between E and G and a <u>perfect fifth</u> between <u>C</u> and <u>G</u>. There's more on intervals on pages 22-23.

3) This example shows a triadic melody:

This extract is from the first movement of Haydn's Trumpet Concerto.

Scalic Melodies Use the Notes of a Scale

1) A <u>scalic</u> melody moves up and down using the notes of a <u>scale</u>.

2) Scalic melodies are <u>similar</u> to conjunct melodies, but they can only move to the <u>next note</u> in the <u>scale</u>. Conjunct melodies can have a few <u>little jumps</u> in them.

3) Like conjunct melodies, scalic melodies sound quite <u>smooth</u>. Here's an example of a scalic melody (it's also from the first movement of Haydn's Trumpet Concerto):

Some melodies contain all of these melodic features...

These different types of melody are pretty <u>easy</u> to spot if you have the <u>music</u> in front of you, but it's a bit <u>harder</u> if you're <u>listening</u> to them. Listen out for them in all types of music and practise <u>identifying</u> them.

Common Melody Structures

Call and response is used a lot in blues, rock and pop, as well as African and Indian music — so it's important that you know what it is. It's used in both instrumental and vocal music.

Call and Response is Like a Musical Conversation

1) Call and response is a bit like question and answer. It takes place either between two groups of musicians, or between a leader and the rest of the group.

2) One group (or the leader) plays or sings a short phrase. This is the call. It's then answered by the other group. This is the response.

3) The call ends in a way that makes you feel a response is coming — e.g. it might finish with an imperfect cadence (see page 37).

4) Call and response is very popular in pop and blues music. Often the lead singer will sing the call and the backing singers will sing the response.

In a 12-bar blues structure (see p.122), the usual pattern of a call and response would be A, A1, B:

A is the call (4 bars)
A1 is the call repeated with slight variations (4 bars)
B is the response (4 bars).

4 bars	4 bars	4 bars
A — CALL	A1 — CALL WITH VARIATION	B — RESPONSE

To make things more complicated, sections A and B can have a 2-bar call and response of their own:

2 bars	2 bars	2 bars	2 bars	2 bars	2 bars
CALL	RESPONSE	CALL	RESPONSE	CALL	RESPONSE
A — CALL		A1 — CALL WITH VARIATION		B — RESPONSE	

Indian and African Music Use Call and Response

1) In Indian music, call and response is usually used in instrumental music. One musician will play a phrase and it'll either be repeated or improvised upon by another musician.

2) African music uses call and response in religious ceremonies and community events. The leader will sing first and the congregation will respond.

3) Call and response is also used in African drumming music. The master drummer plays a call and the rest of the drummers play an answering phrase.

Some Melodies Form an Arch Shape

1) If a melody finishes in the same way it started, then the tune has an arch shape.

2) The simplest example of this is ABA — where the first section is the same as the last section of the piece. This is extended in some pieces to ABCBA, or even ABCDCBA.

3) This gives a symmetrical melody because the sections are mirrored. It makes the whole piece feel more balanced.

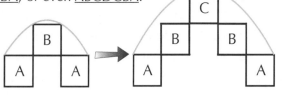

Call and response is used in a lot of music...

...so make sure you can spot it in case it comes up in the exam.
Try not to confuse arch-shaped melodies with rondo form — Section A only returns once in an arch.

Common Forms

The <u>movements</u> of big works like <u>symphonies</u>, <u>sonatas</u> and <u>concertos</u> often follow <u>set structures</u> — e.g. <u>sonata form</u>, <u>minuet and trio</u> or <u>scherzo and trio</u>.

A Piece in Sonata Form has Three Main Sections

The <u>first movement</u> of a symphony, sonata or concerto is usually in <u>sonata form</u> — e.g. <u>Tchaikovsky's Violin Concerto No.1 in D</u>. The <u>last movement</u> sometimes is as well. Sonata form has <u>three</u> main sections:

EXPOSITION	DEVELOPMENT	RECAPITULATION
Themes are "exposed" — heard for the first time.	Themes go through a number of interesting <u>twists</u> and <u>turns</u>.	Themes are "recapped" — played again.

1) The <u>exposition</u> has two <u>contrasting themes</u>. It ends in a <u>different</u> (but related) key to the one it started in.

2) The <u>development</u> keeps the piece <u>interesting</u> — the themes are taken through lots of <u>variations</u>.

3) The <u>recapitulation</u> pulls it all <u>together</u> again — the themes from the exposition are <u>repeated</u>. They're usually <u>changed</u> slightly — e.g. the composer might add <u>ornaments</u> or <u>shorten</u> them a bit.

Pieces in sonata form often start with a short <u>introduction</u> — usually in the <u>dominant key</u>.

Composers sometimes use <u>bridge sections</u> between the themes and <u>links</u> between the main sections. They usually add a <u>coda</u> — a short section that's a bit <u>different</u> to the rest of the piece and finishes it off <u>nicely</u>.

See Section 2 for more on related keys.

A Minuet and Trio has Contrasting Sections

1) The <u>third movement</u> of four-movement symphonies and sonatas is often in <u>minuet and trio form</u>.

2) A minuet is a <u>French dance</u> with <u>three beats</u> in a bar.

3) The <u>trio</u> is <u>another minuet</u> in a <u>contrasting</u> but <u>related</u> key — often the <u>dominant</u> or <u>relative minor</u>. It's often written for <u>three instruments</u> (which is why it's called a trio).

4) After the trio, the <u>first minuet</u> is played again. This is <u>ternary form</u> — ABA (see p.80).

MINUET	TRIO	MINUET

5) Some of the movements of Handel's <u>Water Music</u> are good examples of minuets.

Later Works Used a Scherzo Instead of a Minuet

1) In <u>later</u> symphonies and sonatas, the <u>third movement</u> is often a <u>scherzo and trio</u> instead of a <u>minuet and trio</u>. <u>Beethoven</u> was one of the <u>first composers</u> to use a scherzo in his pieces — the third movement of his <u>Violin Sonata No. 5 in F</u> (often called 'Spring') is a scherzo. In <u>Schubert's</u> Piano Quintet '<u>The Trout</u>', the third movement is a scherzo and trio.

2) A scherzo and trio is very <u>similar</u> to a minuet and trio — except that a scherzo is <u>faster</u> and more <u>light-hearted</u>. Scherzo means '<u>joke</u>' in Italian.

3) In a four-movement piece, the scherzo is normally the <u>fastest</u> and most <u>playful</u>.

4) If a symphony or sonata only has <u>three</u> movements, it's often the <u>scherzo</u> or <u>minuet</u> that's <u>missed out</u>.

Don't worry, I'll be there in a minuet...

You need to learn the <u>names</u> and <u>features</u> of the different sections of each of these forms — and how they <u>relate</u> to each other. Drawing <u>diagrams</u> might help you remember — try using different colours.

Common Forms

Strophic form, through-composed form and da capo arias are all popular structures used in songs. Cyclic form is usually found in large works like symphonies, but it's also used in some big vocal works.

In *Strophic Form* Each *Verse* has the *Same Tune*

1) In strophic form, the same section of music is repeated over and over again with virtually no changes.

2) Strophic form is used in Classical, folk, blues and pop music.

3) In strophic songs, the music for each verse is the same, but the lyrics change in every verse. Hymns are a good example of this.

4) Strophic form can be thought of like this: A, A1, A2, A3, etc. — the same section is repeated but with a small change (the lyrics).

5) The first part of Led Zeppelin's 'Stairway to Heaven' is in strophic form.

In *Through-Composed Form* Each *Verse* is *Different*

1) Through-composed form is the opposite of strophic form — the music changes in every verse.

2) Every verse of lyrics has different music to accompany it, so there's no repetition.

3) Verses can have different melodies, different chords, or both.

4) This form is popular in opera, as the changing music can be used to tell stories. Verses sung by different characters can be completely different.

5) A lot of film music is through-composed — the music changes to reflect what's happening on-screen.

Baroque Composers Used *Ternary Form* in *Arias*

1) An aria is a solo in an opera or oratorio (see p.84).

2) Arias from the Baroque period (1600-1750) are often in ternary form (see p.80). Arias like this are called 'da capo arias'. Handel wrote lots of these.

After repeating Section A and Section B you come to the instruction da capo al fine. It means "go back to the beginning and play to where it says fine". The fine is at the end of Section A. That's where the piece finishes.

fine   da capo al fine

‖: SECTION A :‖ ‖: SECTION B :‖

Works in *Cyclic Form* Have a *Common Theme*

1) Pieces in cyclic form have common themes in all the movements. These themes link the movements together.

2) Big works like sonatas, symphonies and concertos are sometimes in cyclic form.

3) The linking themes vary in different ways, e.g. they might be played on different instruments, played faster or slower, or played in a different key in different movements. You'll still be able to recognise them though.

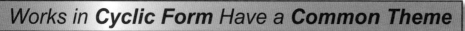

4) An example of a common theme in a piece in cyclic form is the four-note theme of Beethoven's Fifth Symphony. It appears in all the movements of the symphony.

5) Film music often has a theme — a bit of melody that keeps popping up throughout the film. The main theme from 'Star Wars®' (by John Williams) is really easy to recognise.

Don't mind me — I'm just passing through...

Film music can make a huge difference to a scene. Dario Marianelli's music for the film 'Atonement' and Hans Zimmer's score for 'Gladiator' really help set the scene and create tension and emotion.

Common Forms

Continuo and ground bass are both types of bass part. A cadenza is played by a soloist.

A *Continuo* is a *Bass Part*

1) A continuo (or basso continuo) is a continuous bass part. Most music written in the Baroque period has a continuo that the harmony of the whole piece is based on.

2) The continuo can be played by more than one instrument, but at least one of the continuo group must be able to play chords (e.g. a harpsichord, organ, lute, harp, etc.). A cello, double bass or bassoon could also be used. The most common combination was a harpsichord and a cello.

3) Continuo parts were usually written using a type of notation called figured bass. Only the bass notes were written on the stave, but numbers underneath the notes told the performers which chords to play. The continuo players would then improvise using the notes of the chord.

4) If there weren't any numbers written, the chord would be a normal triad (the root, the third and the fifth). A 4 meant play a fourth instead of the third, and a 6 meant play a sixth instead of the fifth. A 7 meant that a 7th should be added to the chord.

means

> *Some versions of Handel's Water Music still have the continuo written in figured bass.*

5) The improvisation is called a realization — the performer would 'realize' a continuo part.

Ground Bass Pieces Have *Repetition AND Variety*

1) A ground bass is a repeated bass part (sometimes called an ostinato) that's usually four or eight bars long. It can be played by the left hand on a harpsichord or piano, or by the cello and double bass in a chamber orchestra.

2) The tune is played over the ground bass part. First you hear the main tune, then a load of variations. The variations are played as one continuous piece — there are no gaps between them.

3) The ground bass part can be varied too. You change the starting note but keep the pattern the same.

First time round, the ground bass tune starts on C.

Later on you get the same tune starting on G.

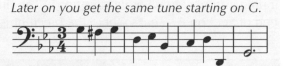

4) The ground bass piece gets more and more complex as it goes on. It can be developed by adding extra, decorative notes to the melody, using more advanced harmonies and adding more instruments to give a richer texture.

A *Cadenza* is Where a *Soloist* can *Show Off*

1) A cadenza is a bit of music that's played by a soloist, usually in the middle of a concerto (see p.89).

2) Almost all concertos have a cadenza — it allows the soloist to show off their technique.

3) Cadenzas started out as improvisations on the main themes of a piece, but now most of them are written out by the composer. However, different musicians will interpret the cadenza in their own way.

Right, that's this page done — better continuo onto the next one...

Listen to a couple of different musicians' performances of Haydn's Trumpet Concerto in E flat major — the cadenzas will sound different in each one, even though the soloists are playing the same notes.

Popular Song Forms

It's not just <u>Classical</u> music that follows set <u>structures</u> — <u>pop songs</u> do as well.

Pop Songs Usually Have an Intro

Pop tunes almost always start with an <u>intro</u>. It does <u>two jobs</u>:

- It often uses the best bit from the rest of the song to <u>set the mood</u>.
- It grabs people's <u>attention</u> and makes them <u>sit up and listen</u>.

Most Pop Songs Have a Verse-Chorus Structure

<u>After</u> the intro, the structure of most pop songs goes <u>verse-chorus-verse-chorus</u>.

- All the verses usually have the <u>same tune</u>, but the <u>lyrics change</u> for each verse.
- The chorus has a <u>different tune</u> from the verses, usually quite a catchy one. The lyrics and tune of the chorus <u>don't change</u>.
- In a lot of songs the verse and chorus are both <u>8 or 16 bars long</u>.

'I Can't Get No Satisfaction' by the Rolling Stones has a verse-chorus structure.

The old verse-chorus thing can get repetitive. To avoid this most songs have a <u>middle 8</u>, or <u>bridge</u>, that sounds different. It's an <u>8-bar section</u> in the <u>middle</u> of the song with <u>new chords</u>, <u>new lyrics</u> and a whole <u>new feel</u>.

The song ends with a <u>coda</u> or <u>outro</u> that's <u>different</u> to the verse and the chorus. You can use the coda for a <u>big finish</u> or to <u>fade out gradually</u>.

Pop Songs Can Have Other Structures Too

For example:

CALL AND RESPONSE

This has <u>two bits</u> to it. <u>Part 1</u> is the call — it asks a musical <u>question</u>. <u>Part 2</u>, the response, responds with an <u>answer</u> (p.49).

RIFF

A <u>riff</u> is a <u>short section</u> of music that's <u>repeated</u> over and over again (a bit like an <u>ostinato</u> — see p.82). Riffs can be used to build up a <u>whole song</u>. <u>Each part</u>, e.g. the drums or bass guitar, has its own riff. All the riffs <u>fit together</u> to make one section of the music. They often <u>change</u> for the <u>chorus</u>.

'Take a Bow' by Rihanna is an R&B ballad.

BALLADS

These are songs that tell <u>stories</u>. Each verse usually has the <u>same rhythm</u> and <u>same tune</u>.

32-BAR SONG FORM

This breaks down into <u>four 8-bar sections</u>. Sections 1, 2 and 4 use the <u>main theme</u>. Section 3 uses a <u>contrasting theme</u>, making an AABA structure. The 32 bars are repeated like a chorus. The <u>verse</u> is only played <u>once</u> — it's usually slowish and acts more like an <u>introduction</u>.

Verse — chorus — verse — chorus — tea break — chorus...

It's not just pop songs that follow these structures — <u>songs from musicals</u> do too. Have a listen to <u>'Defying Gravity'</u> from the musical <u>'Wicked'</u>, <u>'I'm Reviewing the Situation'</u> from <u>'Oliver!'</u> and <u>'Any Dream Will Do'</u> from <u>'Joseph and the Amazing Technicolour Dreamcoat'</u> and look for the structures.

Improvisation

Improvisation isn't just making up whatever you like. There's actually quite a bit more to it.

Lots of *Jazz* is *Improvised*

1) Improvisation is where a performer makes up music on the spot.
   There's often an improvised solo section in jazz pieces.

2) The improvisations aren't totally random though — the soloist will be told which chords to improvise over. This is often a 12-bar blues chord pattern (see p.122). Some improvisations use a mode (see page 21) instead of a chord pattern.

3) The soloist will know which notes are in each chord, but sometimes they'll play clashing notes to keep the solo interesting. If they're using a mode, they'll use the notes of the mode in their solo.

4) They might also use bits of the main melody of the piece as a starting point, then develop it into a much more complex phrase.

5) Some performers pinch bits of other tunes in their solos — it keeps the audience entertained when they spot them.

6) Rock songs will often include an improvised guitar solo — e.g. Led Zeppelin's 'Stairway to Heaven'.

Improvisation Uses Lots of *Different Techniques*

1) Performers use lots of different musical ideas and techniques in their solos
   — it gives them a chance to show off.

2) Improvisations will often be syncopated to make them feel 'jazzy'.
   Triplets and dotted rhythms can help the tunes flow (see p.11).

3) Ornaments (like passing notes and appoggiaturas) make the tunes more exciting
   (see p.35). Blue notes (see p.121) are often used in jazz improvisations.

4) A wide range of dynamics (see p.13) and accents (see p.14) also help keep the solos interesting.

Indian Music Uses *Improvisation* Too

1) Improvisation isn't just used in Western music — it's an important part of Indian music as well.

2) The improvisations are based on a raga — a set of notes (usually between 5 or 8) that are combined to create a particular mood. There are hundreds of different ragas. Each one is named after a different time of day or season and is supposed to create an atmosphere like the time or season it's named after.

3) Raga performances are improvised, but based on traditional tunes and rhythms.
   These are never written down — they are passed on from generation to generation aurally.

4) The improvised melody is often played on an Indian instrument called a sitar (see p.167), but it's sometimes performed by a singer instead. They only use the notes of the raga.

5) The melody is played over a drone — a long held-on note that provides the harmony (see p.169).

These are the notes of the raga vibhasa, a dawn raga. The melody would be improvised using these notes over a drone.

I'll improvise my way through the listening exam...

In all types of improvisation, it's really important that the performer knows their scales (or mode or raga). So even though practising your scales is about as exciting as watching jelly set, it's well worth doing.

Warm-up and Exam Questions

Warm-up Questions

1) Describe each of the following melody structures:

   Conjunct   **Disjunct**   **Triadic**   **Scalic**

2) What are the **three** main sections of a piece in Sonata form?

3) What is a ground bass, and what instruments often play these parts?

4) Give **two** examples of types of music where improvisation is used.

Exam Question

If there are bits you get stuck on in this question, reread the last few pages, then try again.

Play the extract **four** times, leaving a short pause between each playing.

Track 28

a) Here is part of the melody from the extract.

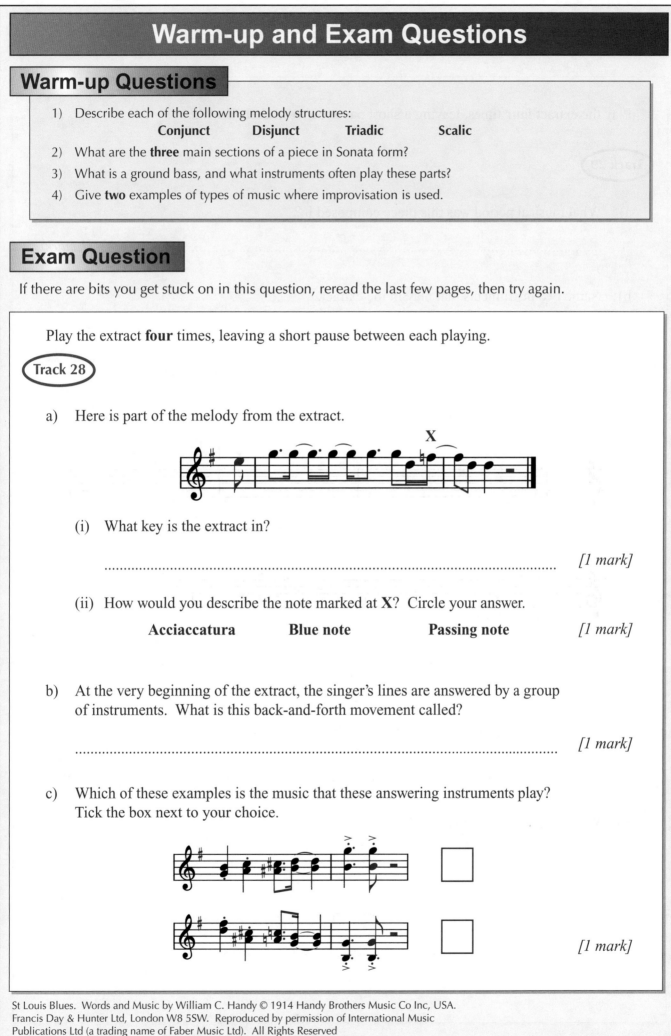

   (i)   What key is the extract in?

   .... *[1 mark]*

   (ii) How would you describe the note marked at **X**? Circle your answer.

   Acciaccatura   **Blue note**   **Passing note**   *[1 mark]*

b) At the very beginning of the extract, the singer's lines are answered by a group of instruments. What is this back-and-forth movement called?

   .... *[1 mark]*

c) Which of these examples is the music that these answering instruments play?
   Tick the box next to your choice.

   [1 mark]

Exam Question

Play the extract **four** times, leaving a short pause between each playing.

Track 29

a) What musical period was this piece composed in?

    .... *[1 mark]*

b) Name two instruments that play in the extract.

    ....

    .... *[2 marks]*

c) The melody at the start of the extract is shown below.

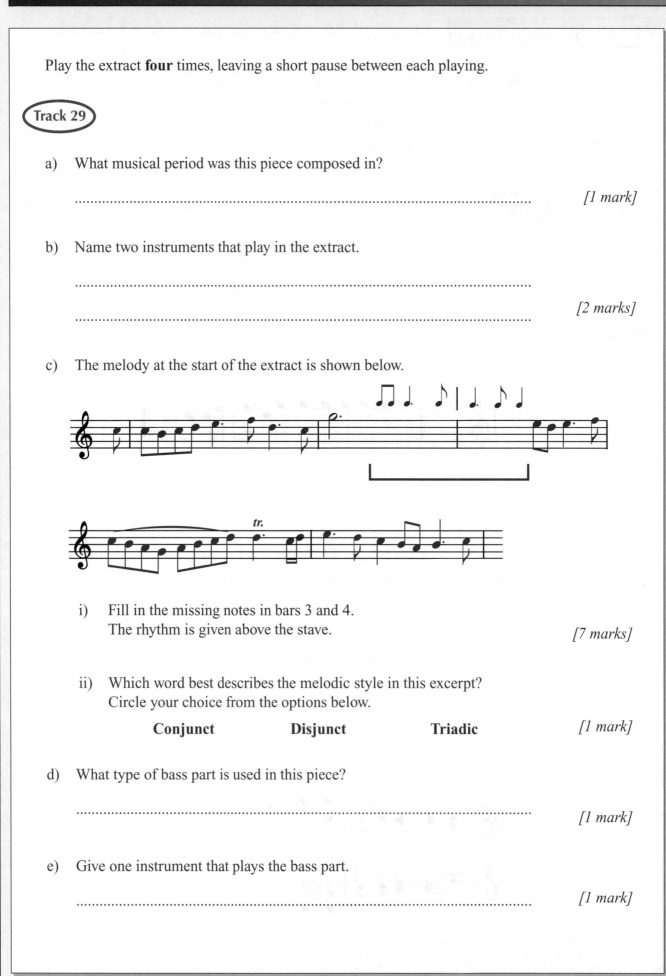

    i) Fill in the missing notes in bars 3 and 4.
        The rhythm is given above the stave. *[7 marks]*

    ii) Which word best describes the melodic style in this excerpt?
        Circle your choice from the options below.

        Conjunct   **Disjunct**   **Triadic**   *[1 mark]*

d) What type of bass part is used in this piece?

    .... *[1 mark]*

e) Give one instrument that plays the bass part.

    .... *[1 mark]*

Revision Summary for Section Three

You need to know a lot more about melodies and structures than being able to whistle a few tunes — you'll need to be familiar with all the terms used in this section so you can use them when you need to describe melodies and musical structures in the exam. If you're not sure about any, go back and have another look over the section. And then to really cement this knowledge into your head, go through these questions until you can answer them without looking back.

1) Explain what is meant by each of the following words that are used to describe melodies:
   a)   conjunct,
   b)   disjunct,
   c)   triadic,
   d)   scalic.

2) What is call and response?

3) Name two types of music that use call and response.

4) Explain what is meant by an arch-shaped melody.

5) What happens in each of the following three different sections in sonata form:
   a)   exposition,
   b)   development,
   c)   recapitulation?

6) Describe minuet and trio form.

7) What is a scherzo?

8) Name two composers who have written scherzos.

9) What's the difference between strophic and through-composed form?

10) Give an example of a type of music that's often written in through-composed form, and explain why this form is used.

11) What's a da capo aria?

12) What is cyclic form?

13) What is basso continuo?

14) Explain how figured bass works.

15) Describe the structure of a ground bass piece.

16) What's a cadenza?

17) Why do pop songs have an introduction?

18) Describe verse-chorus structure.

19) What is a riff?

20) Name three other structures often used in pop songs.

21) Name two different types of music that use a lot of improvisation.

22) Name three different things performers can do to keep improvised solos interesting.

Brass Instruments

You probably know a lot about your instrument. It's also a good idea to know about the instruments other people play so you can understand what they're up to. Brass first.

Brass Instruments are All Made of Metal

1) Brass instruments are horns, trumpets, cornets, trombones and tubas.

2) They're all basically a length of hollow metal tubing with a mouthpiece (the bit you blow into) at one end and a funnel shape (the bell) at the other.

3) The different shapes and sizes of these parts gives each brass instrument a different tone and character.

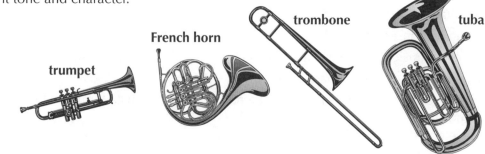

trumpet   French horn   trombone   tuba

You Get a Noise by 'Buzzing' Your Lips

1) To make a sound on a brass instrument, you have to make the air vibrate down the tube.

2) You do it by 'buzzing' your lips into the mouthpiece. You squeeze your lips together, then blow through a tiny gap so you get a buzzing noise.

3) You have to squeeze your lips together tighter to get higher notes.

4) Notes can be slurred (played together smoothly) or tongued (you use your tongue to separate the notes).

Brass Instruments Use Slides and Valves to Change Pitch

1) Squeezing your lips only gets a limited range of notes. To get a decent range, brass instruments use slides (like on a trombone) or valves (like on a trumpet).

2) The slide on a trombone is the U-shaped tube that moves in and out of the main tube. Moving it out makes the tube longer so you get a lower note. Moving it in makes the tube shorter so you get a higher note.

3) Horns, trumpets and cornets use three buttons connected to valves. The valves open and close different sections of the tube to make it longer or shorter. Pressing down the buttons in different combinations gives you all the notes you need.

Brass Players use Mutes to Change the Tone

1) A mute is a kind of bung that's put in the bell of a brass instrument. It's used to make the instrument play more quietly and change the tone. You wouldn't usually use one all the way through a piece — just for a short section.

2) Different shapes and sizes of mute change the tone in different ways, e.g. the wah-wah mute gives the instrument a wah-wah sound.

Brass instruments aren't always made of brass...

If you get brass in a listening test and need to say what instrument it is, remember that the bigger instruments generally play lower notes and the smaller instruments usually play higher notes.

Woodwind Instruments

Some people get woodwind and brass muddled up. If you're one of them, learn the difference.

Woodwind Instruments Used to be Made of Wood

Woodwind instruments got their name because they all use air — wind — to make a sound and once upon a time were all made of wood. Nowadays some are still made of wood. Others are made of plastic or metal. These are the main ones:

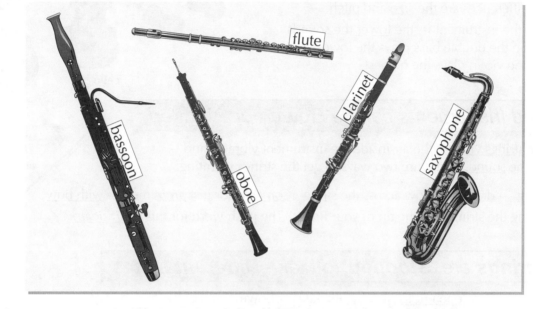

flute

bassoon

oboe

clarinet

saxophone

Woodwind Instruments Make Sound in Different Ways

To get a sound from a wind instrument, you have to make the air in its tube vibrate. There are three different ways woodwind instruments do this:

1) Edge-tone instruments — flutes and piccolos. Air is blown across an oval-shaped hole. The edge of the hole splits the air. This makes it vibrate down the instrument and make the sound.

2) Single-reed instruments — clarinets and saxophones. Air is blown down a mouthpiece which has a reed (a thin slice of wood/reed/plastic) clamped to it. The reed vibrates, making the air in the instrument vibrate, and creating the sound.

3) Double-reed instruments — oboes and bassoons. The air passes between two reeds, tightly bound together and squeezed between the lips. The reeds vibrate and you get a sound.

> Like brass instruments, woodwind instruments can be slurred or tongued as well.

Different Notes are Made by Opening and Closing Holes

1) Wind instruments are covered in keys, springs and levers (or just holes for some instruments). These operate little pads that close and open holes down the instrument.

2) Opening and closing holes effectively makes the instrument longer or shorter. The shorter the tube, the higher the note. The longer the tube, the lower the note.

I can't see the woodwind for the clarinets...

Flutes and saxophones are made of metal but they're still woodwind instruments. If you're still confused remember that woodwind instruments sound more breathy than brass instruments.

Orchestral Strings

Orchestral strings are the <u>heart</u> of the orchestra — or so string players would have you believe.

The **Double Bass**, **Cello**, **Viola** and **Violin** are Very Alike

These are all <u>made</u> and played in a <u>similar way</u>.
The main differences are the <u>size</u> and <u>pitch</u>.

The <u>bigger</u> the instrument is, the <u>lower</u> the sounds it makes. So the double bass plays the lowest notes and the violin plays the highest.

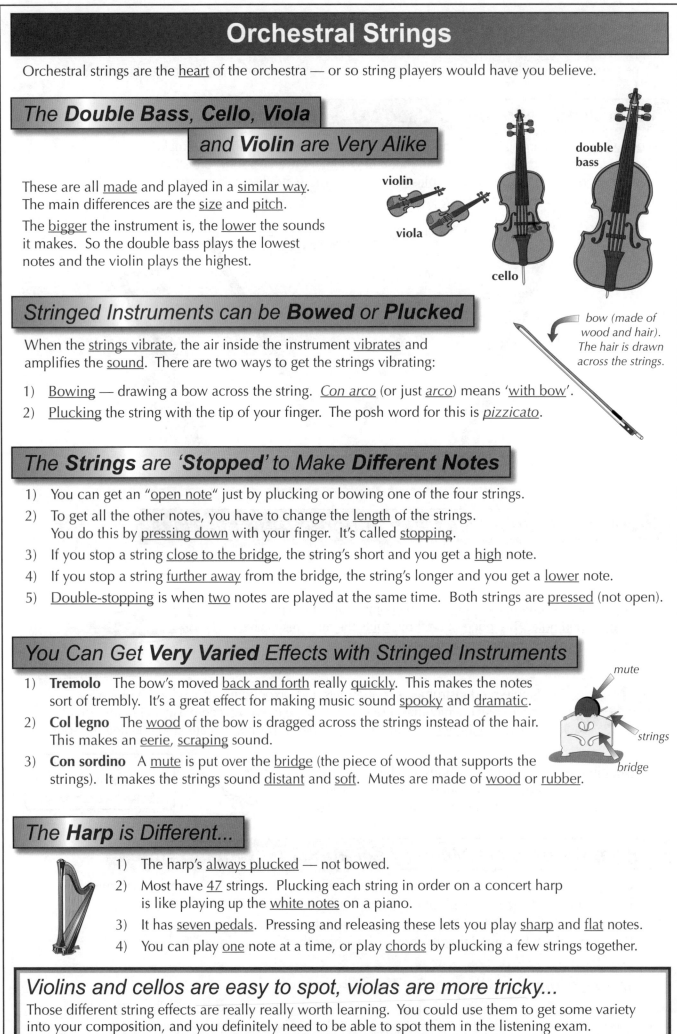

violin

viola

cello

double bass

bow (made of wood and hair). The hair is drawn across the strings.

Stringed Instruments can be **Bowed** or **Plucked**

When the <u>strings vibrate</u>, the air inside the instrument <u>vibrates</u> and amplifies the <u>sound</u>. There are two ways to get the strings vibrating:

1) <u>Bowing</u> — drawing a bow across the string. *Con arco* (or just *arco*) means '<u>with bow</u>'.

2) <u>Plucking</u> the string with the tip of your finger. The posh word for this is *pizzicato*.

The **Strings** are '**Stopped**' to Make **Different Notes**

1) You can get an "<u>open note</u>" just by plucking or bowing one of the four strings.

2) To get all the other notes, you have to change the <u>length</u> of the strings. You do this by <u>pressing down</u> with your finger. It's called <u>stopping</u>.

3) If you stop a string <u>close to the bridge</u>, the string's short and you get a <u>high</u> note.

4) If you stop a string <u>further away</u> from the bridge, the string's longer and you get a <u>lower</u> note.

5) <u>Double-stopping</u> is when <u>two</u> notes are played at the same time. Both strings are <u>pressed</u> (not open).

You Can Get **Very Varied** Effects with Stringed Instruments

1) **Tremolo** The bow's moved <u>back and forth</u> really <u>quickly</u>. This makes the notes sort of trembly. It's a great effect for making music sound <u>spooky</u> and <u>dramatic</u>.

2) **Col legno** The <u>wood</u> of the bow is dragged across the strings instead of the hair. This makes an <u>eerie</u>, <u>scraping</u> sound.

3) **Con sordino** A <u>mute</u> is put over the <u>bridge</u> (the piece of wood that supports the strings). It makes the strings sound <u>distant</u> and <u>soft</u>. Mutes are made of <u>wood</u> or <u>rubber</u>.

mute

strings

bridge

The **Harp** is Different...

1) The harp's <u>always plucked</u> — not bowed.

2) Most have <u>47</u> strings. Plucking each string in order on a concert harp is like playing up the <u>white notes</u> on a piano.

3) It has <u>seven pedals</u>. Pressing and releasing these lets you play <u>sharp</u> and <u>flat</u> notes.

4) You can play <u>one</u> note at a time, or play <u>chords</u> by plucking a few strings together.

Violins and cellos are easy to spot, violas are more tricky...

Those different string effects are really really worth learning. You could use them to get some variety into your composition, and you definitely need to be able to spot them in the listening exam.

Guitars

Guitars are <u>everywhere</u> so it's best to know a bit about how they work.

An *Acoustic Guitar* has a *Hollow Body*

The <u>acoustic guitar</u> makes a sound the same way as the orchestral strings — by vibrating air in its belly.
Slightly different types are used by pop, folk and classical guitarists, but the <u>basic design</u> is similar.

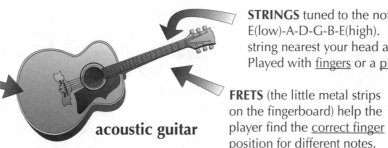

HOLLOW BODY makes the string vibrations <u>resonate</u>, giving a louder sound.

STRINGS tuned to the notes E(low)-A-D-G-B-E(high). Low E is the string nearest your head as you're playing. Played with <u>fingers</u> or a <u>plectrum</u>.

FRETS (the little metal strips on the fingerboard) help the player find the <u>correct finger position</u> for different notes.

acoustic guitar

There are three different kinds of acoustic guitar:

1) The <u>classical</u> or <u>Spanish</u> guitar — has nylon strings (the thickest three are covered in fine wire) and a thick neck.

2) The <u>acoustic guitar</u> — has <u>steel strings</u> and is used mainly in pop and folk music. Its neck is <u>thinner</u> and is <u>strengthened</u> with a metal bar — this supports the higher tension created by the steel strings.

3) The <u>12-stringed guitar</u> — often used in folk music. There are two of each string — this gives a 'thicker' sound which works well for accompanying singing.

Electric Guitars Use an Amplifier and a Loudspeaker

1) An electric guitar has <u>six strings</u>, just like an acoustic guitar, and is <u>played</u> in a similar way.

2) The main difference is that an electric guitar has a <u>solid body</u>. The sound's made louder <u>electrically</u>, using an <u>amplifier</u> and a <u>loudspeaker</u>.

3) A <u>combo</u> — short for combination — is an <u>amplifier</u> and <u>loudspeaker</u> '<u>all in one</u>'.

electric guitar

The Bass Guitar has Four Strings

1) The bass guitar works like a guitar except it usually has <u>four strings</u>, not six.

2) They're tuned to the notes <u>E-A-D-G</u> (from lowest note to highest).

3) It's <u>lower pitched</u> than other guitars because it has <u>thicker and longer</u> strings.

4) Most bass guitars have frets, but there are some — imaginatively named <u>fretless basses</u> — that don't.

Like ordinary guitars, you can get electric or acoustic basses.

Guitar Strings are Picked or Strummed

1) Plucking <u>one string</u> at a time is called <u>picking</u>. <u>Classical</u> and <u>lead guitarists</u> pick the notes of a <u>melody</u>. <u>Bass</u> guitarists almost <u>always</u> pick out the individual notes of a bass line. They <u>hardly ever strum</u>.

2) Playing <u>two or more</u> strings at a time in a sweeping movement is called <u>strumming</u>. It's how <u>chords</u> are usually played. <u>Pop</u> and <u>folk guitarists</u> tend to play <u>accompaniments</u> rather than tunes, so they do more strumming than picking.

3) A <u>plectrum</u> is a small, flat piece of plastic that guitarists can use to pluck or strum with — it works like an extra-long fingernail.

The guitar's a really popular instrument...

Learn those different <u>playing techniques</u> and if you hear them in the exam, use the proper words — <u>picking</u> and <u>strumming</u> — to describe them. Examiners love it when you talk their language.

Keyboard Instruments

The actual <u>keyboard</u> looks much the same on most keyboard instruments, but the wires and mysterious levers <u>inside</u> vary quite a bit. That means the <u>sounds</u> they make vary too.

Harpsichords, Virginals and Clavichords Came First

harpsichord

1) Harpsichords were invented long before pianos. They're still played today but they were <u>most popular</u> in the <u>Baroque</u> and <u>early Classical</u> periods.

2) Harpsichords have quite a <u>tinny</u>, <u>string</u> sound. When you press a key a string inside is <u>plucked</u> by a lever. You can't vary the <u>strength</u> of the pluck, so you <u>can't</u> vary the <u>dynamics</u>.

3) A <u>virginal</u> is a miniature table-top version of a harpsichord. In the sixteenth century, virginals were really popular in England.

4) The <u>clavichord</u> is another early keyboard instrument. Clavichords are small and have a <u>soft</u> sound. The strings are <u>struck</u> with hammers (called "blades"), not plucked, so you can vary the dynamics a little bit.

*The **Most Popular** Keyboard Instrument Now is the **Piano***

1) The piano was invented around <u>1700</u>. The <u>technology</u> is <u>more sophisticated</u> than it was in earlier keyboard instruments. When a key's pressed, a hammer hits the strings. The <u>harder</u> you hit the key, the <u>harder</u> the hammer hits the strings and the <u>louder</u> the note — there's a big range of <u>dynamics</u>.

2) Pianos have a wide range of <u>notes</u> — up to <u>seven and a half octaves</u>.

3) Pianos have <u>pedals</u> that let you change the sound in different ways.

The <u>soft</u> pedal on the left <u>mutes</u> the strings, making a softer sound.

The <u>sustain</u> pedal on the right <u>lifts</u> all the <u>dampers</u>. This lets the sound <u>ring on</u> until you release the pedal.

<u>Grand pianos</u> have a <u>middle pedal</u> too. This lets the player <u>choose</u> which notes to sustain. Modern pianos might have an extra mute pedal for <u>very quiet</u> practising.

*Traditional Organs Use **Pumped Air** to Make Sound*

1) The traditional organ — the <u>massive instrument</u> with hundreds of metal pipes that you see at the back of churches and concert halls — is one of the most <u>complicated</u> instruments ever designed.

2) Sound is made by <u>blowing air</u> through sets of pipes called <u>ranks</u>. The air is pumped in by <u>hand</u>, <u>foot</u> or, on more recent organs, <u>electric pumps</u>.

3) The pipes are controlled by <u>keyboards</u>, called <u>manuals</u>, and lots of <u>pedals</u> which make a keyboard for the player's feet.

4) <u>Pressing</u> a key or pedal lets air pass through one of the pipes and play a note. <u>Longer</u> pipes make <u>lower</u> notes. <u>Shorter</u> pipes make <u>higher</u> notes.

5) Organs can play <u>different types of sound</u> by using differently designed pipes. Buttons called <u>stops</u> are used to select the different pipes. One stop might select pipes that make a <u>trumpet</u> sound, another might select a <u>flute</u> sound...

6) Modern <u>electronic organs</u> don't have pipes. Sound is produced <u>electronically</u> instead. These organs are much <u>smaller</u> and <u>cheaper</u> to build.

You've got to learn it all...

Harpsichords sound <u>jangly</u> compared to pianos so they're easy to tell apart. It's also fairly easy to spot an organ sound, though it's harder to tell whether it's "real" or electronic.

Percussion

A percussion instrument is anything you have to <u>hit</u> or <u>shake</u> to get a sound out of it. There are <u>two</u> <u>types</u>: those that play tunes are called <u>tuned percussion</u>, and the ones you just hit are <u>untuned</u>.

Tuned Percussion Can Play **Different Notes**

XYLOPHONES have <u>wooden</u> bars. The sound is '<u>woody</u>'.

GLOCKENSPIEL — Looks a bit like a xylophone but the bars are made of <u>metal</u>. Sounds <u>tinkly</u> and <u>bell-like</u>.

CELESTA — a bit like a glockenspiel except that you use a <u>keyboard</u> instead of whacking it with a hammer.

TUBULAR BELLS — Each of the <u>hollow steel tubes</u> plays a different note. Sounds a bit like <u>church bells</u>.

TIMPANI — also called <u>kettledrums</u>.

The handles on the side or the foot pedal can be used to tighten or relax the skin, giving <u>different notes</u>.

VIBRAPHONE — This is like a <u>giant glockenspiel</u>. There are long tubes called <u>resonators</u> below the bars to make the notes <u>louder</u> and <u>richer</u>. <u>Electric fans</u> can make the notes <u>pulsate</u>, giving a warm and gentle sound.

There are **Hundreds** of **Untuned Percussion** Instruments

<u>Untuned percussion</u> includes any instrument that'll <u>make a noise</u> — but <u>can't</u> play a tune. These are the instruments that are used for <u>pure rhythm</u>. It's pretty much <u>impossible</u> to learn <u>every</u> untuned percussion instrument, but try and remember the names of these.

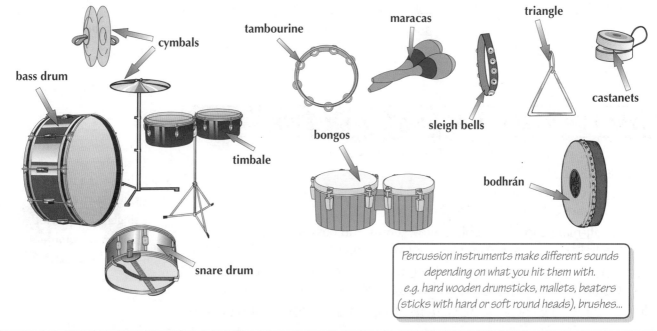

cymbals

bass drum

tambourine

maracas

triangle

castanets

timbale

sleigh bells

bongos

snare drum

bodhrán

Percussion instruments make different sounds depending on what you hit them with. e.g. hard wooden drumsticks, mallets, beaters (sticks with hard or soft round heads), brushes...

You need to learn the names of every instrument you see...

In a band, the drummer's job is to make the song sound like it's going somewhere and keep everyone in time. In an orchestra, the percussion's more there to add <u>special effects</u> — like thundery drum rolls on the timpani or huge clashes of the cymbals. Just make sure you're not sitting right in front of them.

The Voice

There are special names for male and female <u>voices</u> and <u>groups</u> of voices.

Female Singers are Soprano, Alto or Mezzo-Soprano

1) A <u>high</u> female voice is called a <u>soprano</u>. The main female parts in operas are sung by sopranos.

2) A <u>lower</u> female voice is called an <u>alto</u> — short for <u>contralto</u>.

3) <u>Mezzo-sopranos</u> sing in the <u>top</u> part of the <u>alto</u> range and the <u>bottom</u> part of the <u>soprano</u> range.

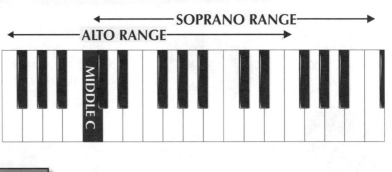

Male Voices are Tenor or Bass

1) <u>Higher</u> male voices are called <u>tenors</u>.

2) <u>Low</u> male voices are called <u>basses</u> (it's pronounced "bases").

3) <u>Baritones</u> sing the <u>top</u> part of the <u>bass</u> range and the <u>bottom</u> part of the <u>tenor</u> range.

4) Men who sing in the <u>female vocal range</u> are called <u>counter-tenors</u>.

5) Some tenors, baritones and basses can push their voices <u>higher</u> to sing some of the same notes as a soprano. This is called <u>falsetto</u> singing.

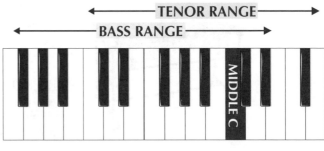

Children's Voices are Either Treble or Alto

1) A <u>high child's</u> voice in the <u>same range</u> as a <u>soprano</u> is called a <u>treble</u>.

2) A <u>low child's</u> voice is called an <u>alto</u>. They sing in exactly the <u>same range</u> as an adult alto.

3) Girls' voices don't change much as they get older. Boys' voices <u>drop</u> to a <u>lower range</u> when they hit puberty.

When Several Voices Sing Each Part It's a Choir

1) A <u>choir</u> is a group of singers. Each part is performed by <u>more than one</u> singer.

2) A <u>mixed voice choir</u> has sopranos, altos, tenors and basses. These are called <u>S.A.T.B.</u> for short.

3) An <u>all-male choir</u> has trebles, altos, tenors and basses — the treble range is the same as a soprano range, so it's basically S.A.T.B.

4) A <u>male voice choir</u> is slightly different — it tends to have two groups of <u>tenors</u>, as well as <u>baritones</u> and <u>basses</u>. No-one sings the higher voice parts.

5) An <u>all-female choir</u> has <u>two groups of sopranos</u> and <u>two groups of altos</u>.

These are the names for smaller groups:
2 singers = a **duet**
3 singers = a **trio**
4 singers = a **quartet**
5 singers = a **quintet**
6 singers = a **sextet**

No excuses — get on and learn all the voices...

The different voices don't just sound different in pitch — they've got different characters too, e.g. sopranos usually sound very clear and glassy, and basses sound more rich and booming.

Wind, Brass and Jazz Bands

In your listening exam, you'll get marks for saying what type of group's playing.
<u>Wind</u>, <u>jazz</u> and <u>brass</u> bands can sound quite <u>similar</u>, so make sure you know the differences.

Wind Bands have Woodwind, Brass and Percussion

1) Wind bands are <u>largish groups</u>, made up of 'wind' instruments —
   woodwind and brass — and percussion instruments.
2) There's <u>no string section</u>. If there was it would be an orchestra...
3) <u>Military bands</u> — the ones that play as they march along — are wind bands.

Brass Bands have Brass and Percussion

1) A brass band is a group of <u>brass</u> and <u>percussion</u> instruments.
2) A typical brass band would have <u>cornets</u>, <u>flugelhorns</u>, <u>tenor</u> and <u>baritone horns</u>, <u>tenor</u> and <u>bass trombones</u>, <u>euphoniums</u> and <u>tubas</u>.
3) The exact <u>percussion instruments</u> depend on the piece being played.
4) Brass bands have been popular in <u>England</u> for <u>years</u>.
5) <u>Contests</u> are organised through the year to find out which bands are 'best'.
   There's a <u>league system</u> similar to football. The divisions are called <u>sections</u>.
   There are <u>five sections</u> and bands are <u>promoted</u> and <u>demoted</u> each year
   depending on how they do at the <u>regional</u> and <u>national</u> contests.

Jazz Bands are Quite Varied

1) Jazz bands have <u>no fixed set of instruments</u>.
2) Small jazz groups are known as <u>combos</u>. A typical combo
   might include a <u>trumpet</u>, <u>trombone</u>, <u>clarinet</u>, <u>saxophone</u>, <u>piano</u>,
   <u>banjo</u>, <u>double bass</u> and <u>drum kit</u> — but there's no fixed rule.
   Combos play in small venues like <u>clubs</u> and <u>bars</u>.
3) Larger jazz bands are known as <u>big bands</u> or <u>swing bands</u>. Instruments are doubled and tripled
   up so you get a <u>much bigger sound</u>. Big bands were really popular in the <u>1930s</u> and <u>1940s</u>.
   They played live at <u>dance halls</u>.
4) A large jazz band with a string section is called a <u>jazz orchestra</u>.

Jazz Bands have a Rhythm Section and a Front Line

In a jazz band, players are either in the <u>rhythm section</u> or the <u>front line</u>.

1) The <u>rhythm section</u> is the instruments responsible for <u>keeping the beat</u> and
   <u>adding the harmony parts</u>. The rhythm section's usually made up of the
   <u>drum kit</u> with a <u>double</u> or <u>electric bass</u>, <u>electric guitar</u> and <u>piano</u>.
2) The instruments that <u>play the melody</u> are the <u>front line</u>. This is usually
   <u>clarinets</u>, <u>saxophones</u> and <u>trumpets</u>, but could also be guitar or violin.

Keep at it — there are only a few more instruments to go...

The examiners are really keen on <u>multiple-choice</u> questions asking what kind of band's playing.
Recognising music styles helps — a jazz band sounds nothing like a brass band.

Chamber Music

Chamber music is music composed for small groups and it's pretty formal stuff.

Chamber Music was Originally 'Home Entertainment'

1) 'Chamber' is an old word for a room in a posh building like a palace or a mansion.

2) Rich people could afford to pay musicians to come and play in their 'chambers'. Musical families could play the music for themselves. The music written for these private performances is what's called chamber music.

3) Nowadays, you're more likely to hear chamber music in a concert hall or on a CD than live at someone's house. Let's face it — most people haven't got the cash to hire musicians for the evening and they've now got stereos instead.

Chamber Music is Played by Small Groups

1) The rooms where musicians came to play were nice and big — but not enormous. Limited space meant that chamber music was written for a small number of musicians — between two and eight.

2) There's a name for each size of group:

Duet = two players
Trio = three players
Quartet = four players
Quintet = five players
Sextet = six players
Septet = seven players
Octet = eight players

Have a look at the names for singing groups on p.64 — they're much the same.

3) With so few people in chamber groups, you don't need a conductor. Instead, one of the players leads. The others have to watch and listen carefully, to make sure the timing, dynamics and interpretation are right.

4) Each part in the music is played by just one person.

Some Chamber Groups are Extra-Popular with Composers

Chamber music is written more often for some instrumental groups than others.
These are some of the most popular types of chamber group:

String trio	— violin, viola, cello
String quartet	— first violin, second violin, viola, cello
Piano trio	— piano, violin, cello (not three pianos)
Clarinet quintet	— clarinet, first violin, second violin, viola, cello (not five clarinets)
Wind quintet	— usually flute, oboe, clarinet, horn and bassoon

Chamber groups are small...

Learn the names for all the different chamber groups. Keep a special eye out for the piano trio and clarinet quintet — they're not what you'd expect. And finally, don't forget there's no conductor.

The Orchestra

If you go to a classical concert, more often than not there'll be an <u>orchestra</u> up there on stage. Loads and loads of classical music has been written for orchestras.

A **Modern Orchestra** has **Four** Sections

If you go and see a <u>modern symphony orchestra</u>, it'll have <u>four sections</u> of instruments — strings (p.60), woodwind (p.59), brass (p.58) and percussion (p.63). The strings, woodwind, brass and percussion always sit in the <u>same places</u>.

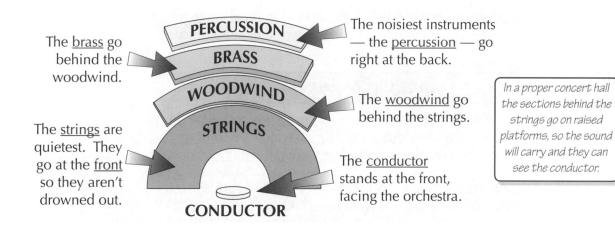

The <u>brass</u> go behind the woodwind.

The noisiest instruments — the <u>percussion</u> — go right at the back.

The <u>woodwind</u> go behind the strings.

The <u>strings</u> are quietest. They go at the <u>front</u> so they aren't drowned out.

The <u>conductor</u> stands at the front, facing the orchestra.

In a proper concert hall the sections behind the strings go on raised platforms, so the sound will carry and they can see the conductor.

The **Conductor** has a **Complete Overview**

1) The conductor has a <u>score</u> — a version of the piece with <u>all the parts</u>. The <u>parts</u> are arranged in a <u>standard order</u>, one on top of the other, so that it's easy to see what any part is doing at any time. Woodwind parts are written at the <u>top</u>, followed by brass, percussion, and strings at the <u>bottom</u>.

2) The conductor <u>controls the tempo</u> by beating time with their hands, or a <u>baton</u> — a pointy white stick that's easy to see. There's a different way of beating time for each time signature.

3) The conductor '<u>cues in</u>' musicians — especially helpful for brass and percussion, who sometimes don't play anything for hundreds of bars, then suddenly have to play a really loud, important bit.

4) The conductor <u>interprets</u> the music. A conductor can decide whether to play one bit louder than another, whether to play a section in a moody or a magical way, and whether to make a piece sound very smooth or very edgy. They're a bit like a <u>film director</u> deciding the best way to <u>tell a story</u>.

An **Orchestra** is Any **Large Group with Strings**

<u>Symphony orchestras</u> (above) are the biggest type of orchestra. There are <u>other</u> smaller kinds too:

1) <u>String orchestra</u> — an orchestra with <u>stringed instruments</u> only.

2) <u>Chamber orchestra</u> — a <u>mini-orchestra</u>. It has a small string section, a wind and brass section with <u>one or two</u> of each instrument (but <u>no</u> tubas or trombones) and a small percussion section.

3) <u>Jazz orchestra</u> — a largish jazz group with an added string section.

You have to do what the conductor tells you...

Copy out the diagram of the orchestra, but don't copy the labels. Close the book and see if you can fill in the different instrument sections in the right places. Then learn all about the conductor.

Music Technology

Modern <u>technological</u> and '<u>virtual</u>' instruments mean that you can make a lot more sounds nowadays.

MIDI lets you **Connect** *Electronic Musical Instruments*

1) <u>MIDI</u> was invented in 1983. It stands for <u>Musical Instrument Digital Interface</u>. It's a way of connecting different electronic instruments.

2) MIDI equipment is connected by <u>MIDI cables</u>.

3) <u>MIDI data</u> is digital information (i.e. in <u>zeroes</u> and <u>ones</u>). It's sent down the MIDI cables. MIDI instruments turn MIDI information into sound (or vice versa).

4) One important <u>advantage</u> of MIDI is that it's allowed <u>musical equipment</u> to be <u>linked</u> with <u>computers</u>, opening up a whole <u>new world</u> of music-making.

Synthesizers Let You **Make New Sounds**

<u>Synthesizers</u> come in <u>different forms</u> — some have <u>keyboards</u> and some <u>don't</u>. The most common ones today are <u>virtual synthesizers</u>, which are <u>software based</u> (see below). The <u>point</u> of them is to let you <u>create</u> sounds. There are <u>different types</u> of synthesizers:

1) <u>Analogue synthesizers</u> were mainly made in the <u>70s</u> and <u>early 80s</u>. They've often got lots of <u>knobs</u> and <u>sliders</u> — you use these to <u>change</u> the sound.

2) <u>Digital synthesizers</u> started to be popular in the <u>80s</u>. Most modern synthesizers are digital, though some of them try to <u>mimic</u> analogue synths. Digital synths usually have <u>fewer</u> knobs and sliders than analogue ones.

3) <u>Software synths</u> started to become popular in the <u>late 90s</u>. Software synths are <u>computer programs</u> (often <u>linked</u> to a <u>sequencer</u> — see below). They often have <u>graphical sliders</u> and <u>knobs</u> that you can move with a <u>mouse</u>. Some of them try to be like analogue and early digital synthesizers. They also try to <u>recreate</u> classic <u>electric instruments</u> like the <u>Hammond organ</u>.

Sequencers Let You **Record**, **Edit** and **Replay** *Music*

1) <u>Sequencer</u> is the posh word for equipment that can <u>record</u>, <u>edit</u> (mess about with) and <u>replay</u> music stored as <u>MIDI</u> or <u>audio</u> information. Modern sequencers are usually <u>computer programs</u>.

2) Many lines (<u>tracks</u>) of music can be <u>played back</u> at the same time.

3) Each track can be given its own set of <u>instructions</u>, e.g. instrument or volume levels.

4) One of the big <u>advantages</u> of a sequencer is that it shows your music as actual <u>notation</u> or as <u>representative boxes</u> — this makes it much easier to change and try out new ideas.

5) Nowadays, most sequencers can record <u>audio</u> (real sounds) as well as the <u>MIDI</u> stuff so you can create <u>MIDI music</u> and then record your own <u>voice</u> or <u>instruments</u> along with it. Most music is recorded using sequencers now.

6) Modern sequencing programs often include <u>synthesizers</u> and <u>samplers</u> as well.

7) <u>Drum machines</u> are special sequencers that play back rhythm patterns using built-in drum sounds.

This can all be a bit confusing...

Some of this stuff is quite <u>technical</u> — but don't panic. You <u>don't</u> need to have an <u>in-depth</u> <u>understanding</u> of how the different types of technology work — as long as you know <u>what</u> they do and what people <u>use them for</u>. You can even have a go at using them in your <u>compositions</u>.

Music Technology

Sampling is a very popular way of putting different sounds into your music.
Samples can be fiddled with and looped to make long repeated sections.

Samplers let you 'Pinch' Other People's Sounds

1) A sampler is a piece of equipment that can record, process (change) and play back bits of sound.

2) These sections of sound are called samples.

3) Samplers are often used to take a bit of a piece of music that's already been recorded to use in some new music.

4) You can sample anything from instruments to birdsong — even weird things like a car horn.

5) Today, samplers are most often used to reproduce the sound of real instruments, such as strings or piano. Most pop music is sampled.

6) Pop stars often use samples of other people's music in their own music — anything from other pop songs to bits from Classical pieces. For example:

- Madonna used a sample of Abba's 'Gimme! Gimme! Gimme! (A Man After Midnight)' in her 2005 hit 'Hung Up'.
- Take That sampled 'Dies Irae' from Verdi's *Requiem* in 'Never Forget' (1995).
- Dizzee Rascal used a sample of 'So You Wanna Be a Boxer' (from *Bugsy Malone*) in his song 'Wanna Be' in 2007.

Samples Can be Added to Other Pieces

1) You don't have to create a piece made up entirely of samples — you can just add one or two, or use a whole range to create a collage of sound. The collage can then be put over the top of a repeating drum and bass loop.

2) DJs and producers often do this when they make a dance remix of a piece.

> REMIX is a term used for a different version of a piece of music.
> They're often used to turn pop or rock tunes into dance music
> — e.g. by speeding them up and giving them a fast drum beat.

3) Samples can be added to a piece by over-dubbing — adding tracks over the top of other tracks. You can record a drum track, then overlay the guitar part, then the vocal part, etc.

DJs Choose, Play and Alter Music

1) DJs (disc jockeys) choose which tracks (lines of music) to play, and change bits of them (e.g. by adding samples). Some DJs also rap over the top of the music.

2) DJs play music in clubs and on the radio.

3) At a live performance in a club, the DJ sometimes adds extra sounds using samples, keyboards or a drum machine to build the piece up.

4) DJs use a mixing desk to combine different tracks and add extra sounds to the music, and a set of decks to play their music.

5) The amplification is important — DJs need to make sure the right parts stand out, and that all parts can be heard. The amplification can be changed in live performances.

The dance remix of Beethoven's 5th was a big hit...

Again, there's lots of technical bits on this page. You might choose to use some samples in your own compositions, but even if you don't, you need to know how other people (like DJs) might use them.

Timbre

When you're listening to music, you can pick out individual instruments because of their unique sound — e.g. a trumpet sounds nothing like a violin. This is all down to a little thing called timbre.

Every Instrument Has its Own *Timbre*

1) Timbre is the type of sound that different instruments make. It's also known as tone colour.

2) Musical notes (and all sounds) are made by vibrations. Different instruments produce vibrations in different ways. For example, on a string instrument, the bow is drawn across the string to make it vibrate. On a brass instrument the vibrations are produced when the player 'buzzes' their lips. The different vibrations make the timbres different.

3) The size and material of the instrument alter the timbre as well — e.g. a cello has a different timbre to a violin because it's bigger, and wooden flutes sound different from metal ones.

4) Timbre can be altered by changing the dynamics and articulation.

Instruments From the *Same Family* Have *Similar Timbres*

Even though each instrument has a unique timbre, it can still sometimes be hard to tell ones from the same family apart. Different families of instruments change the timbre in different ways:

STRING INSTRUMENTS

- String instruments (like the violin, viola, cello and double bass) have a warm sound. Notes are produced by making the strings vibrate, either using a bow or the fingers.
- All string instruments can be played *con arco* (with a bow), *pizzicato* (plucked), *con sordino* (muted) or *sul ponticello* (close to the bridge).
- Double stopping is when two strings are pressed at the same time, so two notes can be played at once.
- Tremolo is a very fast trill between notes — it sounds like trembling.

PIANO

- When you press the keys, a hammer hits the strings inside the piano, making them vibrate.
- The timbre of the piano can be changed by using the soft or sustain pedals.

There's more on families of instruments and types of ensembles on pages 58-67.

WOODWIND INSTRUMENTS

- Wind instruments (e.g. flute, clarinet, oboe and bassoon) have a soft, mellow sound.
- Edge-tone instruments (e.g. flutes) make a softer, breathier sound than reed instruments (e.g. clarinets).
- Clarinets and oboes can alter their timbre by using a technique called 'bells up', where the player points the end of the instrument upwards. This produces a harsher sound.

BRASS INSTRUMENTS

- Brass instruments (like the trumpet, French horn, trombone and tuba) have a bright, metallic sound.
- Playing with a mute (*con sordino*) can change the timbre.

PERCUSSION INSTRUMENTS

- Percussion instruments (e.g. drums and xylophones) make a sound when they're struck.
- What you hit them with can change the timbre — e.g. whether you use sticks, brushes or your hands.

SINGERS

- Singers produce notes when their vocal chords vibrate.
- The speed that they vibrate changes the pitch and the timbre — e.g. bass voices sound very different to sopranos.
- Techniques like vibrato (making the note wobble) can give a richer sound.
- Falsetto singing produces a much thinner sound.

I'm picking up good vibrations...

You may be asked to describe the timbre of different instruments that crop up in your exam.

Timbre

Electronic effects can be used to alter the timbre of some instruments.

There are Lots of Different Guitar Effects

1) There are loads of different ways to change the sound of an electric guitar.
2) These effects are really popular with rock bands, especially during guitar solos.
3) Guitarists use pedals (e.g. a wah-wah pedal) to alter the tone or pitch.
4) They create effects like:

- **DISTORTION** distorts the sound.
- **REVERB** adds an echo to the sound.
- **CHORUS** creates a slightly delayed copy of the original sound and combines the two together, making it sound as if there's more than one player or singer.
- **PHASER** creates a 'whooshing' effect (a bit like the noise an aeroplane flying overhead makes).
- **FLANGER** similar to a phaser, but makes a more intense sound. It's used a lot in sci-fi programmes.
- **PITCH SHIFTING** used to bend the natural note or add another harmony.
- **OCTAVE EFFECTS** creates octaves above or below the note being played.

Synthesised Sounds have Different Timbres to Real Sounds

1) The natural sound of an instrument can be digitally reproduced to create a synthesised sound.
2) Electronic keyboards have different settings, so they can be made to sound like pretty much any instrument, from violins to percussion.

One big difference between real and synthesised sounds is what happens to the timbre when the volume changes. When a real instrument is played louder, it has a different timbre to when it's played quietly. However, a synthesised sound has the same timbre at any volume — it's just the loudness that changes.

Sampling Uses Recordings of Real Instruments

1) The most effective way to recreate the sounds of real instruments is to use sampling.
2) Sampling is where you record an instrument and use the recording (called a sample) in your music.
3) The samples can be altered to create different effects — there are lots of different computer programs that help you do this.
4) Samples can be looped (played over and over again — see p.159), and other samples can be added over the top.
5) Most electronic music produced today uses looping, especially drum patterns.
6) It's not just instruments that can be sampled — you can take samples of anything you like, e.g. traffic noises or doorbells.
7) Lots of pop songs use samples — Kanye West sampled Ray Charles' 'I Got A Woman' in his 2005 hit 'Gold Digger'.

I'd like a sample of that cake please...
Modern pop (and often rock) songs will use really different timbres of sounds to make them stand out from the crowd. Sampling is also often used in dance and R 'n B music to create a catchy hook.

Warm-up and Exam Questions

The questions on these pages are great for finding out what you know — don't ignore them.

Warm-up Questions

1) For each of the words below name an instrument that links with the word:

         slide   **single reed**   **double reed**   **pizzicato**   **wooden bars**

2) Explain each of these words and phrases:

         tremolo   **con sordino**   **tenor**   **falsetto**

3) Explain the difference between a military band, a brass band and a jazz band.

4) List all the instruments that play in a piano trio and a clarinet quintet.

5) Define the following terms:

         MIDI   **sampler**   **remix**   **sequencer**

6) In which period was the harpsichord the most popular keyboard instrument?

7) Name the **three** main types of guitar and briefly describe each of them.

Exam Question

Brush up on your exam technique with this question.

This question is about two extracts, Track 30 and Track 31.
First play Track 30 **three** times, leaving a short pause for writing time between each playing.

Track 30

a) Name the solo woodwind instrument that plays at the beginning.

.... *[1 mark]*

b) What is the other instrument that plays in the extract?

.... *[1 mark]*

Exam Question

c) Tick **one** box to indicate which shape best represents the opening of the melody played by the solo instrument.

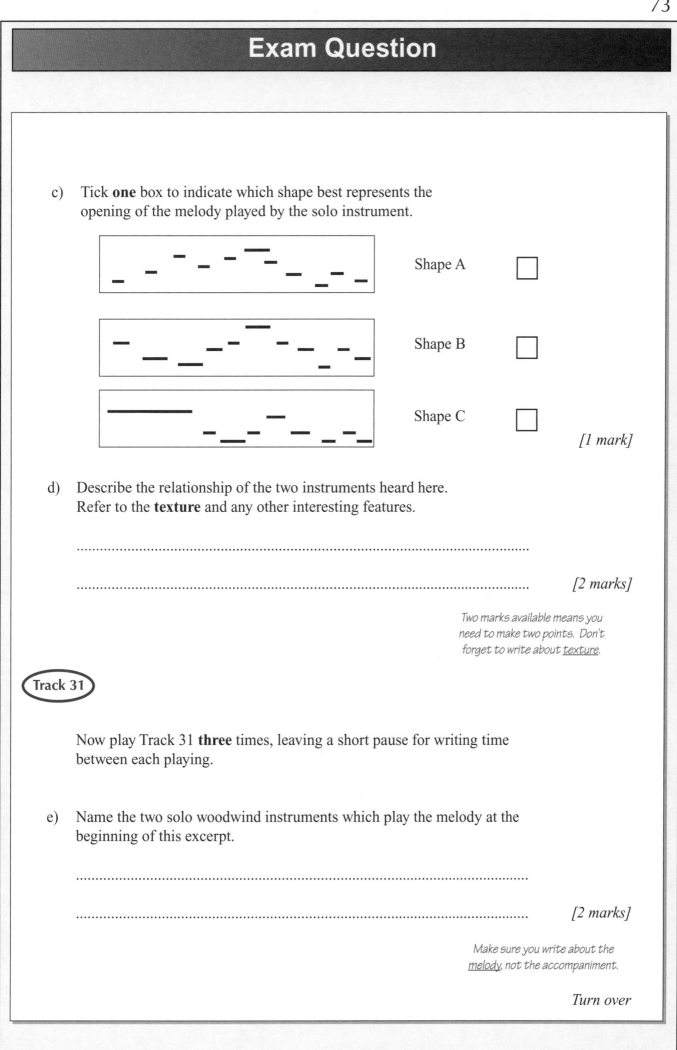

Shape A ☐

Shape B ☐

Shape C ☐

[1 mark]

d) Describe the relationship of the two instruments heard here. Refer to the **texture** and any other interesting features.

....

.... *[2 marks]*

Two marks available means you need to make two points. Don't forget to write about <u>texture</u>.

Track 31

Now play Track 31 **three** times, leaving a short pause for writing time between each playing.

e) Name the two solo woodwind instruments which play the melody at the beginning of this excerpt.

....

.... *[2 marks]*

Make sure you write about the <u>melody</u>, not the accompaniment.

Turn over

Exam Question

f) Name the family of instruments playing throughout this excerpt.

.... *[1 mark]*

g) Ring the word that describes the scale used throughout the excerpt.

major   **minor**   **chromatic**   *[1 mark]*

h) Tick one of the following to represent the backing melody played by the two wind instruments.

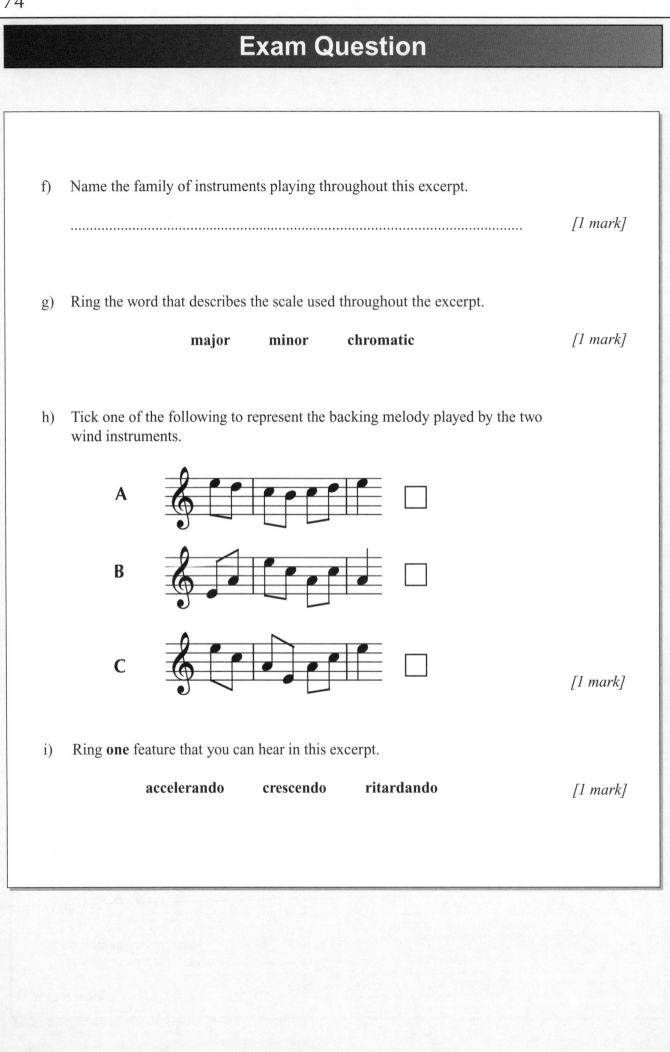

i) Ring **one** feature that you can hear in this excerpt.

accelerando   **crescendo**   **ritardando**   *[1 mark]*

Revision Summary for Section Four

This section should be easy where it's talking about your own instruments. Don't ignore the other instruments. You'll need to know enough about them to be able to describe them in the listening test. And you might need to write parts for other instruments for your composition — it'll be a big help to know what they can and can't do. Go through the questions and check you can answer them all.

1) Name three brass instruments.

2) How do you vary the pitch on a brass instrument?

3) Are all woodwind instruments made of wood?

4) Name three woodwind instruments.

5) What are the three different mouthpieces used on woodwind instruments called? How do they work?

6) What are all those little keys, springs and levers for on a woodwind instrument?

7) What's the smallest orchestral string instrument?

8) What's the biggest string instrument that you play with a bow?

9) What makes a harp different from the other string instruments? Give three differences.

10) Where would you put a mute on a bowed string instrument and what effect would it have?

11) How do you make different notes on a string instrument?

12) How many strings are there on:
   a) an acoustic guitar   b) an electric guitar   c) a bass guitar?

13) What do you call those metal bits on the fingerboard of a guitar? Do you get them on a bass?

14) What's the proper word for twanging a guitar string with a plectrum?

15) Name three different keyboard instruments.

16) What's the biggest type of keyboard instrument?

17) What's the most popular keyboard instrument?

18) How could you tell you were listening to a church organ and not a harpsichord?

19) Name three tuned percussion instruments and six untuned percussion instruments.

20) What's the highest type of singing voice?

21) What's the lowest type of singing voice?

22) What do you call a boy's voice when it's got the same range as a soprano?

23) How can you tell the difference between a wind band and a brass band?

24) How can you tell the difference between a wind band and a jazz orchestra?

25) What are the two sections of a jazz orchestra called, and what are their jobs?

26) Why's chamber music called chamber music?

27) How many people are there in: a) a trio   b) a sextet   c) a quartet   d) an octet?

28) How many clarinets are there in a clarinet quintet?

29) Sketch a plan of a standard symphony orchestra. Label the different sections and the conductor.

30) What sections are there in a string orchestra, chamber orchestra and jazz orchestra?

31) How is MIDI information stored?

32) What do sequencers do?

33) What are samples? How can they be used in tracks?

34) Explain how the sound is produced on:
   a) a string instrument   b) a piano   c) a brass instrument?

35) Name four different guitar effects.

The Great Choral Classics

Choirs have been around for ages. They vary in size from just a <u>few</u> singers to <u>hundreds</u>, and perform anywhere from <u>school halls</u> and <u>churches</u> to <u>concert halls</u>, <u>theatres</u> and <u>cathedrals</u>.

Choral Music has Been Around for Over 600 Years

1) The first choral pieces were sung in <u>churches</u> in the <u>14th century</u>.
   Before that, monks used to sing <u>plainsong</u> (a unison chant).

2) Most choral music in <u>Renaissance</u> and <u>Baroque</u> times was <u>sacred</u> (<u>church</u> music).

3) <u>Masses</u> were sung in Catholic churches. They were part of the church service.
   A <u>requiem</u> was a <u>mass</u> for the <u>dead</u>.

4) <u>Oratorios</u> are <u>Bible stories</u> set to music. Masses, requiems and oratorios are all <u>sacred</u> music.

5) <u>Bach</u> and <u>Handel</u> became famous for their <u>masses</u> and <u>oratorios</u>.
   They're made up of <u>choir</u> sections and <u>solo</u> sections.

6) The main <u>secular</u> (<u>non-church</u> music) choral music were <u>choruses</u> in <u>operas</u>. Operas told
   <u>love stories</u> and were performed <u>on stage</u>. The chorus <u>explains</u> what's happening in the story.

Choirs Were Originally All Male

1) <u>Baroque choirs</u> were fairly <u>small</u> — they'd sometimes have just <u>one singer</u> on each part.
   All parts were sung by <u>men</u> (women were <u>banned</u> from singing in church).

2) Most choir music was written for <u>4 different voices</u>: <u>treble</u> — a <u>boy soprano</u>, <u>countertenor</u> (or <u>alto</u>)
   — a <u>falsetto</u> (<u>high-pitched</u>) voice, <u>tenor</u> — a <u>high male</u> voice, <u>bass</u> — a <u>low male</u> voice.

3) By the <u>Victorian era</u>, choirs were <u>huge</u> — they'd often have over 100 members. Singing in a choral
   society was a <u>popular Victorian hobby</u>. Lots of these societies still exist today — a famous one is
   the <u>Huddersfield Choral Society</u>, which was started in 1836.

4) Some choirs were <u>mixed-sex</u>, with music arranged for SATB voices: <u>soprano</u> — a <u>high female</u> voice,
   <u>alto (or contralto)</u> — a <u>lower female</u> voice, <u>tenor</u> — a <u>high male</u> voice, <u>bass</u> — a <u>low male</u> voice.

5) <u>All-female</u> choirs are usually <u>SSAA</u> (2 soprano parts and 2 alto parts) or <u>SSA</u> (2 soprano parts and one
   alto part). <u>Male voice</u> choirs are often <u>TTBB</u> (2 tenor and 2 bass parts).

6) <u>Soloists</u> can also be <u>mezzo-sopranos</u> (lower than a soprano but higher than an alto) or <u>baritones</u>
   (lower than a tenor but higher than a bass).

Messiah is a Famous Oratorio by Handel

1) <u>Messiah</u> tells the story of <u>Jesus' life</u>.

2) It's written for <u>SATB soloists</u>, <u>SATB choir</u> and a <u>full orchestra</u>. At the time Handel wrote it, all the
   parts would have been sung by <u>men</u>.

3) Handel wrote it for a <u>small choir</u>, but in <u>Victorian</u> times, Messiah would have been performed by
   <u>hundreds</u> of singers.

4) Much of the Messiah is <u>melismatic</u> (a <u>single syllable</u> of text is sung over
   a <u>succession</u> of notes). In the chorus '<u>For Unto Us a Child is Born</u>',
   the <u>soprano</u> part has a run of <u>57 notes</u> for the word '<u>born</u>'.

> The opposite of melismatic is <u>syllabic</u>, where every <u>syllable</u> is sung to a <u>single note</u>.

Tenor

Crook - ed

5) Handel also uses <u>word-painting</u> — where the music <u>matches</u> the words.
   E.g. the word '<u>crooked</u>' is <u>split</u> over four notes each time it is sung,
   making it <u>sound</u> crooked.

6) The most famous bit of the Messiah is probably the '<u>Hallelujah Chorus</u>'.

Operas, oratorios — there's Masses of stuff on this page...

Imagine the <u>impact</u> of a massive choir singing the <u>Hallelujah Chorus</u> — sounding <u>majestic</u> and <u>powerful</u>.
Quite appropriate for words like '<u>King of Kings</u>', '<u>He shall live forever</u>' and of course '<u>Hallelujah</u>'.

The Great Choral Classics

Big choral works aren't stuck in the past — there are lots of modern pieces too.

Choral Singing is Still Popular Today

1) 20th and 21st century choirs are generally quite small compared to the large Victorian choirs, though they'll often have around 80 members. Some can have as many as 130 members.

2) Lots of 20th century choral works are written for chamber choir and chamber orchestra. These are just small versions of choirs and orchestras (they're called 'chamber' because they used to perform in rooms or chambers, rather than a concert hall). Chamber choirs normally have 20-25 members.

3) Chamber choir pieces may have been a reaction against 19th century composers, who often composed pieces for massive choirs.

4) Professional choirs normally perform in concert halls. Amateur choirs will often perform in school halls or churches (even if they're not singing religious music).

Modern Choir Pieces are Varied and Experimental

1) Composers like Schoenberg, Messiaen and Penderecki experimented with atonal music (music that's not written in a key), discordant sounds and clashing harmonies. These were difficult for choirs to sing and audiences found them harder to listen to.

2) English composer Benjamin Britten wrote a War Requiem using Latin words from the Requiem Mass (a mass for the dead) together with war poems by Wilfred Owen. It's written for soprano, tenor and baritone soloists, chorus, boys' choir, orchestra and portable organ (though the last movement needs a full-size organ).

> Music written in the first half of the twentieth century falls into the Modern period (music written after that is Post-Modern). Schoenberg and Stravinsky were Modernist composers. Modernist music includes Serialism and Neo-Classicism.

3) Vaughan Williams, another English composer, wrote a lot of choral works. He also arranged popular English folk songs for choirs.

Carmina Burana is a Famous 20th Century Choral Work

1) Carmina Burana was written by Carl Orff. It's based on 24 medieval poems.

2) The poems are on secular topics like money, drink, gambling and lust. Most of them are in Latin.

3) It was written in Nazi Germany. It was immediately popular, even though it was quite controversial — it went against the values the Nazis were trying to promote. After the Second World War it was seen as 'Nazi music' — but people still liked it.

4) The most famous piece of Carmina Burana is called 'O Fortuna'. It starts and ends the whole thing.

5) It's written for a huge orchestra, a main choir (SATB), a chamber choir (SATB) and a boys' choir. The chamber choir sits within the main choir — it's a choir within a choir. There's a lot of solo parts.

6) Carmina Burana needs 8 timpani and loads of percussion. It's very dramatic.

7) This piece has lots of time changes. In 'O Fortuna', it changes from 7 beats to 5 to 4. The rhythms follow the words and make it sound very exciting.

8) The texture is mainly homophonic (all parts moving together in chords).

9) The chorus mostly sing in unison, parallel thirds or major or minor triads — primitive harmonies compared to the experimental style of other composers at the time.

10) Carl Orff wanted Carmina Burana to be performed with lots of speech, movement and dance. He called this idea Theatrum Mundi. It made the work even more dramatic and expressive. It's hardly ever performed like this today.

An orchestra, 8 timpani and 3 choirs — pretty loud then...

'O Fortuna' is about the Roman goddess of fortune. It's been used in adverts, films and TV programmes (like Only Fools and Horses and The Simpsons™). It's normally played when something's a bit scary.

The Great Choral Classics

20th and 21st century composers like John Rutter and Karl Jenkins have written pieces for choirs of all ages. It's the 'pop' of the choral world — more accessible than stuff by Schoenberg or Messiaen.

John Rutter is a Well-Known 20th and 21st Century Composer

1) John Rutter is an English composer and conductor who was born in 1945.

2) He's written lots of choral pieces — hymns, carols, and anthems. Many of these are arrangements of existing works. His longer compositions include a Requiem, Gloria and Mass of the Children.

3) Rutter's setting of Psalm 150 was sung at the Queen's Golden Jubilee in 2002. It was commissioned specially for the occasion. It was performed in St Paul's Cathedral — he wrote it for a traditional church choir. It sounds like a fanfare and celebration.

Rutter did his Own Thing

1) In the 1960s, Rutter took no notice of what other composers were doing — he virtually ignored Serialism and Minimalism (two fashionable ways of composing at that time). Instead, he wrote songs that had more in common with traditional English and French choral music.

2) He was influenced by American songwriting — especially songs from musicals (p.115-116). He wanted hummable tunes that people would want to sing. This was quite a change from the weird experimental stuff some other composers were doing.

3) His Requiem shows how he combines traditional ideas with new ideas. As well as the usual Latin words, he also includes two psalms sung in English. The most famous bit of it is probably the Pie Jesu. It's written for a soprano or treble soloist with a light accompaniment. The rest of the choir sing at the end of the solo sections.

> Other famous settings of the Pie Jesu have been done by Fauré, Andrew Lloyd Webber and Karl Jenkins.

4) Rutter uses different types of accompaniment for his pieces. Some have full orchestral parts, some are strings only, and some are written for brass. Most of his songs have a simple piano or organ accompaniment as well.

Sir John Tavener and Karl Jenkins are Also Popular

1) Sir John Tavener is another famous English composer. Some of his choral works are settings of poems by William Blake. He was also inspired by religious ideas.

2) One of his best known pieces is 'Song for Athene' — it was performed at Princess Diana's funeral in 1997. It's a very sad piece.

3) Tavener's music tends to be more discordant and modern-sounding than Rutter's.

4) Karl Jenkins is a Welsh composer. His works include Requiem and The Armed Man: A Mass For Peace. His music has interesting rhythmic ideas and it's easy to listen to.

5) Jenkins' most famous work is probably Adiemus. It's a large vocal work that's been used on adverts. The words are in a made-up language. Their meaning isn't important because he's treating the voices like instruments — he was more concerned about the sound of the vocal parts.

6) Adiemus was originally written for an all-female choir and features female soloists. It sounds like ethnic or world music.

I can't believe it's not Rutter...

Rutter's Gloria has an unusual accompaniment — it's written for a brass ensemble, organ, timpani and percussion. It sounds very grand and glorious, though there are some quiet sections in the middle.

Baroque and Classical Music

Baroque and classical music are similar but not the same. Here's a rough guide to both types...

Baroque Composers Used Major and Minor Scales

Baroque
1600–1750

1) From about 1600, Western composers stopped writing modal (p.21) music.

2) Instead they used major and minor keys to write tonal music. This was a big change. In Western countries, most music is still tonal, hundreds of years later.

3) Modulating (switching between keys — see p.38) turned out to be a good way of creating contrast in music.

4) Composers developed new structures for organising music using modulation and contrast, e.g. binary, ternary and rondo forms (see next page).

Baroque has a Recognisable Sound

Baroque music's pretty easy to recognise. These are the main things to look out for in the Listening:

1) The dynamics change suddenly. Each bit is either loud or soft. You won't hear any gradual changes in volume — no crescendos or diminuendos. This is called terraced or stepped dynamics.

2) The melody's built up from short musical ideas (called motifs), so you get a fair bit of repetition.

3) The harmonies are simple, with a fairly narrow range of chords — mainly I and V.

4) The melody is packed with ornaments, added in to make it sound more interesting (see p.83).

5) The texture's often contrapuntal (polyphonic — see p.39).

Most Baroque Music had a Basso Continuo

1) A basso continuo is a continuous bass part. It's played throughout a piece, and the chords are based on it.

2) It was often played on an organ or harpsichord (harpsichords were popular Baroque instruments). It could also be played by more than one instrument — e.g. cellos, double basses and bassoons.

3) Other Baroque instruments are the flute, recorder, oboe, bassoon and orchestral strings (violins, violas, cellos and double basses).

Baroque Turned into Classical Music

Classical music grew out of Baroque, so it's similar but not the same.

1) Classical tunes are very balanced. They tend to have equal four-bar phrases, split into a two-bar question and a two-bar answer.

2) Classical music uses fewer ornaments.

3) Classical composers still wrote in binary, ternary, and rondo forms, but they also came up with a new structure called sonata form (p.91).

4) The dynamics are more subtle, using crescendos and diminuendos, not just changing suddenly.

5) New instruments and groups changed the sound:

Classical
1750–1820

- The piano was invented in about 1700. It became much more popular than the harpsichord because you could vary the dynamics. Classical composers include the piano in a lot of their music.

- The clarinet was invented around this time too.

- Orchestras got bigger — they had more woodwind, trumpets and horns, and larger string sections.

What was life like before the piano was invented...

In the listening exam they might ask who wrote the piece on the CD. If you're stuck, try one of these:
Baroque — Bach, Handel, Vivaldi or Purcell; Classical — Mozart, Haydn or Beethoven.

Baroque and Classical Structures

Baroque and Classical composers used standard structures to give their melodies a <u>shape</u>.

Music in **Binary** Form has **Two Sections**

1) <u>Binary</u> means something like '<u>in two parts</u>' — there are <u>two bits</u> to a tune in <u>binary form</u>.
2) Binary form's usually used for <u>Baroque dances</u>, e.g. bourrée, menuet, gavotte, sarabande and gigue.
3) Each section is <u>repeated</u>. You play Section A twice, and then Section B twice, so it goes <u>AABB</u>.
4) Section B <u>contrasts</u> with Section A — the two bits should sound <u>different</u>.
5) The contrast's often made by <u>modulating</u> to related keys. Pieces in a <u>minor</u> key usually modulate to the <u>relative major</u>, e.g. A minor to C major. Pieces in a <u>major</u> key usually modulate to the <u>dominant</u> key (V), e.g. C major to G major.

Ternary Form has **Three Sections**

1) There are <u>three sections</u> in music with ternary form. Each section <u>repeats</u>, so it goes AABBAA.
2) Section A ends in the <u>home key</u>, normally with a <u>perfect cadence</u> (see pages 36-37). This makes it sound like a <u>complete piece</u> in itself.
3) In Section B the music modulates to a <u>related key</u>, like the <u>dominant</u> or <u>relative minor</u>, and then <u>goes back</u> to the <u>home key</u> before it ends.
4) The last section can be <u>exactly the same</u> as Section A, or a slightly <u>varied</u> version. If it <u>is</u> varied, you call it <u>A1</u> instead of A.

Baroque Composers Used Ternary Form in **Arias**

An <u>aria</u> is a solo in an <u>opera</u> or <u>oratorio</u> (big vocal works — see page 101). Arias in the <u>Baroque period</u> (1600-1750) are often in ternary form — they are often called a 'da capo aria'. <u>Handel</u> wrote lots of these.

After repeating Section A and Section B you come to the instruction <u>da capo al fine</u>. It means "go back to the beginning and play to the end". To tell you where the end is it says <u>fine</u> at the end of Section A.

Classical Composers Used Ternary Form in **Symphonies**

1) In a Classical symphony (see pages 90-91), the <u>third movement</u>'s often in a ternary form called <u>minuet and trio</u>. The trio's in a different (but related) key <u>for contrast</u>.
2) They're sandwiched together to give the <u>whole movement</u> a ternary structure.

There are no repeats when the music goes back to the minuet.

Rondo Form can Have **Any Number** of Sections

1) <u>Rondo</u> means <u>going round</u>. A rondo starts with a main idea in <u>Section A</u>, moves into a <u>new section</u>, goes round again to <u>A</u>, moves into another <u>new section</u>, goes round again to <u>A</u>... as many times as you like. The <u>new section</u> after each Section A always <u>contrasts</u> with A.
2) Section A is known as the <u>main theme</u> or <u>refrain</u>. The contrasting structures are called <u>episodes</u>.

3) The main theme is always in the <u>home key</u>. Each <u>episode</u> tends to modulate to a <u>related key</u> for contrast.

Baroque and Classical Structures

Variations are pieces which start with one pattern or tune, and then change it in different ways. There are two main structures for variation. In the Baroque and Classical periods composers really loved them. They're called 'theme and variation' and 'ground bass'.

Theme and Variation Form *Varies the Melody*

1) In theme and variation form, the theme's usually a memorable tune.

2) The theme's played first. There's a short pause before the first variation's played, then another pause before the next variation. Each variation is a self-contained piece of music. There can be as many or as few variations as the composer wants.

3) Each variation should be a recognisable version of the main theme, but different from all the others.

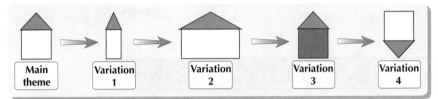

You can vary a tune in loads of simple ways:

1) Start off with a basic theme...

Posh name — ornamentation

2) Add notes to make the tune more complex.

3) Remove notes to simplify the tune.

4) Change the metre — say, from two beats in a bar to three.

5) Add a countermelody — an extra melody over the top of the theme.

6) You can also change the tempo, change the key (from major to minor or vice versa), change some or all of the chords or add a different type of accompaniment, e.g. a Classical 'Alberti bass' pattern instead of block chords.

Ground Bass Form *Varies Ideas Over a **Fixed Bass Part***

Ground bass is a continuous set of variations — there are no pauses. The main theme (called the ground) is a bass line which repeats throughout the piece. Varying melodies and harmonies which become gradually more complex are played over the ground. There are two types of Baroque dance that are in ground bass form — the chaconne and passacaglia. They're quite slow and stately.

Freshly ground bass — it goes all powdery...

Neither of these structures is horribly complicated — but it's easy to get one muddled up with another. These are good pages to learn painstakingly thoroughly so you can be sure you know what's what.

Baroque and Classical Melody Patterns

Look out for these patterns in your <u>listening</u> exam, and try to use some in your <u>compositions</u>.

Melodic Inversion — Turning the Tune **Upside Down**

1) <u>Melodic inversion</u> makes a melody sound very different, but not totally different.

2) You keep the <u>same intervals</u> between the notes, but they go in the <u>opposite direction</u>, i.e. down instead of up, and up instead of down. Basically you turn the tune on its head.

The first melody goes <u>up a major third</u> from C to E, then up a minor third to G.

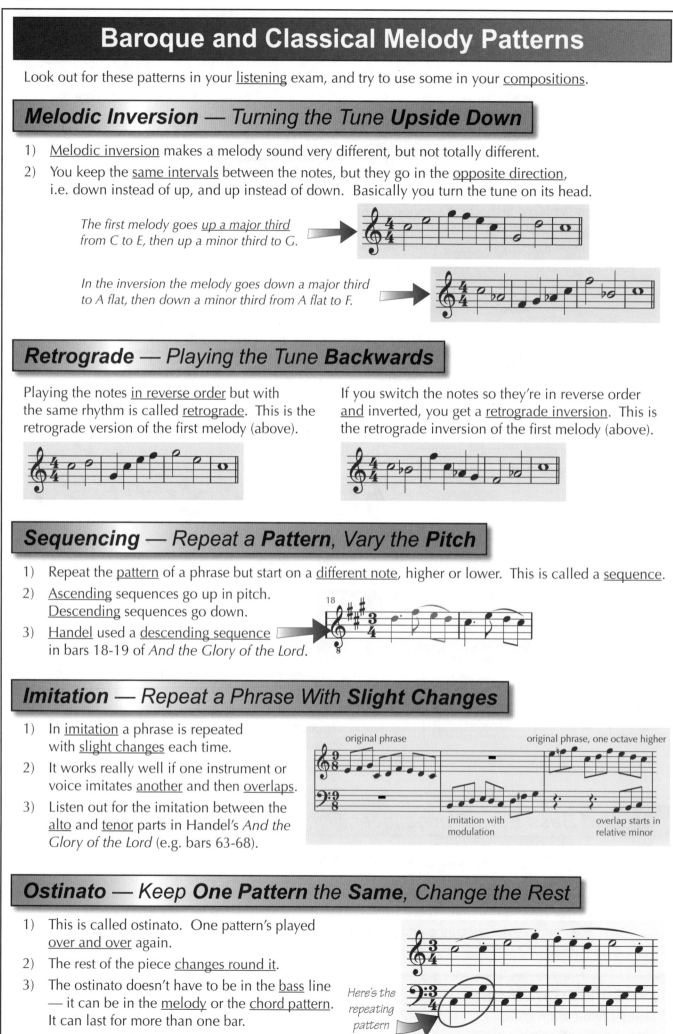

In the inversion the melody goes down a major third to A flat, then down a minor third from A flat to F.

Retrograde — Playing the Tune **Backwards**

Playing the notes <u>in reverse order</u> but with the same rhythm is called <u>retrograde</u>. This is the retrograde version of the first melody (above).

If you switch the notes so they're in reverse order <u>and</u> inverted, you get a <u>retrograde inversion</u>. This is the retrograde inversion of the first melody (above).

Sequencing — Repeat a **Pattern**, Vary the **Pitch**

1) Repeat the <u>pattern</u> of a phrase but start on a <u>different note</u>, higher or lower. This is called a <u>sequence</u>.

2) <u>Ascending</u> sequences go up in pitch. <u>Descending</u> sequences go down.

3) <u>Handel</u> used a <u>descending sequence</u> in bars 18-19 of *And the Glory of the Lord*.

Imitation — Repeat a Phrase With **Slight Changes**

1) In <u>imitation</u> a phrase is repeated with <u>slight changes</u> each time.

2) It works really well if one instrument or voice imitates <u>another</u> and then <u>overlaps</u>.

3) Listen out for the imitation between the <u>alto</u> and <u>tenor</u> parts in Handel's *And the Glory of the Lord* (e.g. bars 63-68).

original phrase

original phrase, one octave higher

imitation with modulation

overlap starts in relative minor

Ostinato — Keep **One Pattern** the **Same**, Change the Rest

1) This is called ostinato. One pattern's played <u>over and over</u> again.

2) The rest of the piece <u>changes round it</u>.

3) The ostinato doesn't have to be in the <u>bass</u> line — it can be in the <u>melody</u> or the <u>chord</u> pattern. It can last for more than one bar.

Here's the repeating pattern

Baroque and Classical Melody Patterns

Another way of livening up a melody that was <u>very popular</u> with Baroque composers was adding in <u>ornaments</u>. Ornaments are fiddly <u>little notes</u> that stand out a bit from the main tune.

A *Trill* is Lots of *Tiny Quick Notes*

1) In Baroque music the trill starts one note <u>above</u> the written note then goes quickly back and forth between the written note and the note you started on.

2) In Classical music the trill starts <u>on</u> the written note and goes up to the note above.

3) Sometimes a trill ends with a <u>turn</u> (see below).

4) A <u>sharp</u>, <u>flat</u> or <u>natural</u> sign above the trill symbol tells you if the note to trill to is sharp, flat or natural.

This is how you play a trill in classical music...

OR

The trill lasts the same length of time as the written note.

An *Appoggiatura* is an *Extra Note* in a *Chord*

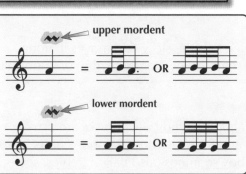

1) The appoggiatura starts on a note that <u>clashes</u> with the chord, then moves to a note that <u>belongs</u> in the chord.

2) The two notes are usually just one <u>tone</u> or <u>semitone</u> apart.

3) It normally takes <u>half the time value</u> of the note it 'leans' on.

Squeezing in a *Tiny Note* is Called *Acciaccatura*

"Acciaccatura" means <u>crushing in</u>. An acciaccatura is a note that's squeezed in before the main note and played <u>as fast as possible</u>.

Mordents and Turns are Set Patterns of Notes

Mordents

Mordents <u>start off</u> like trills.

The difference is they <u>end</u> on the written note, which is played a bit <u>longer</u> than the trilled notes. There are loads of different mordents but these two are the most common.

upper mordent

= OR

lower mordent

= OR

Turns

Start on the note <u>above</u> the written note, then play the <u>written note</u>, followed by the note <u>below</u> the written note. End back on the <u>written note</u>.

For an <u>inverted turn</u> play the note <u>below</u> the written note, the written note, the note above that and finally the written note.

OR OR =

I've done my bit — now it's your turn...

Take a look at page 35 for more on decoration. All the stuff in this section is about how they put the <u>melody line</u> together. If you want to find out more about writing <u>harmonies</u>, have a look at Section 2.

Baroque Choral Music

Baroque composers wrote a lot of <u>choral music</u> — some of it's still performed <u>today</u>.

Choral Music is Sung by Choirs and Soloists

Choral music can be <u>sacred</u> (religious) or <u>secular</u> (non-religious).

SACRED MUSIC

MASS	Part of the <u>Catholic church service</u> set to music.
REQUIEM	Mass for the <u>dead</u>.
CHORALE	A <u>hymn</u>.
ORATORIO	Religious version of an <u>opera</u>, often telling <u>Bible stories</u>.
CANTATA	Vocal pieces made up of two or three <u>arias</u>, separated by <u>recitatives</u> (see below).

SECULAR MUSIC

OPERA		A <u>story</u> set to music with <u>singing</u> and <u>acting</u>. Most operas were divided up into three parts (or '<u>Acts</u>').
		The main types of Baroque opera were:
	<u>Opera Seria</u>	(serious, often mythological themes),
	<u>Opera Buffa</u>	(lighter, more everyday themes)
	<u>Opéra Comique</u>	(like Opera Buffa, but with some spoken recitatives),
	<u>Operetta</u>	(not big enough to be a proper opera).
CANTATA	You can get secular cantatas as well.	

Operas, Oratorios and Cantatas Have 3 Main Types of Song

1) ARIA

An <u>aria</u> is a <u>solo vocal piece</u> (backed by the <u>orchestra</u>). It gives the <u>main characters</u> the chance to show what they're thinking and <u>feeling</u>. In England and France, they could be called '<u>airs</u>' instead.

2) RECITATIVE

A <u>recitative</u> is a song which <u>tells the story</u> and <u>moves it along</u>.
The rhythm of the words tends to imitate the <u>rhythm</u> of normal speech.

3) CHORUS

A <u>chorus</u> is sung by the <u>chorus</u> (a <u>choir</u>). Choruses are usually written for <u>SATB</u> choirs (Sopranos, Altos, Tenors and Basses). Most Baroque choirs were <u>all male</u> — the highest parts would be sung by <u>boy sopranos</u> (also called <u>trebles</u>, see p.76).

Oratorios are Religious Versions of Operas

1) Oratorios often tell <u>Bible stories</u>, or tales with a <u>religious</u> or <u>moral</u> theme.
2) They're <u>not</u> usually <u>acted out</u> with <u>scenery</u> and <u>costumes</u> (like operas are).
3) They normally have an <u>instrumental accompaniment</u>.
4) They can be performed in <u>concert halls</u> as well as <u>churches</u>.

Anyone for a sing-song then...

Make sure you know the <u>difference</u> between <u>sacred</u> and <u>secular</u> music, and can give examples of each. Being able to <u>describe</u> the different <u>types</u> of songs in operas, oratorios and cantatas will be useful too.

Handel — And the Glory of the Lord (Messiah)

Now it's time to meet <u>And the Glory of the Lord</u> from Handel's oratorio '<u>Messiah</u>'.

Handel was a German Composer

1) <u>George Frideric Handel</u> was born in <u>Germany</u> in <u>1685</u>. From about <u>1710</u>, he lived in <u>England</u>. He died in <u>London</u> in <u>1759</u> and is buried in <u>Westminster Abbey</u>.

2) He was popular with <u>Queen Anne</u>, <u>George I</u> and <u>George II</u> — he composed '<u>Zadok the Priest</u>' for the <u>coronation</u> of George II, and it's been played at every coronation since then. He also wrote music for the <u>Calvinist</u> church in Germany and the <u>Church of England</u>.

3) Handel wrote loads of music, including lots of <u>oratorios</u> and <u>operas</u> (see p.101). As well as <u>choral music</u>, he also wrote many <u>orchestral</u> pieces — one of the most famous is the '<u>Water Music</u>'.

'Messiah' is a Famous Oratorio

1) Handel wrote '<u>Messiah</u>' in <u>1741</u>. It only took him about 3 weeks to compose it (though he did <u>pinch</u> a few bits from his <u>earlier compositions</u>).

2) It became popular with <u>audiences</u> because of its <u>uplifting choruses</u> — like the *Hallelujah Chorus*.

3) It was also popular with <u>other composers</u> — <u>Mozart</u> even <u>arranged</u> his own version of it.

4) 'Messiah' was originally supposed to be performed at <u>Easter</u>, but now it's usually sung at <u>Christmas</u>.

5) The <u>libretto</u> (text) was put together by <u>Charles Jennens</u>, who took words from the <u>Old</u> and <u>New Testaments</u>. Most of the words are from the <u>King James Bible</u>.

6) It was written for <u>SATB choir</u>, <u>SATB soloists</u> and a full <u>Baroque orchestra</u>. Handel wrote parts for <u>oboes</u>, <u>bassoon</u>, <u>trumpets</u>, <u>timpani</u>, <u>strings</u> and <u>basso continuo</u> — often a <u>harpsichord</u> (see p.62). Mozart's later arrangement added <u>flutes</u>, <u>clarinets</u>, <u>French horns</u>, <u>trombones</u> and an <u>organ</u>.

It's Divided up into Three Parts

1) Like an <u>opera</u>, 'Messiah' is divided into <u>three sections</u>:

   - The first section describes the <u>prophecies</u> about <u>Jesus' birth</u>.
   - The middle section is about the <u>persecution</u> and <u>crucifixion</u> of Jesus.
   - The last section is about his <u>resurrection</u>.

2) In each section, there are lots of <u>different pieces</u> — there's a mix of <u>arias</u>, <u>recitatives</u> and <u>choruses</u>. There's also a <u>duet</u> and some <u>instrumental</u> sections. There are arias and recitatives for <u>soprano</u>, <u>alto</u>, <u>tenor</u> and <u>bass</u> soloists. The famous *Hallelujah Chorus* is at the <u>end</u> of the <u>2nd</u> section.

The First Chorus is And the Glory of the Lord

1) The <u>chorus</u>, *And the Glory of the Lord*, is the <u>fourth</u> piece in the <u>first</u> section of 'Messiah'.

2) It comes after an <u>aria</u> sung by a <u>tenor</u>, and before a <u>bass recitative</u>.

3) It's the <u>first</u> chorus you hear in the oratorio.

4) The chorus is made up of the lines '<u>And the glory of the Lord shall be revealed</u>', '<u>And all flesh shall see it together</u>' and '<u>for the mouth of the Lord hath spoken it</u>'. These phrases are <u>repeated</u> throughout the piece (the first is <u>broken up</u> into two parts — 'And the glory of the Lord' and 'shall be revealed', so there are actually <u>four</u> separate phrases).

5) For most of this chorus, the orchestra <u>doubles</u> the vocal parts — <u>instruments</u> often play in <u>unison</u> with the <u>singers</u>.

Handel — And the Glory of the Lord (Messiah)

Have a <u>listen</u> to the piece and make sure you can <u>spot</u> all the bits mentioned on this page.

And the Glory of the Lord is in a *Major Key*

1) Most of *And the Glory of the Lord* is in <u>A major</u>, though it does <u>modulate</u> (change key) a few times. It goes to <u>E major</u> twice, and <u>B major</u> once. It sounds <u>happy</u> and <u>joyful</u>.

2) The <u>texture</u> in most of the piece is <u>homophonic</u> (all the parts move together). Some bits are <u>polyphonic</u> (parts weaving in and out of each other). For example, in bars 91-107, all four vocal parts are singing <u>different tunes</u> at the <u>same time</u>.

3) The piece is marked *Allegro* — it's <u>quick</u> and <u>lively</u>. It's in <u>3/4</u>, but in some places (e.g. bars 9-10), it <u>feels</u> like it's in <u>2/4</u> — this is called a <u>hemiola</u>.

There are *Four* Main *Musical Ideas*

1) *And the Glory of the Lord* (like most of the choruses in 'Messiah') is made up of a few <u>musical ideas</u> (or <u>motifs</u>). Handel usually <u>introduces</u> these motifs very <u>simply</u> — just sung by <u>one part</u>, then <u>weaves</u> them into the rest of the music. The <u>four motifs</u> in this chorus go with the <u>four phrases</u> on p.85.

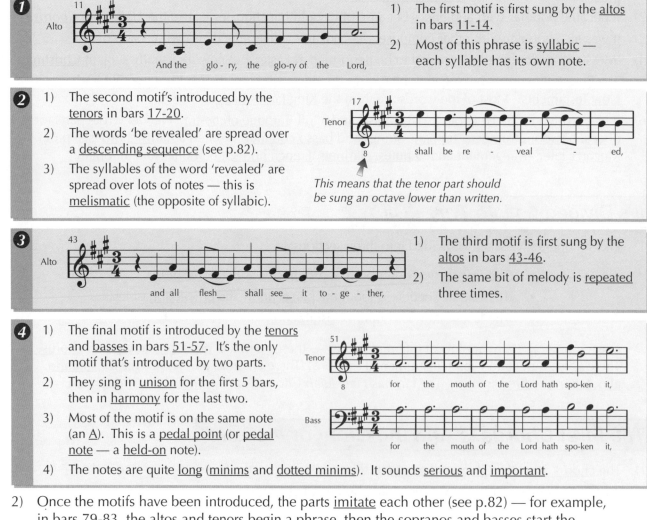

1

Alto — And the glo-ry, the glo-ry of the Lord,

1) The first motif is first sung by the <u>altos</u> in bars <u>11-14</u>.

2) Most of this phrase is <u>syllabic</u> — each syllable has its own note.

2

1) The second motif's introduced by the <u>tenors</u> in bars <u>17-20</u>.

2) The words 'be revealed' are spread over a <u>descending sequence</u> (see p.82).

3) The syllables of the word 'revealed' are spread over lots of notes — this is <u>melismatic</u> (the opposite of syllabic).

Tenor — shall be re - veal - ed,

This means that the tenor part should be sung an octave lower than written.

3

Alto — and all flesh__ shall see__ it to - ge - ther,

1) The third motif is first sung by the <u>altos</u> in bars <u>43-46</u>.

2) The same bit of melody is <u>repeated</u> three times.

4

1) The final motif is introduced by the <u>tenors</u> and <u>basses</u> in bars <u>51-57</u>. It's the only motif that's introduced by two parts.

2) They sing in <u>unison</u> for the first 5 bars, then in <u>harmony</u> for the last two.

3) Most of the motif is on the same note (an <u>A</u>). This is a <u>pedal point</u> (or <u>pedal note</u> — a <u>held-on</u> note).

4) The notes are quite <u>long</u> (<u>minims</u> and <u>dotted minims</u>). It sounds <u>serious</u> and <u>important</u>.

Tenor — for the mouth of the Lord hath spo-ken it,

Bass — for the mouth of the Lord hath spo-ken it,

2) Once the motifs have been introduced, the parts <u>imitate</u> each other (see p.82) — for example, in bars <u>79-83</u>, the altos and tenors begin a phrase, then the sopranos and basses start the same phrase (at a <u>different pitch</u>) one bar later. The parts <u>overlap</u> — they're singing in <u>canon</u>.

3) The last four bars of the piece are marked *Adagio* — they're much <u>slower</u>. It finishes with a <u>plagal cadence</u> (chord IV followed by chord I — see p.37). It makes the piece <u>sound</u> like it's finished.

Pedal as fast as you can...

Remember that lots of <u>religious</u> pieces end with a <u>plagal cadence</u> — <u>chord IV</u> followed by <u>chord I</u>.

The Classical Orchestra

After Baroque came Classical music. You need to know what a Classical orchestra was like.

Orchestral Music was Written for **Wealthy Audiences**

1) The Classical period began around 1750. Then, composers worked for royalty and aristocrats. They were paid to write music for official events, church services and plain old entertainment. Composers had to write music that their patrons (employers) would approve of.

2) Later in the Classical period, society changed. Middle-class people had more money and wanted entertainment. Public concert halls were built, where people could go to listen to music.

3) Famous Classical composers like Haydn and Mozart worked for patrons, but they also put on concerts in the new concert halls.

4) By the 1800s, composers could earn quite a bit of money from ticket sales at concert halls. This gave them more freedom — they could write for the tastes of concert-goers instead of just pleasing their patrons.

Orchestras **Grew** During the **Classical Period**

1) At the start of the Classical period, composers wrote for smallish orchestras — mainly strings, with horns, flutes and oboes. There'd be two horns and one or two woodwind.

2) Later on, the woodwind section grew — clarinets were invented during the Classical period, and were included in the orchestra. Mozart was the first composer to use the clarinet in a symphony. Bassoons were introduced too.

3) Trumpets were added to the brass section, and timpani were included in the percussion section.

4) In some early Classical music, there'd be a harpsichord (see p.62), but after a while composers stopped using it. The harpsichord was there to fill in the harmonies, but it wasn't really needed once the extra woodwind had been added.

5) This is a fairly typical layout for a later Classical orchestra:

TIMPANI		
FRENCH HORNS		TRUMPETS
FLUTES		CLARINETS
	OBOES	BASSOONS
SECOND VIOLINS	VIOLAS	DOUBLE BASSES
FIRST VIOLINS		CELLOS

Classical Orchestras Mostly Used **Stringed Instruments**

1) The most important section in a Classical orchestra is the strings. They're the dominant sound in most Classical music. The violins generally play most of the tunes.

2) The wind instruments play extra notes to fill out the harmony. When they do get the tune, they mostly double the string parts.

3) You do hear the occasional wind solo. Orchestral pieces called concertos (p.89-90) feature one or two solo instruments accompanied by an orchestra.

4) In later Classical music, the woodwind section started to have a more independent role. They'd sometimes play the tune alone, and there'd be more solos. The strings were still really important though.

You've got to know how it all fits together...

Orchestras grew in size because composers in the Classical period began to include more parts for different instruments. This gave rise to a greater variety of music later in the Classical period.

The Classical Style

A whole page about the features of Classical music... enjoy.

Classical Melodies Have a Clear, Simple Structure

Classical music sounds clearer and simpler than music from other periods. This is partly because the tunes are structured in a very straightforward way, with short, balanced 2- or 4-bar phrases.

Here's an extract from Haydn's *Clock Symphony*:

And here's a bit from Mozart's *Symphony No. 40* in G minor, with the same balanced question and answer phrasing:

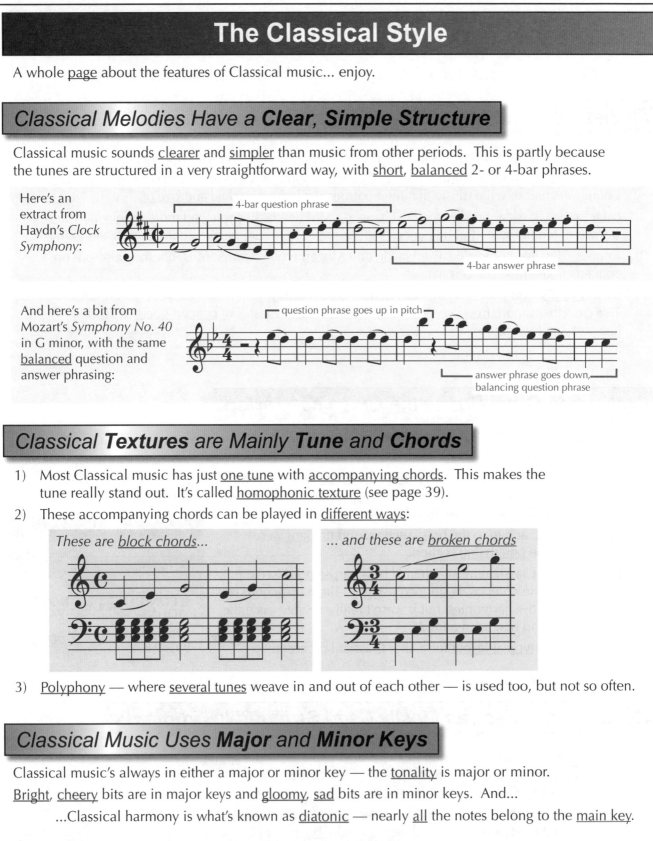

Classical Textures are Mainly Tune and Chords

1) Most Classical music has just one tune with accompanying chords. This makes the tune really stand out. It's called homophonic texture (see page 39).

2) These accompanying chords can be played in different ways:

These are block chords...

... and these are broken chords

3) Polyphony — where several tunes weave in and out of each other — is used too, but not so often.

Classical Music Uses Major and Minor Keys

Classical music's always in either a major or minor key — the tonality is major or minor.
Bright, cheery bits are in major keys and gloomy, sad bits are in minor keys. And...

...Classical harmony is what's known as diatonic — nearly all the notes belong to the main key.

The Beat is Obvious and Easy to Follow

1) The metre in Classical music is very regular. You can happily tap your foot in time to the music.

2) The tempo stays constant — the speed of the beat stays pretty much the same all the way through, without massively speeding up or slowing down.

Classical style — a wig, tailcoat and breeches...

Knowing these key features is useful if you're asked to describe music from the Classical period. Make a list of them all, then learn it. Keep going back over it to check you know them off by heart.

Classical Structures

Concertos, sonatas and symphonies were very popular in the Classical period.
Take your time and make sure that you're familiar with each one of these structures.

Concertos are Played by a Soloist and Orchestra

1) Concertos, symphonies and sonatas were popular Classical forms.

2) A concerto is a piece for a soloist and orchestra. The soloist has most of the tune, and can really show off. The orchestra does get the tune too — they're not just an accompaniment.

3) A concerto usually has three movements — quick, slow and quick.

4) They often have a bit called a cadenza (p.52), where the orchestra stops and the soloist manically improvises to show everyone how brilliant they are.

5) Piano and violin concertos were most popular in the Classical period, though some composers wrote clarinet, horn and trumpet concertos too.

6) An example of a Classical concerto is Haydn's Trumpet Concerto.

Baroque Concertos Were a Bit Different

1) In the Baroque period (about 1600-1750), concertos were written as a type of chamber music (see p.66). They were performed in quite small spaces — so pieces were often written for fewer than eight musicians.

> E.g. Vivaldi's original arrangement for 'Spring' from 'The Four Seasons' was for a main violin, a string quartet (which usually includes two violins, a viola and a cello), and a harpsichord.

2) Another type of Baroque concerto was the concerto grosso — a piece for a small group of soloists (called the concertino) contrasted with the rest of the orchestra (the ripieno) and the basso continuo (see p.79).

Later Concertos Used a Full Orchestra

1) After about 1700, composers began to experiment with new instruments (the piano and the clarinet were introduced in the 18th century). The size of the orchestra increased and concertos were longer.

2) The most important section of the orchestra in a Classical concerto is the strings — violins often play the tune.

3) Wind instruments play extra notes to fill out the harmony. They would tend to double up the string parts.

The four seasons — salt, pepper, vinegar and ketchup...

You need to make sure you know all about concertos for your exam. Cover up this page and jot down the key features of this Classical structure — if you can't remember them, have another look at this page until you can. After that, you'll be ready to move on to sonatas and symphonies on the next few pages.

Classical Structures

Almost done with concertos — then it's on to symphonies and sonatas.

Classical Concertos Have a Standard Structure

All concertos follow the same basic plan.
The three movements traditionally have the following characteristics:

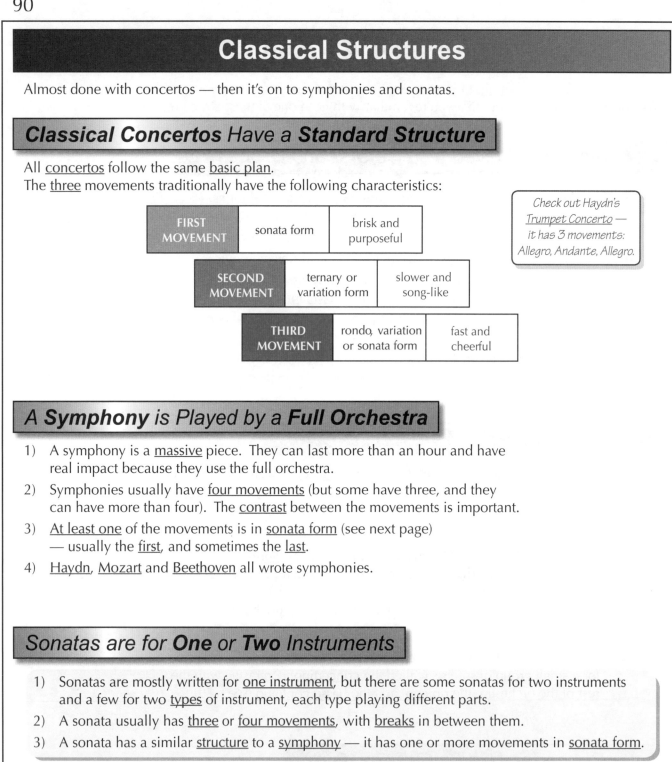

FIRST MOVEMENT	sonata form	brisk and purposeful

SECOND MOVEMENT	ternary or variation form	slower and song-like

THIRD MOVEMENT	rondo, variation or sonata form	fast and cheerful

> Check out Haydn's *Trumpet Concerto* — it has 3 movements: *Allegro, Andante, Allegro.*

A Symphony is Played by a Full Orchestra

1) A symphony is a massive piece. They can last more than an hour and have real impact because they use the full orchestra.

2) Symphonies usually have four movements (but some have three, and they can have more than four). The contrast between the movements is important.

3) At least one of the movements is in sonata form (see next page) — usually the first, and sometimes the last.

4) Haydn, Mozart and Beethoven all wrote symphonies.

Sonatas are for One or Two Instruments

1) Sonatas are mostly written for one instrument, but there are some sonatas for two instruments and a few for two types of instrument, each type playing different parts.

2) A sonata usually has three or four movements, with breaks in between them.

3) A sonata has a similar structure to a symphony — it has one or more movements in sonata form.

Classical Composers Wrote Overtures and Suites Too

1) An overture is a one-movement piece for orchestra.

2) Overtures are written as introductions to larger works like operas and ballets.

3) They use ideas, moods and musical themes from the main work to prepare the audience.

4) Classical orchestral suites are another offshoot of ballets and operas.

5) A suite is an orchestral arrangement of the music used to accompany the action on stage, put together as a separate piece of music and played at concerts.

Classical composers churned out a lot of music...

Classical composers were real masters of form and structure. They liked their music to be carefully constructed and beautifully balanced, with helpful hints to what was coming next. How kind of them.

Classical Structures

Sonata form is a really important structure in Classical music — most sonatas and symphonies had at least one movement in sonata form.

A Piece in Sonata Form has Three Main Sections

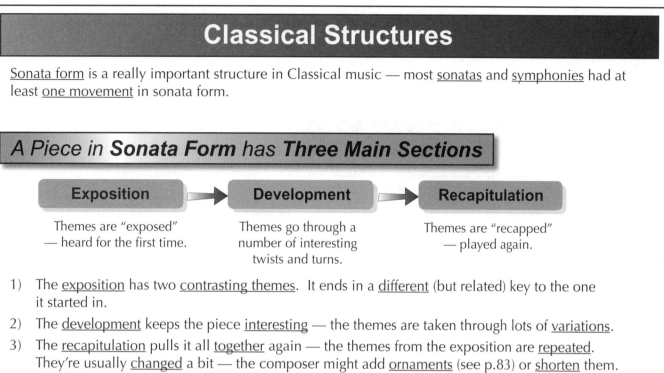

Exposition	Development	Recapitulation
Themes are "exposed" — heard for the first time.	Themes go through a number of interesting twists and turns.	Themes are "recapped" — played again.

1) The exposition has two contrasting themes. It ends in a different (but related) key to the one it started in.

2) The development keeps the piece interesting — the themes are taken through lots of variations.

3) The recapitulation pulls it all together again — the themes from the exposition are repeated. They're usually changed a bit — the composer might add ornaments (see p.83) or shorten them.

4) Composers sometimes use bridge sections between the themes and links between the main sections. They usually add a coda to finish off the piece neatly as well.

Musical Signposts Tell You What's Coming Next

The most obvious clue that a new section is starting in Classical music is a change of key.

Classical composers were also keen on dropping advance hints that a new section was about to start. These hints are called musical signposts. They're not all that easy to spot at first, but with a bit of practice you should get the hang of it:

1) Bridge passages lead smoothly into the new theme and also help prepare the new key.

2) Cadences (p.36-37) clearly mark the end of a phrase or section, and they come at the end of a piece too. When they do, the chords used in the cadence are repeated several times, to let the audience know it's all over.

There are Standard Forms for 4-Movement Compositions

Sonatas and symphonies all follow the same basic plan. These are the traditional forms used by composers for each of the movements.

This one's left out of sonatas in three movements.

FIRST MOVEMENT	sonata form	brisk and purposeful
SECOND MOVEMENT	ternary or variation form	slower and songlike
THIRD MOVEMENT	minuet or scherzo	fairly fast and dance-like
FOURTH MOVEMENT	rondo, variation or sonata form	fast and cheerful

It's complicated, but that's no excuse for not knowing it...

Sonata form is very sophisticated. Don't get muddled up between sonata form and sonatas. Sonatas use sonata form for the first movement, and sometimes the last one too, but not the second.

Mozart — 1st Movement from Symphony No. 40 in G minor

Make sure you're <u>familiar</u> with the first movement of Mozart's *Symphony No. 40* —
<u>listen</u> to it <u>over and over again</u> until you can <u>whistle</u> it in your <u>sleep</u>.

Mozart was an Austrian Composer

1) <u>Wolfgang Amadeus Mozart</u> was born in <u>Salzburg</u>, <u>Austria</u> in <u>1756</u>.
   He died in <u>Vienna</u> in <u>1791</u>.

2) He was taught <u>performance</u> and <u>composition</u> by his father, <u>Leopold Mozart</u>,
   who was also a composer.

3) Wolfgang showed his <u>musical talent</u> at a very <u>young</u> age — he composed his
   first piece of music when he was just <u>5 years old</u>. By the time he was <u>10</u> he
   had <u>toured Europe</u>, performed for <u>kings</u> and <u>queens</u> and written his first <u>opera</u>.

4) He went on to write over <u>600</u> pieces of music, including <u>operas</u>, <u>masses</u>,
   <u>symphonies</u> and <u>concertos</u>. He also wrote smaller works, like <u>chamber music</u>
   and <u>string quartets</u>.

5) He's still considered to be one of the <u>greatest composers</u> that ever lived.

He Wrote Lots of Symphonies

1) Mozart wrote over <u>40</u> symphonies in his short life.

2) He wrote most of his symphonies before he was <u>25</u>, then took a <u>break</u> from them — he could
   make <u>more money</u> from composing <u>concertos</u>, and get a <u>better reputation</u> from writing <u>operas</u>.

3) He <u>returned</u> to symphonies later on — <u>Symphony No. 40</u> was written in <u>1788</u>.
   It's one of only two of his symphonies in a <u>minor key</u> (*Symphony No. 25* and *Symphony No. 40*,
   both in <u>G minor</u>).

4) He wrote *Symphony No. 40* and <u>two</u> others in just <u>6 weeks</u>.

Symphony No. 40 was Written for a Small Orchestra

1) This symphony is written for a <u>fairly small orchestra</u> — there's <u>no percussion</u> at all,
   and the only brass instruments are the <u>French horns</u> (there are no <u>trumpets</u>).

2) The original version didn't have <u>clarinets</u> because they'd only just been invented.
   Mozart wrote <u>another, later version</u> that included them.

It has Four Movements

Like most symphonies, *Symphony No. 40 in G minor* has <u>four movements</u>. What's <u>unusual</u>
is that Mozart uses <u>sonata form</u> (see p.91) for <u>three</u> movements, instead of just one or two.
The <u>names</u> of the movements are just the <u>tempos</u>.

FIRST MOVEMENT	*Molto Allegro* (very fast) — sonata form.
SECOND MOVEMENT	*Andante* (walking pace) — sonata form.
THIRD MOVEMENT	*Allegretto* (in between *andante* and *allegro*) — minuet and trio form (see p.80).
FOURTH MOVEMENT	*Allegro assai* (very, very fast) — sonata form.

Mozart wrote operas, masses, symphonies, concertos...

If you're reading this book, it's a safe bet that you will have heard of this Mozart chap. If not, then
this is the page for you. Read it, learn it, and then cover it up and try to write a mini-essay on it...

Mozart — 1st Movement from Symphony No. 40 in G minor

This movement is in sonata form. Make sure you know the three different sections of this form (see p.91).

Bars 1-100 are the Exposition

FIRST SUBJECT (BARS 1-28)

1) The first idea lasts from bar 1 to bar 9 (there's no introduction), then the second idea is heard in bars 9-14. Bars 1-5 are shown on p.88. Both ideas are played by the violins (the two parts are playing in octaves).

2) The first three notes of the first idea are repeated throughout the first subject — the second idea starts with these notes but a 6th higher.

3) This movement is marked *p* (*piano*) at the start, which is very unusual for a Classical symphony — they normally have a loud opening.

4) It's in G minor, but it modulates (changes key) to B♭ major when the subject is repeated in bars 20-28.

TRANSITION or BRIDGE PASSAGE (BARS 28-43)

1) This section is *f* (*forte*) all the way through, with lots of *sfz* (*sforzandos*) from bar 34.

2) This section begins in B♭ major, but extra chromatic notes (notes that don't fit in the key) add tension.

3) The violins play a descending sequence from bars 30-33, over a lower string tremolo with sustained notes from the upper woodwind.

SECOND SUBJECT (BARS 44-72)

1) The second subject's in B♭ major, though Mozart uses a lot of chromatic notes in this bit.

2) The strings play the theme first, then the woodwind repeat it at bar 52.

3) Mozart uses ornaments (see p.83) for the first time here — the woodwind play trills in bar 65.

CODETTA (BARS 72-100)

1) A codetta is like a mini coda — it's used to finish off the exposition section.

2) There's lots of imitation (see p.82) between the clarinet and the bassoon.

3) The key changes back from B♭ major to G minor at the end of this bit.

4) The whole of the exposition is repeated.

The Development Section is Bars 101-164

> All the music in the development section is based on the first idea from the exposition.

1) The harmonies are more chromatic in this bit.

2) The development section begins in F♯ minor, but it explores many different keys — e.g. bars 118-128.

3) From bar 140, Mozart uses lots of pedal points (see p.86).

Bars 164-299 are the Recapitulation

1) The first subject (bars 164-184) is exactly the same as in the exposition.

2) The bridge passage is much longer this time — it lasts from bar 184 to bar 227. It passes through quite a few keys — including E♭ major, F minor and D major. It's polyphonic — in bars 202-210, there's a sequence being played in canon between Violin I and the lower strings.

3) The second subject (bars 227-260) is shared between the woodwind and the strings. Now it's in G minor, and there are some ascending chromatic notes in the bass parts from bar 245.

4) The coda (bars 260-299) is an extended version of the codetta. It finishes with four G minor chords — it's really obvious that the movement's finished.

A codetta is a baby coda...

Make yourself really familiar with this movement — pay attention to the different features of each bit.

Warm-up and Exam Questions

Use the warm-up questions to get your brain in gear before attempting the Exam question.

Warm-up Questions

1) Name **two** instruments that were included in the Classical orchestra that were not used in orchestras of the Baroque period.

2) What is a concerto?

3) What is the standard structure of a Classical concerto?

4) What are the **three** main sections of a piece in sonata form?

5) Name **two** Classical composers.

Exam Question

Here's another exam-style question for you to try.

Track 32 is an extract from Mozart's *Rondo in D Major*.
Play the extract **five** times, leaving a short pause for writing between each playing.

Track 32

The score shows the first 16 bars of the melody.

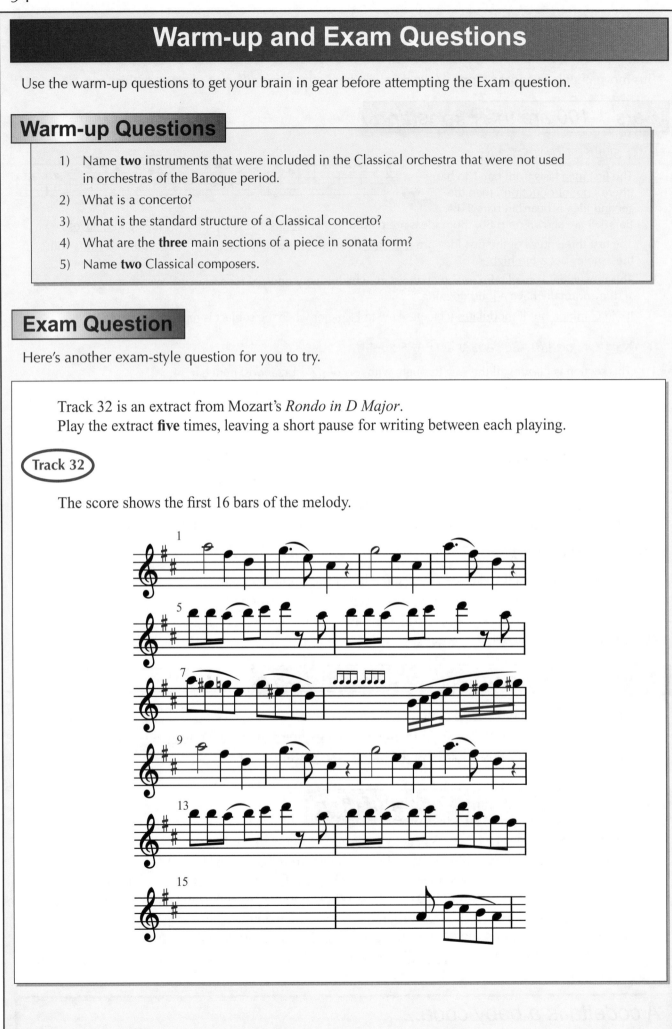

Exam Question

a) Name the types of ornamentation heard in the following bars:

    (i)   Bars 1 and 3

    .... *[1 mark]*

    (ii) Bars 5 and 6

    .... *[1 mark]*

b) Name the musical device used in the melody in bars 1 to 4.

    .... *[2 marks]*

c) What is the cadence at bars 15 to 16? Underline your answer.

        imperfect   **perfect**   **plagal**   **interrupted**   *[1 mark]*

d) Write the time signature of the music on the score.   *[1 mark]*

e) In bar 8 of the score, fill in the missing notes of the melody,
using the rhythm supplied.   *[8 marks]*

f) Describe **two** ways in which the section following bar 16 contrasts with it.

    ....

    .... *[2 marks]*

The Romantic Period

The Romantic period was about how passionate emotions can be expressed through art and music.

The **Romantic Period** was in the **19th Century**

1) The Romantic period was from about 1820-1900 (but there's a bit of an overlap between different musical periods).
2) Writers, artists and composers at this time were portraying feelings and nature in their work. They wanted to show contrasts — like love and hate, happiness and grief, and life and death.
3) As well as being inspired by the natural world, they were fascinated by supernatural ideas.
4) Composers wrote music based on poems and paintings, and also used their music to tell stories.
5) Tchaikovsky, Brahms and Chopin were all Romantic composers. Some of Beethoven's later pieces also fitted into the Romantic period.

Romantic Music is More **Dramatic** Than Classical

1) Romantic composers used a wide range of dynamics, with lots of sudden changes — in one bar, the music could change from *ppp* to *fff* and back again. They also used a lot of sforzandos and accents as well — it made the music very dramatic.
2) To make the music more expressive, composers gave extra instructions — as well as tempo markings, they would include instructions like *dolce* (sweetly), *amoroso* (lovingly) or *agitato* (agitated).
3) There were more tempo changes — a piece might change speeds lots of times within the same section. Musicians in this period used *rubato* as well — it means 'robbed time' and it's when performers speed up a little in one phrase and slow down in another to make up for it. It gives them the freedom to be more expressive.
4) Composers added extra notes to chords to make the harmonies more interesting — they used 7ths, 9ths, 11ths and 13ths (9ths, 11ths and 13ths are just 2nds, 4ths and 6ths but an octave higher). They helped create dissonance (clashing notes), which let them show emotions like pain and misery.
5) There was a lot of virtuoso playing — composers wrote technically difficult music to give performers the chance to show off. It was very exciting to watch and listen to. Rachmaninoff and Liszt wrote solo piano music that had to be written on four staves as there were so many notes to play.
6) Lots of Romantic composers were very proud of the countries they came from — they used folk tunes and dance rhythms from their homelands to show their national pride. Tchaikovsky used the French and Russian national anthems in his 1812 Overture.

The Orchestra **Developed** in the **Romantic Period**

1) Orchestras got much bigger — extra instruments were added to all sections of the orchestra, especially woodwind and percussion.
2) Brass instruments were able to play more notes as they now had valves.
3) All these changes meant that composers could write music with a larger range of texture, timbre and dynamics.
4) The development of the piano (see the next page) meant that it became a much more popular and important instrument. Lots of piano music was written in the Romantic period.

If music be the food of love — play on...

Make sure you know some key features of Romantic music — you'll need to be able to spot them in the exam. Listen out for dynamic contrasts and interesting harmonies in Chopin's *Raindrop* prelude.

The Romantic Period

The piano was definitely one of the most important instruments in the Romantic period.

The **Piano Developed** in the **Romantic Period**

The piano's been around since the 18th century, but the developments in the 19th century made it really popular with Romantic composers.

SIZE: the piano changed shape a bit and got bigger (and louder). This meant it had a bigger dynamic range.

KEYS: the number of keys (and notes) increased to just over 7 octaves. Composers now had a larger range in pitch to compose for.

PEDALS: both pedals (the sustain pedal that holds notes on and the soft pedal) became more effective. Some modern pianos have three pedals — the third pedal allows some notes to be held on while others are not.

STRINGS: the strings inside were both thicker and longer, making a fuller tone. They were also pulled tighter, so they were more tense.

FRAME: the frame used to be made of wood, but was now made of metal (to cope with the new strings). This made it easier to transport them.

HAMMERS: the hammers were given a felt covering (instead of a leather one). This made the tone softer and more rounded.

Melodies Were the **Focus** of Piano Pieces

1) In Romantic piano pieces, the melody was the most important part. Melodies were often marked *cantabile* — to be played in a singing style.

2) There were lots of virtuosic sections and cadenzas (see p.89) to give the pianist chance to show off.

3) The music had a large range of dynamics, articulation and tone. Pianists had to use the pedals a lot to get the right sounds.

4) The accompaniment was often broken chords (see p.88), but unlike many Classical pieces, the broken chords would be spread across several octaves.

Preludes Were Popular Piano Pieces

Preludes were originally the bit of music that came before the main piece. During the Romantic period, they had become popular as stand-alone pieces.

1) Debussy wrote preludes for piano. There's one in his *Suite Bergamasque*.

2) Liszt and Rachmaninoff wrote some very tricky piano preludes.

3) Chopin wrote a set of 24 piano preludes, one in each of the 24 keys. They're all pretty short — the longest is only 90 bars long, and the shortest lasts for just 13 bars. They don't follow set structures, though there are motifs (short musical ideas) that crop up in more than one prelude.

I'll have soup as a prelude to my dinner...

Pianos were popular because they were so versatile — with a range of over seven octaves, composers had fewer limitations when they were composing. The newly-developed piano could play a range of dynamics, and the pedals could be used to change the tone of the instrument too. Perfect for Romantics.

Chopin — Prelude No. 15 in D flat Major

Chopin's *Prelude No. 15 in D flat Major* is also known as the *Raindrop* prelude.

Chopin *was a* Polish Composer

1) Frédéric Chopin was born in Poland in 1810 — lots of his music uses Polish folk tunes and dance rhythms. He died in Paris in 1849.

2) He made a name for himself in Vienna before moving to Paris.

3) As well as composing, he also performed and taught music.

4) He composed a lot of piano music, and had a reputation as a 'tragic' Romantic composer, because he was ill a lot, and died young.

The Raindrop Prelude *is in* Ternary Form

1) *Prelude No. 15 in Db Major* is quite short (it's only 89 bars long) but can be divided up into four main sections. The first, Section A lasts from bars 1-27, and Section B from bars 28-75. A short bit of Section A is repeated in bars 76-81, then the piece finishes with a coda in bars 81-89. Unlike some of the other preludes, it has a clear structure — it's in ternary form (see p.80).

2) Section A is in Db major, while Section B is in C♯ minor. Enharmonically, C♯ minor is the tonic minor of Db major (as Db is the enharmonic equivalent of C♯). Chopin explores other keys in both sections — this is typical of Romantic music.

3) It's called the *Raindrop* prelude because of a repeated quaver Ab in the left-hand part (it changes to a G♯ when the key changes to C♯ minor). This note is repeated throughout the piece.

Section A Introduces the 'Raindrop'

1) This prelude is marked sostenuto — it doesn't just mean sustained here, but it should also have a slow, held back tempo. The pianist has to use the pedal a lot — it helps sustain the notes.

2) You can hear the 'raindrop' note in the first bar, and it continues throughout the piece.

3) The first melodic phrase lasts 4 bars and is marked *p* (*piano* — quiet). The first three notes of the melody are descending — like raindrops. In the bar 3, the melody is harmonised in 6ths. These four bars are repeated with no changes (except for the last beat of the phrase, which leads into the new phrase). There's an ornament (see p.83) in the fourth bar — it's a turn written out in full. The turn isn't played in the 8th bar.

4) Another melodic idea starts in the last two quavers of bar 8. It's a four-bar melody and the key moves towards Ab minor. It's followed by a variation of the tune.

5) From bars 14-20, the 'raindrop' note is played on an F, not an Ab.

6) The melody goes through Bb minor (the relative minor of Db major), then back to Db major for the last few bars of this section, where you can hear the opening melody again.

Raindrops keep falling on my piano...

Try following the phrases marked on the score as you listen to the piece. Section B's coming up next...

Chopin — Prelude No. 15 in D flat Major

This page carries on with the <u>analysis</u> of the *Raindrop* prelude — it picks up at <u>Section B</u>, which starts at bar 28 and finishes at bar 75.

Section B is in C♯ Minor

1) Section B is very <u>different</u> to Section A. It's in a <u>minor key</u>, and sounds much more <u>dramatic</u>.

2) The <u>melody</u>'s in <u>crotchets</u> in the <u>bass part</u>. The melody is played <u>underneath</u> the 'raindrop' notes — in this section, they're <u>G♯s</u>. It's marked *sotto voce*, which means '<u>in an undertone</u>' — it should be <u>soft</u> and <u>quiet</u>.

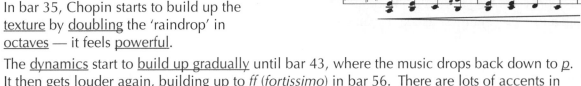

3) In bar 35, Chopin starts to build up the <u>texture</u> by <u>doubling</u> the 'raindrop' in <u>octaves</u> — it feels <u>powerful</u>.

4) The <u>dynamics</u> start to <u>build up gradually</u> until bar 43, where the music drops back down to *p*. It then gets louder again, building up to *ff* (*fortissimo*) in bar 56. There are lots of <u>accents</u> in Section B (see bars 40-43 and 56-59). This is quite a <u>contrast</u> to Section A, which was *p* all the way through with no accents.

5) In bars 60-63, the melody is quite <u>similar</u> to the start of Section B, but some of the <u>note lengths</u> have been <u>augmented</u> (made longer). This makes it feel <u>slow</u> and <u>heavy</u>.

6) In bars 64-67, the <u>repeated G♯s</u> in the top line form an <u>inverted pedal</u> (a <u>pedal point</u> is one that is <u>held on</u> or repeated, usually in the <u>bass part</u>. An inverted pedal is a <u>held note</u> in the <u>top part</u>).

7) Although this section's in <u>C♯ minor</u>, Chopin <u>explores</u> other keys — the <u>harmonies</u> pass through <u>G♯ minor</u> and <u>F♯ minor</u>.

8) Bar 75 (the last bar of Section B) is a <u>transition bar</u> between Section B and the repeat of Section A. The last 4 quavers of bar 75 prepare for the <u>key change</u> in the next bar.

Part of Section A is Repeated

1) In bar 76, the piece <u>returns</u> to the key of <u>D♭ major</u> and repeats Section A.

2) The <u>opening phrase</u> is played again, just with a slightly different <u>ornament</u> — it's more <u>chromatic</u>, and has 10 notes instead of 7.

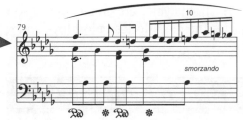

3) Chopin suggests that the piece is coming to the end by using the term *smorzando* (which means '<u>dying away</u>') in bar 79.

4) In bar 81, the melody is <u>cut short</u> to make way for the <u>coda</u>.

The Coda Finishes the Piece

1) The <u>coda</u> starts on the last beat of bar 81, and lasts until bar 89 (the end of the piece). The <u>melodic line</u> in bars 81-83 has the <u>highest notes</u> of the prelude. These are also the <u>only</u> bars that are <u>not</u> accompanied by the 'raindrop' quavers.

2) In bar 84, the 'raindrops' <u>come back</u> on the dominant note (A♭) until the final tonic (D♭) chord.

3) The coda starts off *f* then drops down to *p*. The final two bars are *pp* (*pianissimo*), the <u>quietest</u> part of the whole piece.

4) The piece <u>slows down</u> towards the end with a gentle *ritenuto*.

The Raindrop Prelude uses a range of dynamics...

Listen for the <u>contrasts</u> between Section A and Section B. Make sure you can spot the <u>key changes</u> and the <u>changes in dynamics</u>. Section B sounds a lot more <u>dramatic</u> than Section A, which is quite <u>calm</u>.

Romantic Songs — Lieder

'Lied' is the German word for 'song'. It's pronounced LEED.
If you're talking about more than one Lied you say Lieder (not 'Lieds').

Lieder are Romantic Songs

1) A Lied's a song for one singer and a piano. The piano part's not just a background accompaniment — it adds a lot to the story-telling of the piece. Lieder were really popular in Europe during the Romantic period — a bit like the pop songs of today.

> The Romantic period lasted from about 1820-1900 and included composers like Beethoven, Schubert, Chopin and Wagner. Romantic music was very expressive and dramatic.

2) The words of a Lied are really important. They're usually based on German poems from the 18th and 19th centuries. Lieder usually tell a story — they're often dramatic and full of emotion. The music illustrates the words, so you can tell when it gets sad or scary (like music in a film).

3) Some Lieder are through-composed (see p.57). This means that the music is different in each verse. Others have a strophic (p.57) structure, where the verses all have the same tune. There are lots of motifs — little bits of music that represent an idea, character or place. The motifs are repeated throughout the songs so you can follow what's happening. Sometimes the motifs match the words — in Schubert's 'Gretchen at the Spinning Wheel', the piano mimics the sound of the spinning wheel.

4) Schubert is one of the best known composers of Lieder. Other composers include Schumann, Beethoven and Brahms. Most well-known Lieder composers were German or Austrian.

Lieder Can be Put Together in Song Cycles

1) Sometimes a collection of Lieder would be put together in song cycles by the composer. These are just groups of songs on the same theme.
2) Schubert's most famous song cycles are 'Winter Journey' and 'The Fair Maid of the Mill'.
3) Both cycles are collections of songs based on the poems of a German poet called Müller. They tell stories of lost love and rejection.

'The Erl King' is a Good Example of a Lied

1) 'The Erl King' is a Lied by Schubert, based on a poem by Goethe, a German poet.
2) It tells the story of a father carrying his dying child on horseback. The child can see the Erl King, a spirit of death.
3) It's a very tragic song — the boy dies at the end.
4) There are 4 characters in the story: the father, his son, the Erl King and the narrator.
5) Schubert uses the music to create different characters. Each character sings at a different pitch so that you can tell them apart when one tenor sings all 4 parts.
6) The piano part's very dramatic — the repeated triplets sound like the horse's galloping hooves.

Franz Schubert — Lieder of the pack...

Don't forget, in Lieder, the piano part's more than just an accompaniment. The words are often (but not always) in German, so if you hear German with a piano accompaniment, it's probably a Lied.

Opera and Oratorio

Opera and oratorio are forms you'll need to know for <u>listening</u>. If you write a whole oratorio for your composition, the examiners will be so impressed they'll probably fall down in a <u>faint</u>. Very undignified.

Operas are Like **Plays** Set to **Music**

1) The <u>main characters</u> are played by <u>solo singers</u>.

2) The main characters are supported by a <u>chorus</u> and an <u>orchestra</u>.

3) The story is <u>acted out</u> — usually with <u>lavish sets</u>, <u>costumes</u> and <u>special effects</u>.

4) In some operas <u>every single word</u> is sung — in others there's a bit of <u>talking</u> from time to time.

5) Some operas have really serious, <u>tragic</u> themes. Others are more light-hearted and <u>comic</u>. These are the names for the main types.

6) The words of an opera are called the '<u>libretto</u>'. This is often written by a 'librettist' working alongside the composer.

Grand opera	serious, set entirely to music
Opéra comique	some spoken dialogue
Opera buffa	comic opera
Opera seria	formal, serious opera

In Opera There are **Three Types** *of* **Singing**

ARIA

1) An <u>aria</u> is a <u>solo</u> vocal piece, backed by the orchestra.

2) Arias are used to go into the <u>emotions</u> of the main characters.

3) The arias have the <u>memorable</u>, <u>exciting tunes</u>. They're <u>challenging</u> for the performers and let them show their vocal <u>tone</u> and <u>agility</u>.

RECITATIVE

1) <u>Recitative</u> is a half-spoken, half-singing style used for some <u>conversations</u>.

2) <u>Recitativo secco</u> is recitative that's <u>unaccompanied</u> or backed by <u>simple chords</u>.

3) <u>Recitativo stromentato</u> or <u>accompagnato</u> is recitative with orchestral backing. The accompaniment's used to increase the <u>dramatic tension</u> of the words.

CHORUS — A bit where the <u>whole chorus</u> sings together.

Oratorio is the **Religious** *Version of Opera*

1) An oratorio has <u>arias</u>, <u>recitatives</u> and <u>choruses</u> just like an opera.

2) Oratorios usually have a <u>religious theme</u>. They're based on <u>traditional stories</u>, sometimes from the Bible.

3) Oratorios don't usually have scenery, costumes or action — they're <u>not acted out</u>.

4) Oratorios were written mainly for <u>concert</u> or <u>church</u> performance.

COMPOSER	LIVED	FAMOUS ORATORIO
Carissimi	1605-1674	Jephte
Handel	1685-1759	Messiah
Hadyn	1732-1809	The Creation
Berlioz	1803-1869	L'Enfance du Christ
Mendelssohn	1809-1847	Elijah
Elgar	1857-1934	The Dream of Gerontius
Walton	1902-1983	Belshazzar's Feast

Smaller Vocal Pieces

These songs are shorter than operas, but you still need to know their <u>forms</u>.

Lots of Music Was Written to be *Sung* in *Church*

CANTATA

Some things in a <u>cantata</u> are similar to <u>oratorio</u>. The performers are <u>solo singers</u>, a <u>chorus</u> and an <u>orchestra</u>. There's <u>no scenery</u> and <u>no acting</u> and they were written to be performed in a <u>church</u> or <u>concert hall</u>.

The <u>difference</u> is that the <u>words</u> are taken from books or poems — they're not specially written. Most cantatas have a religious theme — but <u>not all</u> of them.

CHORALE

<u>Chorales</u> are hymns. They have <u>simple language</u> and a melody that's <u>easy to sing</u>. <u>J.S. Bach</u> wrote lots of them. Here's a bit from a chorale he put in *St. Matthew's Passion*.

O Lord, who dares to smite Thee?

MOTET & ANTHEM

A <u>motet</u>'s a short piece written to be performed by the <u>choir</u> in church. They're written for <u>Roman Catholic</u> churches and the words are often in <u>Latin</u>. Motets are <u>polyphonic</u> — see p.39.

An <u>anthem</u> is very similar to a motet except they're written for <u>Protestant</u> churches, so the words aren't in Latin.

MASS

The <u>mass</u> is the name of a Roman Catholic church service — these parts of the mass are sung by the choir, or the choir and soloists:

- Kyrie — *Lord have mercy...*
- Gloria — *Glory be to God on high...*
- Credo — *I believe in one God...*
- Sanctus — *Holy, holy, holy...*
- Benedictus — *Blessed is He...*
- Agnus Dei — *O Lamb of God...*

(Some of them are quite long, so I've only given you the starting bits.)

Musical settings of the Mass were originally written to be <u>used in church</u>, but nowadays they're played in concerts, too. The text is usually in <u>Latin</u>.

Madrigals and *Lieder* are *Non-Religious*

Most madrigals were written in the <u>1500s</u> and <u>1600s</u>. They're about love or the countryside — or both. Most have <u>no accompaniment</u> and each person sings a <u>different part</u>. Madrigals often use <u>imitation</u> (see p.82).

Now is the month of May-ing, When mer-ry lads are play-ing; Fa la la la la la la la la, Fa la la la la la la.

A <u>lied</u>'s a <u>song</u> for <u>one singer</u> and a <u>piano</u>. Both parts are equally important. The words really matter too — they're usually based on <u>poems</u>. Lieder were massively popular in the <u>German Romantic</u> period (late 18th to early 19th century) — there's more about them on p.100.

To wan-der is the mil-ler's joy, to wan-der

From The Wandering Miller by Schubert. He wrote over 600 lieder.

They don't seem to have mentioned karaoke...

Several more types of music to learn about here, but then that's it for this section. Cover the page and see if you can remember them all — if not, back to the top of the page and read 'em again..

Revision Summary for Section Five

What you need to take away from this section are the facts about Baroque, Classical and Romantic music — it's really important that you know how they were different from each other. Have a go at these questions to check that you're up to speed. You know what to do — keep going through them until you can answer them all without needing to look back through the section.

1) What are the four main voices in a mixed sex choir?

2) Describe the terms melismatic, syllabic and word-painting.

3) What type of music does John Rutter write?

4) Give the approximate dates of the Baroque and Classical periods.

5) How do the dynamics change in Baroque music?

6) What is a basso continuo and what instruments would normally play it?

7) Which Baroque structure can be described as AABBAA?

8) In theme and variation form, what is the theme?

9) What is the main difference between theme and variation form and ground bass form?

10) Explain what each of these terms means:

   a) melodic inversion   b) retrograde   c) ostinato.

11) Name three different ornaments used by Baroque composers and explain what they are.

12) What is an appoggiatura?

13) What are the three main types of songs in Baroque choral music?

14) Write down three features of an oratorio.

15) In what year did Handel write 'Messiah'?

16) What are the three sections of 'Messiah' about?

17) Describe where the *And the Glory of the Lord* chorus comes in 'Messiah'.

18) Write down the words that make up the *And the Glory of the Lord* chorus.

19) Describe the way the key modulates in *And the Glory of the Lord*.

20) Write down two features of the last four bars of *And the Glory of the Lord* which make the piece sound finished.

21) What is the most important section in a Classical orchestra?

22) Classical music usually has a homophonic texture. What does this mean?

23) What are the three main sections in sonata form?

24) What instruments did Mozart write *Symphony No. 40* for?

25) What is the first movement of *Symphony No. 40* called and what form is it in?

26) How does Mozart develop the Exposition in bars 101-164 of *Symphony No. 40*?

27) Write down four ideas which inspired Romantic composers.

28) Why is Chopin's *Prelude No. 15 in D flat Major* known as the *Raindrop* prelude?

29) Briefly describe the structure of the *Raindrop* prelude.

30) What key is Section A of the *Raindrop* prelude in? What key is Section B in?

31) What's a Lied?

32) Where do the words of Lieder usually come from?

33) Name two composers of Lieder.

34) What are the words of an opera called?

35) What are the three main singing styles in an opera?

36) Write down one difference and one similarity between opera and oratorio.

37) What's the difference between a motet and an anthem?

38) Write down the six main parts of a mass.

Expressionism

In the 1900s composers started changing the way music was written.
They dumped Classical-style tonal music — they hardly ever used major and minor scales.

Romantic Composers Started the Move Away From Tonality

The big changes to music in the twentieth century didn't just appear suddenly.
They developed from changes that were already happening during the Romantic period.

1) Classical music is tonal — the key a melody's written in gives it a definite character.

2) Romantic composers used a lot of chromatic notes
   and chords — notes and chords that didn't belong
   to the main key of a melody.

   > The Romantic period runs roughly
   > from 1820 to 1900 — it fills the
   > gap between Classical music and the
   > twentieth century. There's more about
   > the Romantic period on p.96-97.

3) The Romantics put in so many chromatics that their music
   started to lose the character of the main key.

4) By the twentieth century a lot of music sounded like it didn't
   belong to any key at all. Music that doesn't sound like it comes
   from any particular key is called atonal.

The change from tonal to atonal music doesn't sound that dramatic on paper, but it was a really
big change. The old forms like binary, ternary and rondo (see p.80 for more on these) relied
on fixed keys to create contrast between the different sections. Now fixed keys were gone,
so were all the old ways of structuring music.

Arnold Schoenberg's Music Was Expressionist

1) Arnold Schoenberg was born in Vienna, Austria, in 1874. He was a composer, conductor
   and teacher at the University of Vienna. His early music had a late-Romantic feel.
   He followed composers like Wagner by adding lots of chromatics to his piece.

2) In the early twentieth century he became interested in the ideas of expressionist painters like
   Wassily Kandinsky. Expressionists believed that art should express your inner feelings without
   being restricted by conventional forms. The practical result of this in Kandinsky's paintings was
   abstract shapes and moody colours.

3) In Schoenberg's music the practical result was his move towards atonal music (his earlier music
   was tonal). He felt traditional tonal music was too restrictive. It couldn't express the full range
   of human emotions — especially not the more unhappy ones. His music had lots of dissonance
   (clashing notes) that didn't resolve (move to a non-clashing note) straight away.

4) One of Schoenberg's first atonal pieces, *Three Piano Pieces*, was first performed in 1909.

   EXPRESSIONIST MUSIC:
   * is intensely emotional
   * has angular, spiky melodies
   * has lots of dissonance (chords with clashing notes)
   * is mainly atonal (doesn't sound like it's in a particular key)
   * has contrasting dynamics
   * doesn't really have cadences, repetition or sequences
   * is always changing — it never sticks with any one musical idea for long

5) Schoenberg invented serialism (see p.107-108) in 1923.

Chromatics, chromatics — nothing but chromatics...

Make sure you know the difference between tonal and atonal music, and can identify it when you hear it.

Arnold Schoenberg — Peripetie

Schoenberg's music sounds a bit <u>weird</u>. You need to know the <u>features</u> that <u>make it</u> weird.

Schoenberg's Music Changed From *Tonal* to *Atonal*

1) Schoenberg wrote a string sextet called '<u>Verklärte Nacht</u>' in 1899.
It's <u>tonal</u>, but has lots of <u>chromaticism</u> in it.

2) His first <u>orchestral</u> work was '<u>Pelleas und Melisande</u>' in 1903.

3) He wrote a suite called '<u>Five Orchestral Pieces</u>' ('Fünf Orchesterstücke') in 1909.
One movement's called *Peripetie* — (it's covered in more detail on the next page).
By this point, most of Schoenberg's work was <u>atonal</u>, including this suite.

4) In '<u>Pierrot-Lunaire</u>' (1912), an atonal piece for soprano and chamber orchestra,
Schoenberg used a <u>half-singing</u>, <u>half-speaking</u> vocal technique (<u>Sprechstimme</u>) to deliver
gruesome lines. Movements have cheery titles like *Homesickness*, *Song of the Gallows*
and *Decapitation*. At one point, Pierrot drills into another character's brain.

5) '<u>5 Pieces for Piano</u>' (1923) was one of his first <u>serial</u> works (see p.107).

Peripetie is an *Expressionist* Piece

1) *Peripetie* is the <u>fourth</u> movement of Schoenberg's '<u>Five Orchestral Pieces</u>'. It was originally
written in 1909, but he <u>revised</u> it in 1922 and 1949. It's an example of one of Schoenberg's
<u>Expressionist</u> pieces.

2) He didn't want to give each movement a <u>title</u>, but gave in because his publisher thought it was
a good idea. He deliberately chose names that didn't <u>give away</u> too much about the piece
— he thought the <u>music</u> should <u>speak for itself</u>. The other movements are called
Premonitions, *The Past*, *Summer Morning by a Lake: Chord Colours* and *Obbligato Recitative*.

3) *Peripetie* comes from a Greek word that means '<u>sudden changes</u>'. It's very <u>different</u> to the one
before it, and there are lots of <u>changes</u> of <u>timbre</u> and <u>texture</u> within the piece (see next page).

Peripetie Was Written for a *Big Orchestra*

1) By the end of the Romantic period, orchestras were <u>huge</u>.
They'd often have full <u>woodwind</u> sections and lots of <u>percussion</u>.

2) Schoenberg wrote his '5 Orchestral Pieces' for a <u>big</u> orchestra.
It allowed him to make lots of <u>contrasts</u> in <u>texture</u>, timbre and <u>dynamics</u>.

3) *Peripetie* needs a massive <u>woodwind</u> section — it's written for <u>quadruple woodwind</u>.
Quadruple woodwind is <u>three flutes</u> and a <u>piccolo</u>, <u>three oboes</u> and a <u>cor anglais</u>,
<u>three clarinets</u> and a <u>bass clarinet</u> and <u>three bassoons</u> and a <u>contrabassoon</u>.

4) It also needs a big <u>brass</u> section — <u>six horns</u>, <u>three trumpets</u>, <u>four trombones</u>
and a <u>tuba</u>. There's lots of <u>percussion</u> as well, including <u>timpani</u>, <u>cymbals</u> and
a <u>xylophone</u>. The <u>string</u> section was fairly standard though.

5) When Schoenberg <u>revised</u> the piece in <u>1949</u>, he <u>changed</u> the instrumentation a bit.
He used <u>fewer</u> instruments, <u>reducing</u> the number of clarinets, oboes, bassoons,
horns and trombones. This made it a bit more <u>accessible</u> for <u>smaller</u> orchestras.

6) The parts are <u>tricky</u> — lots of instruments play <u>very high</u> or <u>very low</u>.
There are big <u>leaps in pitch</u> too, sometimes more than an <u>octave</u>.

Bigger orchestras allow more expressive and dramatic music...

Schoenberg was a bit of a <u>revolutionary</u> — he wrote music in a very different style to composers that
came before him. Unfortunately this means there's more for you to learn, so keep at it...

Arnold Schoenberg — Peripetie

'Peripetie' is only a short piece (it lasts about 2 minutes), but Schoenberg manages to cram a lot into it.

It Has an **Unusual Structure**

1) Schoenberg didn't use a conventional structure — there isn't an obvious melody. He uses melodic fragments and complicated, fragmented rhythms. Each fragment is based on a hexachord — a group of six notes from the 12 different semitones. The six semitones not used in the hexachord are called the complement.

2) It's atonal (not written in a key). Schoenberg uses the hexachords to create dissonances (clashing notes).

3) *Peripetie*'s almost in rondo form (see p.80) — the same melodic idea returns a few times. Some people say it's a free rondo. The sections are different lengths, and the textures and tempos change in each section.

4) This movement's marked *Sehr rasch* (very fast) and it's only 66 bars long. Schoenberg gives other instructions during the piece, like *heftig* (passionate) and *ruhiger* (calmer).

5) It's an example of Klangfarbenmelodie (a German word that means 'tone-colour-melody'). The name was made up by Schoenberg, and it's a technique he used to break up a melody by passing it round different parts. It gives the tune variations in the timbre (tone colour).

The **Instrumentation** Changes in Each **Section**

The free rondo structure is made up of five sections — ABA'CA" (A' and A" are variations on Section A).

SECTION A (BARS 1-18) Every instrument in the orchestra gets to play in Section A, but only for a bar or two at a time. The instruments play in groups — the clarinets, bass clarinet and bassoons play one melodic fragment, followed by the trumpets and trombones, and so on — the little bits of tune are passed around the orchestra. This section starts off very loud, but drops down to *pp* in bar 6.

SECTION B (BARS 18-34) Again, all the instruments in the orchestra get to play in this section, but this time most parts play alone. They're all playing different rhythms, and the parts overlap. Towards the end of this section, almost every instrument's playing at the same time, though not the same rhythms — it has a very thick texture. Section B starts off very quietly, but the dynamics build up quickly.

SECTION A' (BARS 35-43) The hexachord from bar 8 is played again by the horns.

SECTION C (BARS 44-58) This section has a thin texture — there are solo lines for the cello and double bass. There are a few loud semiquaver triplets, but most of this section is calm and quiet.

SECTION A" (BARS 59-66) *Peripetie* finishes with another variation of Section A. The instrumentation builds up from just the clarinets and strings until the whole orchestra plays a *fff* chord in bar 64. The piece finishes with a *pp* chord in the horns and double bass.

There Are Lots of **Contrasts**

1) *Peripetie* is a very dramatic piece. Schoenberg uses lots of sudden changes in texture, dynamics and timbre to make it sound exciting.

2) There's a wide range of extreme dynamics — from *pp* to *fff*. The dynamics change very quickly.

3) There are sudden changes of texture. In some places, lots of instruments play different parts, all weaving in and out of each other (polyphony or counterpoint). At other points, the texture is much thinner and you can hear a solo instrument, like a clarinet or flute.

4) Schoenberg changes the timbre a lot as well. There are quick changes between families of instruments, like woodwind, strings and brass. This changes the sound of the piece.

5) He uses lots of different note lengths — from demi-semiquavers to semibreves.

Serialism

Not content with trying out a new sound, Schoenberg also worked out a completely new <u>theory</u> to help him compose longer, more interesting pieces.

Schoenberg **Replaced** Tonality With **Serialism**

1) Once Schoenberg had done away with the conventions of using major and minor keys he needed to find a new way to <u>structure</u> his music. The method he came up with was called <u>serialism</u>.

2) Serialism meant putting some element of the piece into a <u>series</u> or <u>order</u> — it could be a set order of <u>volume changes</u> or a particular set of <u>notes</u> — his first works concentrated on ordering the notes.

3) To compose a piece, Schoenberg would start by arranging the <u>12 chromatic notes</u> of an octave into a <u>set order</u>. It was known as the <u>12-Tone System</u>. The initial arrangement is called the <u>Prime Order</u>:

The Prime Order is **Rearranged**

The <u>next step</u> in creating a piece of music is to <u>rearrange the prime order</u>.
Schoenberg had several fixed ways of doing this...

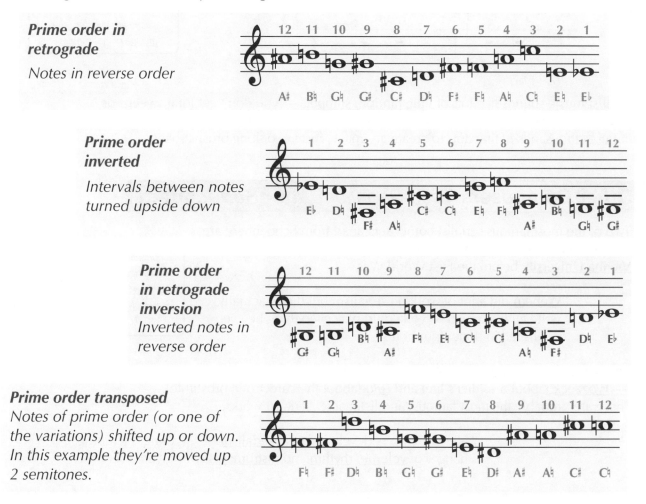

Prime order in retrograde
Notes in reverse order

Prime order inverted
Intervals between notes turned upside down

Prime order in retrograde inversion
Inverted notes in reverse order

Prime order transposed
Notes of prime order (or one of the variations) shifted up or down. In this example they're moved up 2 semitones.

The four different versions of the Prime Order can be <u>transposed</u> — each one can start on any of the twelve different notes. This creates <u>48</u> different sets of notes to work with. These sequences of notes are called <u>rows</u> — they're written out horizontally, not vertically (like chords)

Serialism

Once you've got the alternative orders it's time to do some <u>actual composing</u> — deciding what rhythms to use, how to construct your chords, what <u>sounds good</u>...

The **Snippets of Melody Combine** as a Complete Piece

Once Schoenberg had all his variations on the prime order, he could use these patterns of notes as <u>building blocks</u> to create a complete piece of music.

1) Notes from the prime order, or variations, could be played in the <u>bass line</u> or <u>melody</u> and in <u>any octave</u>.

2) Notes could be combined to make <u>motifs</u> — memorable bits of melody that reappear through the piece.

3) Groups of notes from the prime order and variations could be piled up to make <u>chords</u>. Notes that were next to each other in the original rows would be played all at once by different instruments. This is called <u>verticalisation</u> — notes that were written out horizontally in the rows would be written out <u>vertically</u> in the score.

4) The prime order could be designed to create decent-sounding chords with <u>triads</u>.

5) The prime order could also be designed to create <u>cluster chords</u> with notes really close together.

cluster chord

FAC triad

> Serialist music is very complicated to write so most pieces are only for <u>small groups</u> of instruments.

Serialist music sounds like lots of little <u>random snippets</u> — you don't get long sweeps of melody or a steady rhythm. It's sometimes described as <u>pointillist</u> after a painting style that uses thousands of tiny dots to create an image, instead of long brushstrokes.

Other Composers Tried Serialism After Schoenberg

Two of the most famous serialist composers apart from Schoenberg are Anton Webern and Alban Berg. They both studied with Schoenberg at <u>Vienna University</u> before the First World War.

> Schoenberg, Webern and Berg are sometimes called the <u>'Second Viennese School'</u> — the first was Haydn, Mozart and Beethoven 100 years before.

<u>Webern</u> did a lot of work on serialism but didn't actually write all that much — you could play everything he ever published in under four hours.

<u>Berg</u> wrote loads compared to Webern, including two operas — *Wozzeck* (about a soldier's life) and *Lulu* (about the career of a prostitute). These are probably the most famous (and listenable) serialist works.

Later composers developed <u>total serialism</u>. Everything, including changes of <u>volume</u>, <u>rhythm</u> and <u>instruments</u>, was given a set order.

Serialist music sounds random but it's very deliberate...

Serialism's not the easiest music to get into, and there's no guarantee you'll ever really take to it however hard you try... but you've got to at least give it a go. You won't know till you've tried.

Minimalism

Minimalist painting is painting with just a few lines or squares. Minimalist <u>music</u> is music that just changes a <u>tiny subtle bit</u> at a time. It's all about slow, gradual changes.

Minimalism Builds Music out of Loops

1) Minimalism is a <u>Western art music</u> style that developed during the <u>1960s</u> and <u>1970s</u>.

2) It's a lot <u>simpler</u> than expressionist music — it's easier to hear what's going on.

3) It's made up of constantly repeated patterns called <u>loops</u>. The loops are <u>short</u> and <u>simple</u>, but the final music can get quite <u>complicated</u> — especially the <u>rhythm</u>.

4) There's <u>no real tune</u> — you can't sing along to minimalist music.

5) The <u>harmonies</u> are made by <u>layering patterns</u> one on top of the other. They take a <u>long time</u> to <u>change</u>.

6) Some of the 'big names' in minimalism are <u>Steve Reich</u> (see p.111), <u>Philip Glass</u> and <u>Terry Riley</u>.

These are the Main Techniques for Changing the Loops

These different ways of changing the loop patterns are used in most minimalist pieces:

Notes are gradually added or taken away

One note is <u>added</u> on each repetition of the pattern — this is called <u>additive melody</u>.

Another similar idea is to <u>replace one note with a rest</u>, or one rest with a note on each repetition.

The notes of the pattern change over time

This technique's called <u>metamorphosis</u> — another word for 'changing'. Tiny changes to <u>one note</u>, or <u>one bit of the rhythm</u>, are made in each repetition.

Often the changes go <u>full circle</u>, so the pattern ends up the <u>same</u> or nearly the same as it was at the start.

Adding or removing notes or rests

Two or more performers start with the <u>same pattern</u>. On each repeat, a note or rest is <u>added</u> or <u>taken away</u> from one of the parts. This changes the <u>length</u> of the pattern in the different parts.

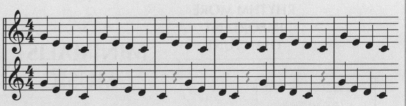

They move gradually <u>out of sync</u> and then gradually back in. The proper name for this is <u>phase shifting</u>.

Classic 90s dance act Orbital used phase shifting on the album Orbital II. In the song Time Becomes, two versions of the phrase "where time becomes a loop" are played simultaneously. They start off in sync, but one's got a bigger gap at the end, so they go gradually out of phase, then gradually back in phase.

Layering different-length patterns together

This one's called '<u>layering</u>'. You play loops of <u>different lengths</u>, e.g. a 4-beat loop and a 5-beat loop, <u>at the same time</u>. You get a similar effect to phase-shifting — the patterns move <u>apart</u> then come back <u>together</u>.

Minimalism

If you've ever seen a film called _The Piano_ then you've heard minimalist music
— the soundtrack's by the British minimalist composer Michael Nyman.

Music Technology Plays a Big Part in Minimalism

Minimalism has always used a lot of <u>electronic</u> bits and bobs to put music together.
When composers first started writing minimalist music in the <u>1960s</u>, they had a bit of a challenge
on their hands, because music technology was a lot less <u>sophisticated</u> than it is today...

1) The repeated <u>loops</u> were played using <u>old-fashioned tape recorders</u> —
   the ones you see in old spy films with two massive wheels for the tape.

2) Composers made <u>loops</u> by carefully <u>cutting</u> a tape so it just had
   the bits of music they wanted, then <u>sticking</u> the cut ends together.

   > _Steve Reich_ and _Terry Riley_ are two of the minimalist composers who came up with this technique for looping.

3) The loop was played by running it <u>out of the tape player</u> and around
   something smooth, like a <u>bottle</u> or <u>mike stand</u>, so it could keep going
   round and round.

4) They didn't just use loops of music. They made loop recordings of <u>words</u>
   and other noises too — it's a bit like modern <u>sampling</u> (p.69).

5) The different loops were put together using <u>multitrack recording</u>. They were
   recorded, one on top of another, to create the layered sound of minimalism.

6) Even <u>live</u> performances of minimalist music often make use of
   <u>recorded backing tracks</u>, played alongside the live instruments.

Minimalism Uses Musical Ideas from All Over the World

Minimalists didn't just sit around in libraries waiting for inspiration to strike.
Most of them have borrowed ideas from <u>other countries</u> and <u>other cultures</u>.

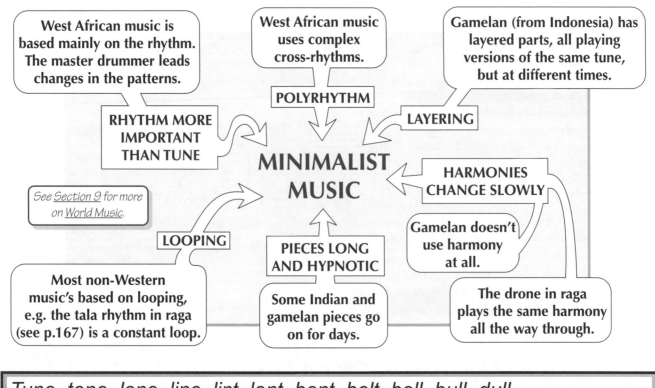

West African music is based mainly on the rhythm. The master drummer leads changes in the patterns.

West African music uses complex cross-rhythms.

Gamelan (from Indonesia) has layered parts, all playing versions of the same tune, but at different times.

POLYRHYTHM

LAYERING

RHYTHM MORE IMPORTANT THAN TUNE

See Section 9 for more on World Music.

MINIMALIST MUSIC

HARMONIES CHANGE SLOWLY

LOOPING

PIECES LONG AND HYPNOTIC

Gamelan doesn't use harmony at all.

Most non-Western music's based on looping, e.g. the tala rhythm in raga (see p.167) is a constant loop.

Some Indian and gamelan pieces go on for days.

The drone in raga plays the same harmony all the way through.

Tune, tone, lone, line, lint, lent, bent, belt, bell, bull, dull...

Minimalism can take a bit of <u>getting used to</u>, because the tune just isn't that important.
It's those tiny continual changes to the <u>rhythm</u> and <u>texture</u> that you're supposed to listen out for.
On the plus side, minimalist music's going to be dead easy to recognise in the Listening exam...

Steve Reich — 3rd Movement from Electric Counterpoint

Steve Reich is an American composer. He's won lots of awards — including a Grammy.

Steve Reich has Composed a Lot of Minimalist Music

1) Reich was born in New York in 1936. He had piano lessons when he was young, then started learning the drums when he was 14.

2) He did a degree in Philosophy, then studied composition with the modernist composer Luciano Berio.

3) His music is influenced by jazz and non-Western ideas, like African drumming (see p.172-174) and Balinese Gamelan (see p.178-180).

4) He had a go at writing serial music (see p.107-108), but preferred writing tonal music (music that's written in a key). After meeting the minimalist composer Terry Riley in the 1960s, Reich began writing minimalist compositions.

He's Written Music for Instruments, Voices and Tape

1) One of his best-known works is a piece called *Different Trains*. It was written in 1988 and is a reaction to the Holocaust. It uses samples of people talking about train journeys, then imitates their voices with instruments.

2) He wrote a piece of music for people clapping (called *Clapping Music*) in 1972. It's for 2 people — one claps a steady rhythm throughout the piece. The other claps the same pattern, but shifts it by one quaver every few bars. It's an example of phase shifting (see p.109).

3) *Vermont Counterpoint* (1982) is for flute and pre-recorded tape.

4) *New York Counterpoint* (1985) is for clarinet and pre-recorded tape. The recorded parts can also be performed by live clarinetists.

Electric Counterpoint is Performed by One Guitarist

1) *Electric Counterpoint* was written for the jazz guitarist Pat Metheny in 1987.

2) It has three movements. The third movement has 7 electric guitars and 2 electric bass guitars, as well as the solo guitar part. The whole piece should be performed by a single guitarist — they play along with a multitrack recording of the other parts (called 'ensemble parts') made before the performance.

3) The movements don't have titles — they're just marked ♩ = 192, ♩ = 96 and ♩ = 192. People tend to call them 'Fast', 'Slow' and 'Fast'. The middle movement's half the speed of the others, so there's a constant pulse. The guitarist shouldn't pause between movements, but go straight from one to the next.

4) The third movement is 140 bars long and lasts about 4 and a half minutes. It's in 3/2 (3 minim beats per bar), but at some points, a few guitars (including the live part) play in 12/8 while the others stay in 3/2. The parts still fit together because both time signatures can be divided into 12 quavers per bar.

5) It's made up of short patterns (or riffs) that are repeated lots of times. A repeated pattern like this is called an ostinato (p.82).

6) The timbre (tone colour, see p.70) of the piece doesn't change much because it only uses guitars and bass guitars, which all have a similar sound. The parts all blend together.

Steve Reich — 3rd Movement from Electric Counterpoint

Just one more page on *Electric Counterpoint* then you're done with minimalism.

Reich Uses **Looping** to Build up **Layers**

1) Each different part is pre-recorded onto a tape loop (or computer loop these days). These parts are overdubbed (recorded on top of one another) using multitracking in a studio to build up the layers. The performer then plays the live part over the top of the recording.

2) The music's repetitive — the same loops are repeated in the ensemble parts (this makes the music sound more hypnotic). At some points (like bars 20-35), the solo guitar's melody is made up of notes that the ensemble parts are playing. It takes its first two notes from guitar 1, its third note from guitar 2, etc.

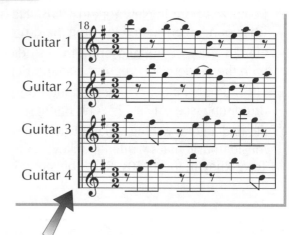

3) Four of the ensemble parts play the same riff throughout the piece. One guitar starts off playing it alone, then the others come in one by one. They all play it at different times — they're in canon (like a round).

4) When it first comes in, guitar 3's part is built up by a technique called note addition (or additive melody — see p.109). It starts off playing just a few notes of the riff, then two or three notes are added each time it's played until the whole riff is heard. It starts in bar 10, but doesn't play the whole riff until bar 15.

Electric Counterpoint is **Polyphonic**

1) As well as the canonic one-bar riff (see point 3 above), Reich builds up another canon between the solo part and the other three ensemble guitars (this first starts in bar 36). They play a repeated strummed chord sequence.

2) The texture is polyphonic (p.39) — it's made up of two or more independent parts being played at the same time. The parts fit together harmonically. The two canons going on at the same time make the polyphony more complex and interesting.

3) The counterpoint is really obvious in the sections where some parts are playing in 3/2 and the others in 12/8 (like bars 82-85). One canon is being played with three (minim) beats in a bar, and the other with four (dotted crochet) beats in a bar.

The Piece **Changes** Between **Two Keys**

1) This movement of *Electric Counterpoint* changes between E minor and C minor. The first modulation (key change) happens about halfway through the piece (in bar 74), but there are another 13 before the end. These key changes happen more frequently as the piece builds up — some only last for two or three bars. The harmony is quite static (the chords don't change very often).

2) Changes in the time signature (from 3/2 to 12/8 and back) in the solo and bass guitar parts happen more often towards the end of the piece as well. It feels like they're switching between three and four beats in a bar. The main part of the piece is in 3/2 though.

3) There are lots of changes in dynamics, mainly in the solo part, which fades in and out during the piece. The four ensemble parts playing the first riff stay at a constant *mf* throughout, but the other parts have some diminuendos. It finishes with a *fortissimo* (*ff*) climax from the solo part.

Warm-up and Exam Questions

You've just met lots of "isms" — Expressionism, Serialism and Minimalism. Time to test how much of it you've remembered. If you struggle with the warm-up questions, re-read the pages before continuing.

Warm-up Questions

1) What does atonal mean?
2) What is the 12-Tone System?
3) Name a serialist composer other than Schoenberg.
4) What is the main musical technique used to create minimalist music?

Exam Question

Here's another exam-style question for you to try — it's a big one, so take a deep breath...

This question consists of **two** extracts, Track 33 and Track 34.
Track 33 is an extract from Peripetie by Arnold Schoenberg.
Play the extract **three** times, leaving a short pause for writing time between each playing.

(Track 33)

a) Which of the following words best describes the tonality of the extract?
Circle your answer.

Tonal   **Atonal**   **Pentatonic**

[1 mark]

b) What period was this piece composed in?
Circle your answer.

1700-1800   **1800-1890**   **1890-1950**

[1 mark]

c) Schoenberg was an Expressionist composer.
State **four** key features of Expressionist music that can be heard in the extract.

....

....

....

.... *[4 marks]*

Turn over

Exam Questions

Track 34 is an extract from a Prelude by J.S. Bach.
Play the extract **three** times, leaving a short pause for writing time between each playing.

(Track 34)

d) Which of the following words best describes the tonality of the extract?
Circle your answer.

Tonal   Modal   Chromatic

[1 mark]

e) i) What name is used to describe the change in harmony in the final cadence of the extract?

.... *[1 mark]*

ii) Describe the features of this type of cadence.

....

.... *[2 marks]*

Play Track 33 and Track 34 again, **twice**.

(Track 33) (Track 34)

f) Compare the texture of the two extracts and explain how they are typical of the musical periods in which they were written.

....

....

....

....

....

.... *[4 marks]*

Songs from Musicals

Musicals are a lighter, more modern version of opera. They've been developing since the 19th century.

Musicals Have *Songs*, *Dialogue* and *Dances*

1) Musicals came from lighter versions of opera, like opéra comique and operetta (see p.84). Towards the end of the 19th century, Gilbert and Sullivan wrote lots of popular comic operas.

2) The type of musicals that are around today started in the 1920s, and developed throughout the rest of the 20th and into the 21st century. They started out on Broadway, a famous theatre street in New York. Some started in London's West End.

3) Musicals use singing, dancing and talking to tell stories.

4) They usually have an orchestra to accompany the singers and play incidental (background) music.

5) Some musicals that started out on the stage have been made into really popular films — like 'Grease', 'West Side Story' and 'Sweeney Todd'. Sometimes, a musical that started life as a film is adapted into a musical performed on stage — like 'Billy Elliot'.

6) Some musicals are based on novels — like 'Wicked' and 'Oliver!'.

Musical Styles are Always *Changing*

Musicals are generally written in the style of the popular music that's around at the time — so musicals from different times sound very different. Earlier musicals were influenced by jazz and swing music (see p.123-124), while lots of musicals from the 1970s onwards used rock music (see p.129). Have a listen to some of these musicals to hear the different styles they use:

1920s-1950s	***COLE PORTER*** 'Paris', 'Anything Goes', 'Kiss Me, Kate', 'Silk Stockings'
1940s-1950s	***RODGERS & HAMMERSTEIN*** 'Oklahoma!', 'South Pacific', 'The King and I', 'The Sound of Music'
1950s-2000s	***STEPHEN SONDHEIM*** 'Follies', 'Sweeney Todd' and lyrics for 'West Side Story'
1960s-1990s	***KANDER & EBB*** 'Cabaret', 'Chicago', 'Kiss of the Spider Woman'
1970s-2000s	***ANDREW LLOYD WEBBER*** 'Joseph and the Amazing Technicolour Dreamcoat', 'Jesus Christ Superstar', 'Evita', 'Cats', 'Phantom of the Opera'
1970s-2000s	***SCHÖNBERG & BOUBLIL*** 'Les Miserables', 'Miss Saigon'

Some *Pop Songs* Start Life in *Musicals*...

Songs from musicals sometimes hit the charts.
In the UK, musicals by Andrew Lloyd Webber and Tim Rice have spawned a few chart hits:

- *Don't Cry For Me Argentina* from 'Evita'.
- *Memory* from 'Cats'.
- *No Matter What* from 'Whistle Down the Wind' (sung by Boyzone).

...While Some *Musicals* are Made Up of *Pop Songs*

On the other hand, sometimes chart hits find their way into musicals — 'Mamma Mia!' was written around a collection of Abba hits, and 'We Will Rock You' is based on the songs of Queen. The plots of these musicals often have nothing to do with the band, but use their songs to tell the story.

Songs from Musicals

Here's how to create that Broadway sound...

Most Musical Songs are Easy on the Ear

Musicals are meant to be <u>entertaining</u> and <u>easy to listen to</u>. This is how they do it...

1) The tunes are easy to <u>sing</u> — audiences tend to prefer songs they can sing along to.

2) The harmony (the chords and stuff) is <u>diatonic</u> — it'll be in either a major or a minor key.

3) The song <u>structure</u> is often <u>simple</u>, with alternating verses and choruses and a middle eight.

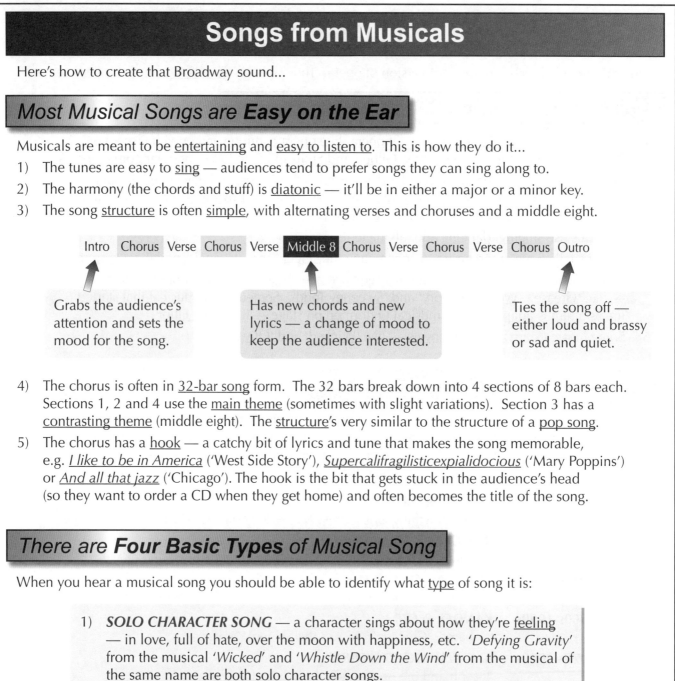

Intro Chorus Verse Chorus Verse Middle 8 Chorus Verse Chorus Verse Chorus Outro

Grabs the audience's attention and sets the mood for the song.

Has new chords and new lyrics — a change of mood to keep the audience interested.

Ties the song off — either loud and brassy or sad and quiet.

4) The chorus is often in <u>32-bar song</u> form. The 32 bars break down into 4 sections of 8 bars each. Sections 1, 2 and 4 use the <u>main theme</u> (sometimes with slight variations). Section 3 has a <u>contrasting theme</u> (middle eight). The <u>structure</u>'s very similar to the structure of a <u>pop song</u>.

5) The chorus has a <u>hook</u> — a catchy bit of lyrics and tune that makes the song memorable, e.g. *I like to be in America* ('West Side Story'), *Supercalifragilisticexpialidocious* ('Mary Poppins') or *And all that jazz* ('Chicago'). The hook is the bit that gets stuck in the audience's head (so they want to order a CD when they get home) and often becomes the title of the song.

There are Four Basic Types of Musical Song

When you hear a musical song you should be able to identify what <u>type</u> of song it is:

1) **SOLO CHARACTER SONG** — a character sings about how they're <u>feeling</u> — in love, full of hate, over the moon with happiness, etc. *'Defying Gravity'* from the musical *'Wicked'* and *'Whistle Down the Wind'* from the musical of the same name are both solo character songs.

2) **DUET** — duets are basically the same as solo character songs, except there are <u>two people</u> singing so you get two different reactions to a situation. *'I Know Him So Well'* from Chess is a great example.

3) **ACTION SONG** — the words of the song tell you what's going on in the <u>plot</u> — they lead you into the next bit of the story.

4) **CHORUS NUMBER** — the whole cast get together and have a <u>big old sing-song</u>. Like at the end of Grease — 'We go together like ramma lamma lamma ka dingedy ding de dong...' and *'You Can't Stop the Beat'* at the end of Hairspray.

All these styles of song developed from opera — solo songs are like <u>arias</u>, action songs are like <u>recitative</u>. The lyrics in a musical song tell part of the story. They're usually <u>written first</u>, so the composer has to fit the music around them.

It's showtime — lets see those jazz hands...

Song structures in musicals are normally a fair bit <u>easier</u> to get the hang of than some of the structures you've come across in classical music. So make sure you know it, and don't forget the <u>four song types</u>.

Leonard Bernstein — Something's Coming

Not all musicals are <u>happy</u> and <u>light-hearted</u>. 'West Side Story' is quite <u>dark</u> and has a <u>sad ending</u>.

Leonard Bernstein Wrote 'West Side Story'

1) <u>Leonard Bernstein</u> was born in Massachusetts in <u>1918</u>. He was an award-winning <u>composer</u> and <u>conductor</u>, as well as a <u>teacher</u> and <u>author</u>. He died in <u>1990</u>.

2) He studied Music at <u>Harvard University</u>, and later studied <u>piano</u>, <u>conducting</u>, <u>orchestration</u> and <u>counterpoint</u> in Philadelphia.

3) He was one of America's most <u>internationally respected</u> musicians. Some of the recordings he made when conducting the <u>New York Philharmonic Orchestra</u> are still considered to be among the best around.

4) '<u>West Side Story</u>' is one of his best known works. He wrote it in <u>1957</u> and it's still performed today.

5) Bernstein also wrote another four <u>musicals</u>, three <u>symphonies</u>, two <u>operas</u>, an <u>operetta</u> and lots of <u>chamber music</u>. He also composed the music for the 1954 film *On The Waterfront*.

'West Side Story' is a Musical

1) 'West Side Story' is set in <u>New York</u> in the <u>1950s</u>. It's about two <u>rival gangs</u>, the <u>Jets</u> (Americans) and the <u>Sharks</u> (Puerto Rican immigrants).

2) It follows the <u>tragic love story</u> of <u>Tony</u>, the best friend of the Jets' leader and <u>Maria</u>, the sister of the Sharks' leader.

3) The story's quite similar to '<u>Romeo and Juliet</u>', though there are some <u>differences</u> — the main one is that Maria (Juliet) <u>doesn't</u> die at the end. Tony (Romeo) does though.

4) It has <u>two acts</u>, with <u>spoken dialogue</u> between the songs. There are <u>solos</u>, <u>duets</u> and <u>action songs</u>. It also has a lot of numbers that are just <u>danced</u> to.

5) 'West Side Story' is a <u>collaboration</u> between <u>Bernstein</u>, <u>Jerome Robbins</u> (the <u>director</u> and <u>choreographer</u> who came up with the idea), <u>Arthur Laurents</u> (the <u>scriptwriter</u>) and <u>Stephen Sondheim</u> (the <u>lyricist</u>).

6) It was quite <u>different</u> to other musicals at the time — it had a <u>sad ending</u>, lots of <u>dance scenes</u> and looked at <u>social problems</u> in America.

It's Written for a Big Orchestra

1) Lots of Broadway musicals from the <u>1950s</u> need a <u>big orchestra</u> — and 'West Side Story' definitely does. It needs players who can <u>double up</u> — play <u>more than one</u> instrument (although not at the same time).

2) The orchestra includes <u>saxophones</u>, <u>piano</u>, <u>electric guitar</u>, <u>mandolin</u> and <u>celeste</u> — as well as the usual <u>wind</u>, <u>brass</u> and <u>string</u> sections. Even these sections were <u>large</u>. It also uses a lot of <u>percussion</u>, including <u>timpani</u>, a <u>glockenspiel</u> and a <u>police whistle</u>.

3) Tony is sung by a <u>tenor</u> (a high male voice), while Maria is sung by a <u>soprano</u> (a high female voice).

4) Bernstein uses <u>Latin American rhythms</u> and <u>instruments</u> (like <u>castanets</u>, a <u>güiro</u> and <u>maracas</u>) to reflect the background of the <u>Puerto Rican</u> gang.

5) He also uses lots of <u>jazz</u> elements — like <u>blue notes</u> and <u>syncopation</u> (see p.121).

6) There are lots of well known songs in 'West Side Story' — like *Tonight*, *America*, *I Feel Pretty* and *Somewhere*.

Two street gangs — both alike in dignity...

Songs from *West Side Story* are used in lots of <u>films</u>, <u>TV programmes</u> and <u>adverts</u> — they have a distinctive style. Learn the different instruments and musical elements that give the music its style.

Leonard Bernstein — Something's Coming

Something's coming — yes, another lovely page on 'West Side Story'. Relax, enjoy and <u>learn</u>.

Something's Coming is Sung by **Tony**

1) *Something's Coming* comes quite <u>early</u> in the show. It's a <u>solo</u> for <u>Tony</u> —
   he's <u>imagining</u> a better future for himself. He sings it <u>before</u> he meets Maria.

2) He's <u>excited</u> about the future — you can hear the <u>excitement</u> in the music.

3) The lyrics talk about a '<u>miracle</u>' coming — this could be <u>meeting Maria</u>. It's <u>dramatic irony</u>,
   as meeting her leads to his <u>death</u>. 'Something's coming' isn't necessarily '<u>something good</u>'.

The Piece Has Lots of **Cross Rhythms**

1) The song's written in <u>3/4</u>, but sometimes it <u>feels</u> like it's in <u>6/8</u> — in the piano part, the <u>left hand</u>
   plays <u>three crotchets</u> while the <u>right hand</u> plays <u>quavers</u> as if it's in <u>6/8</u>. The quavers have <u>accents</u>
   on the <u>first</u> and <u>fourth</u> quavers in the bar — it makes it feel like <u>two dotted crotchet beats</u> in a bar
   (rather than the three crotchets of 3/4).

2) Lots of the parts are playing <u>cross-rhythms</u> (see p.174).

3) Much of <u>Tony's part</u> feels like it's in 6/8 — with <u>two beats</u> in a bar. The <u>accented off-beats</u>
   (like in his first two entries — '<u>could be</u>' and '<u>who knows</u>') give a sense of <u>anticipation</u>,
   which matches his <u>mood</u>.

4) It's a <u>fast</u> song — it's marked ♩ = 176. The <u>quick tempo</u> reflects Tony's <u>excitement</u>.

5) At the start, Tony sings <u>pianissimo</u> (*pp*) in a <u>half-whispering</u> style, with <u>quaver rests</u> between
   words. This gives it a <u>breathless, agitated feeling</u> — he's <u>impatient</u> to leave the gang behind.

6) *Something's Coming*'s in <u>D major</u>. Major keys are often used to reflect <u>happy emotions</u>
   — at this point, Tony's <u>excited</u> and <u>looking forward</u> to the future.

7) The final word '<u>tonight</u>' is <u>echoed</u> later on in the song *Tonight* that he sings with Maria.

8) There are <u>ostinati</u> (repeated patterns — ostinati is the plural of ostinato (p.82)) in lots of parts.
   Listen out for the <u>three crotchets</u> in the <u>bass parts</u> and the <u>accented quaver pattern</u> in
   some other parts. There's <u>imitation</u> (p.82) between instruments too.

Bernstein Uses **Tritones** *in 'West Side Story'*

1) A <u>tritone</u> is an <u>interval</u> of two notes that are <u>three whole tones</u> apart (like F to B). In Medieval
   music they were known as the '<u>diabolus in musica</u>' (the '<u>devil in music</u>') and composers were
   <u>banned</u> from using them in <u>church music</u>.

2) Even today, composers often use tritones when something is <u>evil</u> or <u>scary</u> —
   in the film *Psycho*, a shrill tritone accompanies each <u>stab</u> of the knife in the
   infamous <u>shower scene</u>.

3) Tritones appear in several places in 'West Side Story',
   showing that underneath the <u>love story</u> something <u>bad</u>
   is happening. There's a tritone in the <u>first chord</u>
   of *Something's Coming* — the <u>D</u> and the <u>G#</u>
   in the piano part give it an <u>edgy, unpredictable</u> feeling.

4) They're often used as an <u>appoggiatura</u> (see p.83)
   — that's how Bernstein's used it here.

Tonight, tonight — lots of revision to be done tonight...

This song uses rhythmic features and harmonic devices to create that mood of excited anticipation.
Make sure you understand which techniques are used where and how they create the dramatic effect.

Warm-up and Exam Questions

Warm-up Questions

1) What is a musical?
2) Name the **four** types of songs found in musicals.
3) What is meant by 32-bar song form?

Exam Question

Have a go at this exam-style question.

Track 35 is an extract from the song '*Something's Coming*' from West Side Story.
Play the extract **four** times, leaving a short pause for writing time between each playing.

Track 35

a) Name the woodwind instrument that can be heard in the accompaniment at the start of the extract.

.... *[1 mark]*

b) The trumpets in the extract sometimes play *con sordino*.
Explain what this means and how it affects the sound of the instruments.

....

.... *[2 marks]*

c) What is the interval between the two notes for the opening words 'could be'?
Circle your answer.

major third   **perfect fourth**   **perfect fifth**   **major sixth**   *[1 mark]*

d) Give **two** ways the composer used rhythm to create a sense of anticipation and excitement.

....

.... *[2 marks]*

Revision Summary for Section Six

There were loads of different styles of music in the 20th Century — often with quirky features and new harmonic and rhythmic devices. You need to be able to talk about the features of expressionism, serialism, minimalism and songs from musicals in your exam. So this revision summary is a good place to start — keep going through these questions until you can answer them all without looking back.

1) What are the rough dates of the Romantic period?
2) What are chromatic notes?
3) What is atonal music? How did it affect traditional musical forms?
4) Why did Schoenberg choose to write atonal music instead of tonal music?
5) Write down five features of expressionist music.
6) When did Schoenberg write 'Five Orchestral Pieces'?
7) What does the word *Peripetie* mean in English?
8) What ensemble is *Peripetie* written for?
9) Explain what is meant by hexachord and complement.
10) What does 'tone-colour melody' mean and why does Schoenberg use it in *Peripetie*?
11) What are the three ways that the Prime Order of a piece can be rearranged?
12) When was minimalism developed?
13) Minimalist music is often made up of loops. What are loops?
14) Write down four different ways of changing the loop patterns in minimalist music.
15) Give two ways that music from other countries influenced minimalist music.
16) When did Steve Reich write '*Electric Counterpoint*'?
17) What instruments play the 3rd Movement from '*Electric Counterpoint*'?
18) Explain the process of looping to build up layers used in the 3rd Movement from '*Electric Counterpoint*'.
19) What is polyphonic texture?
20) Which two keys are used in the 3rd Movement from '*Electric Counterpoint*'?
21) Which two time signatures are used in the 3rd Movement from '*Electric Counterpoint*'? What time signature is the main part of the piece written in?
22) What does diatonic mean?
23) What is a hook?
24) What are the four basic types of musical song?
25) When did Leonard Bernstein write 'West Side Story'?
26) Write down the simple plot of 'West Side Story'.
27) What kind of voice is Tony's part written for?
28) What is Tony singing about in *Something's Coming*?
29) What is the effect of the pianissimo (*pp*) at the beginning of *Something's Coming*?
30) What time signature is used in *Something's Coming*? What time signature does it sometimes feel like and why?
31) What key is used in *Something's Coming*?
32) What is a tritone, and why does Bernstein use it in *Something's Coming*?

The Blues

The blues style has been around for years. It first became really popular in the 1920s. That may sound like a long time ago but the blues <u>still</u> has a big influence on pop music today.

African Slaves in America Started Off the Blues

1) In the 1600s and 1700s hundreds of thousands of Africans were captured and sold as <u>slaves</u>. Many were taken to work on plantations in North America.

2) To pass the time and take their minds off their work, which was often brutally hard, they sang <u>work songs</u>, using their tools to give the music a <u>beat</u>. The lyrics were often about the hardship and misery of living as a slave.

3) Over the years, African musical styles like <u>call-and-response</u> singing (p.174) blended with features of European music, especially <u>chords</u>. This combination was the beginning of the <u>blues</u>.

4) Even after slavery was finally abolished in the 1860s, ex-slaves living in the southern states were poor and powerless. The lyrics and tone of their songs carried on being <u>sad</u> and 'blue'.

5) The traditional blues instruments are <u>harmonica</u>, <u>guitar</u>, <u>banjo</u>, <u>violin</u>, <u>piano</u>, <u>double bass</u> and the <u>voice</u>. They're all <u>acoustic</u> — electric instruments hadn't been invented when blues began.

6) In the early twentieth century black Americans started playing the blues in bars and clubs beyond the southern states. By the 1920s blues was massively popular all over America with both white and black audiences.

7) In the 1940s and 1950s a style called <u>rhythm'n'blues</u> (R'n'B) was developed. It's a <u>speeded-up</u> version of blues played on electric guitar and bass.

Blues has its Own Scale

1) You get a blues scale by <u>flattening</u> the <u>third</u> and <u>seventh</u> of any major scale by a semitone. The <u>fifth</u> note is sometimes flattened too.

2) The flattened notes are known as the <u>blue notes</u>.

3) The blue notes are notes that were '<u>bent</u>' in African singing. The singers would 'slide' up or down to a note, giving it a twang and making it slightly <u>flatter</u>.

4) The <u>second</u> and <u>sixth</u> notes are often left out.

Blues Melodies have Swinging, Offbeat Rhythms

1) In normal '<u>straight</u>' rhythm the beats split up into <u>equal halves</u>.

I want chips and egg

I want chips and egg

2) In the blues, the first bit of the beat <u>steals</u> some time from the second bit. The first bit ends up <u>longer</u> and with more <u>oomph</u>. This gives the music a <u>swinging</u> feel.

3) The blues uses lots of <u>syncopation</u>. You get a <u>lively offbeat sound</u> by avoiding the <u>strong beats</u> — it puts the <u>oomph</u> in <u>unexpected places</u>.

Please don't make me beg

The blues have influenced almost all forms of popular music...

The blues doesn't have to be mournful, sad and depressing — it just sounds better that way...

The Blues

There are lots of different types of blues, but the most popular song structure is the 12-bar blues.

Twelve-bar Blues has a Repeated 12-Bar Structure

12-bar blues uses a set chord pattern, 12 bars long. Singers like Bessie Smith and Robert Johnson made the 12-bar blues structure really popular in the 1920s — it's been around ever since and is still one of the most popular styles.

BAR 1	BAR 2	BAR 3	BAR 4
Chord I	Chord I	Chord I	Chord I

BAR 5	BAR 6	BAR 7	BAR 8
Chord IV	Chord IV	Chord I	Chord I

BAR 9	BAR 10	BAR 11	BAR 12
Chord V	Chord IV	Chord I	Chord I

1) The only chords are I, IV and V.

2) The 12-bar pattern is repeated right through the song.

3) You can make the chords even more bluesy by adding the minor 7ths (see p.23).

When the 12-bar structure is repeated, chord V is played in bar 12 instead of chord I. This leads back smoothly to Bar 1.

12-bar blues has had a huge influence on other musical styles including ragtime, jazz, rock and roll and R&B. Loads of pop songs today still use the standard 12-bar structure.

Twelve Bars Break Nicely into Three Lines

The 12-bar chord pattern of 12-bar blues breaks up nicely into three lines, each with four bars. The lyrics of a 12-bar blues song usually stick to three lines for each verse of the song.

Lines 1 and 2 are usually the same. →
Woke up this morning feeling blue.
Woke up this morning feeling blue.

Line 3 is different, but rhymes with lines 1 and 2. →
Feeling sad and lonesome without you.

The words are usually pretty gloomy.

Each line takes up 4 bars, but the words don't always fill up the whole line.

The singer's bit — the call — is followed by an instrument playing an answer — the response — in the gap before the next line.

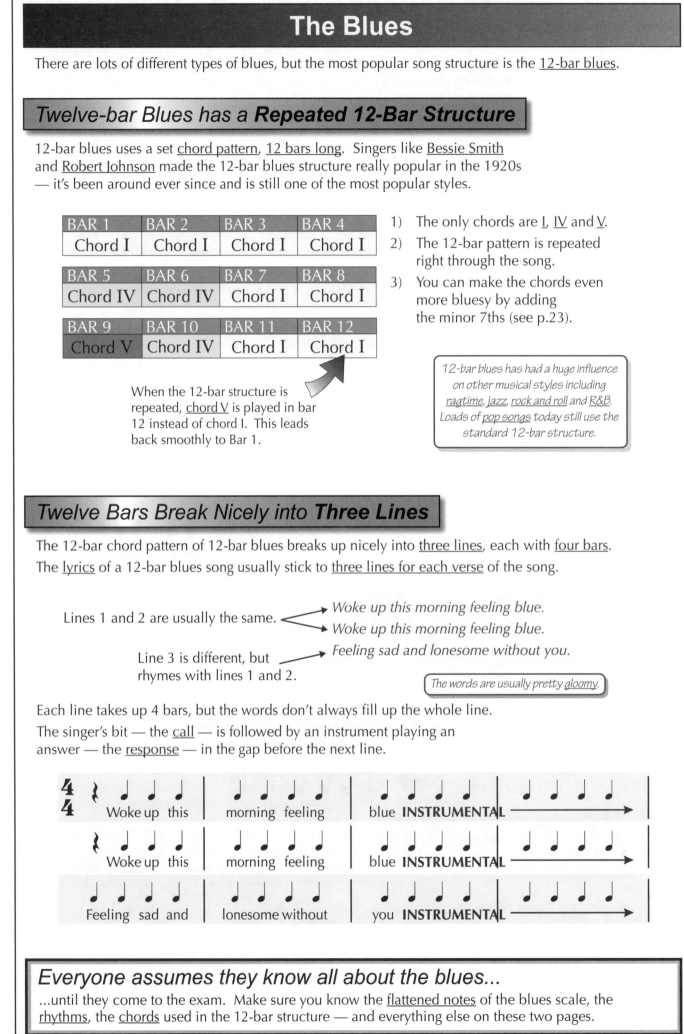

Everyone assumes they know all about the blues...

...until they come to the exam. Make sure you know the flattened notes of the blues scale, the rhythms, the chords used in the 12-bar structure — and everything else on these two pages.

Jazz

Jazz is a pretty massive subject, so I've tried to cram the important bits into these two pages. You'll probably have heard lots of jazz — it's a word used to cover quite a few types of music.

Jazz has its **Roots** in **African American Blues** and **Ragtime**

1) Jazz is a type of music that developed in the USA in the early 20th century. It's a fusion of African and European influences that came from the music of the newly-freed slaves.

2) It started off as Dixieland jazz in New Orleans in the early 1900s. Dixieland jazz is a mix of brass band marches, ragtime (music with lots of syncopated melodies that was often played on the piano) and blues (see p.121-122). Dixieland jazz is polyphonic (different parts move at different times).

3) It was played in brothels and bars — the only places black musicians were allowed to perform because of segregation (black people weren't allowed to use the same places as white people, like schools and bars).

4) In 1920, jazz moved to Chicago. This was the era of the Prohibition (from 1920-1933, alcohol was banned in the United States). Illegal bars (called speakeasies) often had jazz bands playing. Jazz started to get a bad reputation. Some people thought it was immoral.

5) The 1920s were known as 'The Jazz Age' or the 'Roaring Twenties'.

Swing Music was Popular in the 1930s and 40s

1) Swing music is a type of jazz that can be danced to. It's more structured than Dixieland jazz.

2) It's usually quite fast, and rhythms are swung (see p.121). Most pieces are in 4/4. It was meant to be danced to, so it had regular phrases and emphasis on the first and third beats of the bar.

3) Swing is played by a big band (see p.124).

4) It was popular because it was played on the radio — it was a lot more accessible and acceptable than going to the brothels and illegal bars.

5) During the Second World War, swing became less popular because lots of the men who played in the big bands had gone off to war.

6) After the war, bebop (or just bop) developed from swing music. Bebop was fast with lots of improvisation. It had complex harmonies, exciting syncopated rhythms, and irregular phrase lengths. Bebop was much less structured than swing.

Free Jazz Broke all the Rules

1) Free jazz is a type of jazz that developed in the 1950s and 60s. It was a reaction against the limits of swing and bebop.

2) It didn't follow the normal rules of tempo and rhythm — players within the same band would play at different speeds to each other. There wasn't a regular rhythm.

3) There was lots of improvisation — the soloist didn't follow the chords or structure of the rest of the band.

Jazz didn't stop developing in the 60s. In the 60s and 70s new types emerged, like soul jazz, Latin jazz and jazz fusion. Since then, there's been experimental jazz and fusions of jazz with other types of music.

Mmmmmm Jaaazz...

As with the rest of these types of popular music, there's loads of different types of jazz out there — the best thing you can do to appreciate it is to listen to as much as you can get your hands on...

Jazz

Jazz has lots of features that mean you'll <u>recognise</u> it when you hear it — for example, it has a <u>swing</u> to it.

Trumpets, Trombones and Clarinets are Jazz Instruments

1) A typical <u>jazz band</u> would have a <u>trumpet</u>, a <u>trombone</u> and a <u>clarinet</u> on the <u>front row</u>. Later, <u>saxophones</u> were included too. The <u>front row instruments</u> play <u>improvised solos</u>.

2) There'd be a <u>rhythm section</u> with <u>piano</u>, <u>guitar</u>, <u>drums</u> and a <u>double bass</u>.

3) Big bands are made up of <u>saxophones</u>, <u>trumpets</u>, <u>trombones</u> and a <u>rhythm section</u>. The sax section has <u>alto</u>, <u>tenor</u> and <u>baritone saxophones</u> and sometimes <u>clarinets</u>. Some big bands have a <u>singer</u> too.

4) A typical big band would have <u>5 saxophones</u> (2 altos, 2 tenors and a baritone), <u>4 trumpets</u>, <u>4 trombones</u> and a <u>4-piece rhythm section</u> (piano, bass, guitar and drums).

Jazz is Swung and Syncopated

1) Early jazz music was based on a <u>12-bar blues</u> (see p.122).

2) The <u>chords</u> were played by the <u>rhythm section</u> and the <u>front row</u> instruments would <u>improvise</u> over them.

3) Jazz musicians use <u>call and response</u> and <u>blue notes</u> — key features of jazz and blues. Blue notes are <u>flattened 3rds</u>, <u>7ths</u> and sometimes <u>5ths</u> of a <u>major scale</u>.

4) <u>Syncopated rhythms</u> move the strong beat away from the first and third beats of the bar. <u>Swung rhythms</u> (see p.121) are also used.

5) Some musicians use <u>scat</u> — a type of <u>improvised singing</u> with <u>nonsense words</u> and <u>syllables</u>.

Jazz has Lots of Improvisation

1) <u>Improvisation</u> is a really important feature of jazz. It's when a soloist <u>makes up</u> music <u>on the spot</u>.

2) If the band's playing a <u>12-bar blues</u>, the soloist knows which notes fit over the chords. The <u>pianist</u> or <u>guitarist</u> supports the soloist by <u>comping</u> — playing chords under the solo.

3) <u>Improvisations</u> are <u>different</u> every time.

4) The <u>improvised</u> nature of jazz means the same piece can be played in radically <u>different</u> ways — depending on the <u>interpretation</u> of it. Even if a piece is played twice by the same people, it <u>won't</u> sound the same.

5) <u>Swing music</u> has <u>less</u> improvisation — people wanted tunes they could <u>recognise</u>. There are still some sections for a soloist to improvise over, but they're <u>shorter</u>.

6) Jazz <u>songs</u> are a bit different — the singer has <u>less chance</u> to improvise (but they can use <u>scat</u>).

Jazz Music Wasn't Written Down

1) In early jazz (and in some today), the music <u>wasn't written down</u>.

2) There was lots of <u>interaction</u> between the soloist and the band, like <u>call and response</u> — the soloist would play a phrase (the <u>call</u>) and the band would answer it (the <u>response</u>) or the other way around. Sometimes the soloist would <u>repeat</u> ideas heard earlier in the piece and <u>develop</u> them in the solo.

3) The band would follow the <u>band leader</u>. Sometimes the band leader would also be the <u>soloist</u> or the <u>composer</u> — like <u>Louis Armstrong</u>, <u>Duke Ellington</u> and <u>Glenn Miller</u>.

4) Popular jazz pieces are called <u>jazz standards</u>. They're pieces that are part of a band's <u>repertoire</u>. Some jazz standards are '<u>I Got Rhythm</u>', '<u>My Funny Valentine</u>' and '<u>Take The "A" Train</u>'.

Jazz — anything goes...

This page covers some of the key features of jazz. Make sure you can write a mini-essay on this page.

Miles Davis — All Blues

All Blues is from the album '<u>Kind of Blue</u>' — released in <u>1959</u>, it still sells about <u>125 000</u> copies a year.

Miles Davis Changed the Way Jazz was Played

1) Miles Davis was born in <u>1926</u> in <u>Illinois</u>, <u>America</u> and died in <u>1991</u>. He started playing the <u>trumpet</u> when he was a young boy, and went on to become a <u>band leader</u> and <u>composer</u> as well.

2) In the <u>1940s</u>, Miles got fed up of <u>bebop</u> (p.123). He didn't like the <u>constantly changing chords</u> that the <u>improvised solos</u> were based on, so he began composing music using <u>fewer chords</u>. The slower harmonic rhythm meant the soloist could <u>develop</u> their <u>melody</u> more before the chords changed.

3) Miles' solos <u>changed</u> the way jazz was played. He used to:

- improvise using a <u>tuneful melody</u> (that you could sing along to) rather than lots of <u>crazy runs</u>.
- play very <u>lyrically</u> — as though he was <u>singing</u>.
- base his improvisations on <u>scales</u> (or sometimes modes) and an <u>overall key signature</u>, rather than <u>chord changes</u> every <u>bar</u>.
- make the trumpet sound <u>natural</u> and <u>pure</u> (not <u>forced</u> and <u>high-pitched</u>).
- often play in the <u>lower register</u>.

4) Miles was capable of playing <u>technically demanding</u> music, but he preferred a <u>simpler</u> approach.

5) '<u>Kind of Blue</u>' was based on <u>scales</u> rather than <u>chords</u>. It let the musicians <u>improvise freely</u>.

All Blues was Recorded in **One Take**

In *All Blues*, the performers <u>improvised</u> on <u>basic scales</u>. The <u>key features</u> of this piece are:

1) **PITCH** All instruments keep to their <u>middle</u> and <u>lower registers</u>.

2) **DURATION** *All Blues* lasts for more than <u>11 and a half</u> minutes.

3) **DYNAMICS** The piece is generally quite <u>subdued</u> — most of it's <u>moderately loud</u> (*mf*), except for a few louder trumpet bits. The <u>ensemble</u> plays even more <u>quietly</u> when a <u>soloist</u> is playing.

4) **TEMPO** It's marked '<u>jazz waltz</u>' — it should be played at a <u>moderate pace</u>.

5) **TIME SIGNATURE** Unlike most jazz and blues at the time, *All Blues* is in <u>6/4</u> (6 crotchets in a bar).

6) **TIMBRE** The timbre's very <u>mellow</u> (the timbre's the overall <u>sound</u> of the piece). Miles uses a <u>mute</u>, <u>ghost notes</u> (notes that are <u>hinted</u> at, rather than <u>played</u> — they're deliberately <u>weak</u> beats) and <u>rests</u> in his solos to make it more mellow.

7) **TEXTURE** It has a <u>simple</u> texture — the <u>wind instruments</u> play in 3rds and 4ths, while the <u>piano</u> and <u>double bass</u> play a <u>simple riff</u> and <u>chords</u>. The <u>drum</u> keeps a <u>steady beat</u>.

8) **STRUCTURE** *All Blues* uses a standard <u>12-bar blues</u> chord pattern (see p.122) in G which gets <u>repeated</u> throughout the piece. It's played under the <u>solos</u> and the <u>main melody</u>. The chords <u>aren't</u> exactly the same as the traditional 12-bar blues though — they're a bit <u>fancier</u>:

Bar of 12-Bar Blues	1	2	3	4	5	6	7	8	9	10	11	12
Traditional Chords	I	I	I	I	IV	IV	I	I	V	IV	I	I
All Blues Chords	I^7	I^7	I^7	I^7	Im^7	Im^7	I^7	I^7	$V^{7\#9}$	$VI\flat^{7\#9}\ V^{7\#9}$	I^7	I^7

<u>#9</u> means there's an <u>augmented 9th</u> in there — that's a <u>2nd</u>, but <u>up</u> an octave and <u>raised</u> by a <u>semitone</u>.

Miles to go — well, one more page on this piece...

Make sure you know the <u>key features</u> of *All Blues* — and how it was <u>different</u> to the jazz that came before it.

Miles Davis — All Blues

Miles Davis believed that 'less is more' when it came to solos. He made them very lyrical.

All Blues is Mainly Improvised

1) The band's made up of a trumpet, alto saxophone, tenor saxophone, piano, double bass and drums.

2) The trumpet, both saxophones and the piano each have an improvised solo. The two saxes tend to play together when they're not playing solos.

3) When they turned up to the recording session, the band had very little idea what they were going to play. Miles gave them a few scales and melody lines to improvise on. He also gave them brief instructions, then off they went.

4) The whole album was recorded in two sessions, and each piece was recorded in one take.

The Piece is Divided into Sections

1) All Blues has an intro, followed by the head (theme). There are four improvised solos, then the head returns.

2) The drums keep time and the piano plays chords or tremolo chords (except for its improvised solo).

3) The double bass plays Riff A from bar 9 onwards (for most of the piece).

4) The piece finishes with a final coda which fades out. A riff is a modern word for an ostinato — a repeated pattern. It can be in the melody, rhythm or chord pattern.

Riff A — Bass

1) INTRO

The intro is 8 bars long. It's made up of two four-bar sections (called Intro 1 and Intro 2). In Intro 2, the alto and tenor saxes play Riff B in 3rds (they don't play anything in the first four bars).

Riff B — Alto Sax, Tenor Sax

2) HEAD (32 BARS)

The head lasts for 32 bars. A muted trumpet plays a 12-bar theme (the saxes play Riff B in the background). They play Intro 2 followed by the theme again, followed by another repetition of Intro 2.

3) IMPROVISED SOLO SECTIONS

The four solo sections each feature a different instrument — first it's the trumpet, followed by the alto sax, then the tenor sax and finally the piano. All the solos are improvised.

The trumpet solo and both saxophone solos last for 48 bars and the piano solo lasts for 24. After each of the solos, Intro 2 is played (but the piano plays Riff B instead of the saxes — except after the piano solo, when the saxes play it again).

4) HEAD (32 BARS)

The head comes back again — it's the 12-bar theme followed by Intro 2. They play both bits twice.

5) OUTRO

All Blues finishes with a 12-bar outro which fades out. The saxophones are playing Riff B again, but the trumpet introduces a new riff, Riff C.

Riff C — Trumpet

Ghost notes (see p.125)

Learn all the different sections...

Most of the sections of All Blues are quite similar, so just remember what's different in each section.

Warm-up and Exam Questions

Warm-up Questions

1) What are the notes in the blues scale on G?
2) What is syncopation?
3) From what origins did jazz music develop?
4) Name **three** jazz instruments.
5) What is swing music?

Don't be blue — here's another exam question for you.

Exam Question

Play the track **four** times with a short pause between each playing.

Track 36

a) What type of popular music is the extract an example of?

.... *[1 mark]*

b) Which of the following words describes how the melody is played.
Tick the box next to your choice.

Legato ☐

Rubato ☐

Improvised ☐ *[1 mark]*

c) The quavers in this extract are *swung*.
Explain what is meant by the term *swung* quavers.

....

.... *[2 marks]*

Turn over

Exam Questions

d)   What instrument plays the solo in the extract?

.... *[1 mark]*

e)   i)   What instruments are playing the accompaniment during the solo?

.... *[2 marks]*

    ii)   Describe **two** musical features of this accompaniment.

....

....

.... *[2 marks]*

f)   What is the time signature of this extract? Circle the correct answer.

$$\frac{6}{4} \qquad\qquad \frac{4}{4} \qquad\qquad \frac{6}{8}$$

[1 mark]

g)   Describe the overall mood of this piece and explain how this mood is created. Comment on the following musical elements:

- Dynamics

- Pitch

- Tempo

....

....

....

....

....

.... *[4 marks]*

Rock Music

Rock stars must have a pretty nice life, what with the posh hotels, adoring fans and truckloads of money. But it's their music that made them famous, and that's what this page is about.

Rock Music's Based on the 12-Bar Blues

1) Rock music started off in the 1950s. The chord structure's based on the 12-bar blues (see p.122).

2) A rock band was originally made up of a lead electric guitar, a rhythm electric guitar, a lead singer, a bass guitar and a drummer.

3) As rock developed, more instruments were added. Some bands introduced a string section (with violins and cellos), some had brass sections (trumpets and trombones) and some had wind sections (flutes, clarinets, saxophones and oboes). They also brought in keyboards and synthesizers.

4) Musicians used the effects on electric guitars to produce new sounds — like distortion, feedback (the noise you get when you stand too close to a speaker with a guitar or microphone) and reverberation (echo, see p.71).

5) Rock bands use lots of other techniques to get unusual sounds — the band Led Zeppelin used a pounding beat turned up really loud as their main rhythm. They sometimes used violin bows on their guitar strings to get a sustained note.

In the 1970s, Rock Songs Started to Develop

Bands in the 1970s started to develop the basic rock formula to make their songs last longer. Their songs had themes and some even told stories.

- Queen's 'Bohemian Rhapsody' lasts for a whopping 6 minutes. It doesn't have a chorus — it's made up of unrelated sections, including a slow ballad, a guitar solo, an operatic section and a heavy rock section.
- Pink Floyd's 1973 album 'The Dark Side of the Moon' is a concept album — there's a theme that links all the tracks.

Rock Songs Became a Way of Expressing Yourself

1) Lots of rock bands write their own lyrics to songs (as well as the music). They use things like religious themes, protest songs and personal experiences of love.

2) Led Zeppelin, David Bowie and Bob Dylan all use the influences of folk music — they've written whole albums in a folky style.

3) Bob Dylan is also famous for his protest songs — his folky 'Blowin' In The Wind' is used as an anti-war song.

4) The more rock developed, the fewer rules it followed. Songs could be any length, and follow any chord pattern (or none at all). Bands could have any instruments, and the lyrics could be about whatever the band wanted.

5) Costumes were used to help the music along — David Bowie's silver suit and lightning make-up really helped to set the scene for Major Tom (an astronaut who is in a lot of Bowie's songs).

Powerful Guitars Were Important in 1990s Rock

1) A lot of rock bands in the 1990s were guitar-based — they used guitars to create a really powerful sound. Power chords (made up of the tonic and fifth of a chord) were used a lot.

2) Bands like Nirvana, Green Day and Pearl Jam were really popular. They wrote songs about controversial topics (like drugs and mental illness) and often swore a lot.

3) 1990s rock music was fused with other types of music — like grunge, punk and funk.

Jeff Buckley — Grace

Jeff Buckley only actually released one studio album — he died before his second was completed.

'Grace' was Jeff Buckley's Debut Album

1) Jeff Buckley was born in California in 1966. He was a singer-songwriter and guitarist. He became popular in the early 1990s.

2) His early work was influenced by Led Zeppelin and Kiss, two of his favourite bands. He also performed covers of songs by Led Zeppelin, Bob Dylan and Elton John.

3) He released one studio album, 'Grace', in 1994, and was working on a second when he died in 1997 — he drowned whilst swimming in a river. The second album was released in 1998.

- The album 'Grace' includes seven original songs and three covers.
- When it was first released, sales were pretty poor (even though the critics liked it). Since then, it's gone on to sell really well — it's now sold over 2 million copies.
- Grace is an original song on the album written by Jeff Buckley and Gary Lucas.
- Grace is about Buckley moving from L.A. to New York to be with someone he loved. He's not afraid of what lies ahead because he's in love.

Grace has a Folk-Rock Feel

1) Grace has a wide vocal range — at some points, Buckley sings falsetto (higher than the normal male range). He also uses vibrato and scoops up to notes (he starts a note lower then slides up to the written note — this is also called portamento).

2) The piece starts quietly, with just two electric guitars playing (one distorted and one not). There's also an eerie wailing in the background played by a synthesizer (see p.135).

3) The dynamics are increased by bringing in more instruments — after a few bars, the bass guitar and drums come in. By the end, there's a full rock band playing, with heavy drums, screaming vocals and wailing guitars. The instruments don't actually get louder themselves, but more are added to make it more intense.

4) It's in a steady 12/8, with four dotted crotchet beats in a bar. This is quite unusual — most rock songs are in 4/4. It feels faster though, as the guitar plays semiquaver runs at the beginning.

5) It has a fairly typical verse-chorus structure, with a guitar solo towards the end. The intro is repeated after the choruses, and the piece ends with a short outro.

6) There are four main guitar riffs (see p.126) in the piece. The first riff's made up of semiquavers and it's played by the electric guitar in the introduction, then repeated between verses. The electric guitar plays another riff in the verses — this one's made up of broken chords (the notes of the chord, but played separately). The acoustic guitar plays a rhythmic, percussive riff in the verses and choruses. In the final section of the piece, both guitars play a fourth riff, while the vocals build to a screaming climax. The riffs build up the texture of the piece.

7) There are some electronic effects used in the piece — like EQ and delay (see p.136). They also use a flanger to create a swirly sound (flangers are added in a studio).

8) Buckley used unusual chord progressions — he chose chords that he liked the sound of. The main part of Grace is in E minor.

9) Considering this song's supposed to be about love, the lyrics are surprisingly morbid. The line 'wait in the fire' is repeated again and again, and it's followed by 'burn'.

Buckley's Other Works are Also Popular

1) Lots of the other songs on the album were really popular. 'Grace' included a cover of Leonard Cohen's Hallelujah, as well as Lilac Wine and Benjamin Britten's Corpus Christi Carol.

2) His 2nd studio album (released after his death) was called 'Sketches for My Sweetheart the Drunk'.

3) He also released several live albums — like 'Live at Sin-é' (1993) and 'Live from the Bataclan' (1995).

Pop Ballads

Everyone <u>loves</u> a good ballad. So I know you'll enjoy these nuggets of pop wisdom.

Ballads Tell Stories

1) <u>Ballads</u> have been around since at least the <u>fifteenth century</u>. Back then a ballad was a long song with lots of verses that told a <u>story</u>. It's the type of thing that was sung by <u>wandering minstrels</u>.

2) Modern <u>pop</u> and <u>rock</u> ballads still tell stories. Often they're <u>slow</u> and <u>sad</u> and tell some kind of <u>love story</u>. Songwriters like to put a romantic or spooky <u>twist</u> right at the <u>end</u> to keep people listening.

3) Each verse has the <u>same</u> rhythm and tune but different lyrics. You'll hear ballads sung in many different styles — a <u>rock ballad</u> accompanied by <u>heavy drums</u> and <u>amplified guitars</u> sounds pretty different to a <u>folk ballad</u> played on an <u>acoustic guitar</u>.

4) <u>Emotional</u>, <u>slow</u> ballads sung by <u>boy</u> and <u>girl bands</u> such as <u>Take That</u> and <u>The Spice Girls</u> were huge in <u>1990's pop</u> — ballads were the <u>perfect song type</u> to get <u>teenage fans</u> to <u>fall in love</u> with the band.

Singer-Songwriters Write Lots of Ballads

<u>Singer-songwriters</u> are artists who <u>write and sing</u> their own stuff. They tend to <u>accompany themselves</u> on either the <u>guitar</u> or <u>piano</u> and write a fair few ballads. The <u>style</u> of the ballad depends on the singer's own personal style. Here are a few performers who sing ballads — they all sound <u>very</u> different:

1) <u>Bob Dylan</u>'s most famous ballad, released in 1963, is an <u>anti-war song</u> called '<u>Blowing in the Wind</u>'. Bob sings a simple <u>diatonic tune</u> in a <u>major key</u> and accompanies himself on an <u>acoustic guitar</u> with simple strummed chords giving the song a folky feel. All the verses have the same music and the same <u>last line</u> — 'The answer my friend is blowing in the wind, the answer is blowing in the wind'. The repeated line works like a <u>mini-chorus</u>.

2) <u>Sting</u> just about always writes his own songs. He accompanies himself on <u>bass guitar</u>, but he's also backed by his <u>band</u>. Sting's music takes a lot from <u>soul</u> and <u>jazz</u>. '<u>Seven Days</u>' is a particularly jazzy ballad — it's in <u>5/4 time</u> and uses <u>major seventh chords</u>, as well as notes from the <u>blues scale</u>.

3) <u>Kate Bush</u> bases the story of her ballad '<u>Wuthering Heights</u>' on the book with the same name. No one else in pop sounds quite like Kate Bush — she sings in a <u>wailing</u>, <u>ghostly manner</u>.

Elton John
- Elton John has <u>written</u> many <u>famous ballads</u>. He accompanies most of his songs on the <u>piano</u>.
- His accompaniments combine <u>rhythmic chords</u> and <u>snippets of the tune</u> to keep the music interesting.
- Elton's '<u>Your Song</u>' was his first pop success. In this piece he blends <u>soul</u>, <u>folk</u> and <u>jazz styles</u> and mixes <u>vocals</u> with <u>piano</u>, <u>acoustic guitar</u> and <u>string accompaniment</u>.
- He also wrote '<u>Candle in the Wind</u>' which was originally a <u>love ballad</u> about Marilyn Monroe. Marilyn's real name was Norma Jean, so the first line goes "Goodbye Norma Jean..." For Princess Diana's funeral he changed the words to "Goodbye England's Rose..."
- Elton has <u>influenced</u> a lot of <u>singer-songwriters</u> and helped to make pop ballads <u>popular</u>.

The Accompaniment Complements the Voice

VOICE The <u>story</u> is the most <u>important part</u> of a ballad — e.g. Snow Patrol's '<u>Set the Fire to the Third Bar</u>', and The Script's '<u>Man Who Can't Be Moved</u>'. <u>Vocals</u> are <u>clear</u> and <u>unhidden</u> by the <u>accompaniment</u>.

ACCOMPANIMENT The <u>accompaniment</u> generally <u>reflects</u> the themes of the vocals. There's usually a lot of <u>repetition</u> or <u>inversion</u> of <u>motifs</u> that are sung in the main melody. The <u>texture</u> of the accompaniment often varies to make the <u>dynamics</u> (crescendos and diminuendos) more dramatic. Sometimes there's an <u>instrumental</u> section where an instrument (maybe a saxophone or electric guitar) does a <u>variation</u> on the tune.

Borrow a lighter and wave it in the air...

Ballads should be really easy to spot in the exam — because the tune gets repeated over and over again.

Pop Ballads

I shouldn't let my own prejudices stop you striving after the truth, but ballads are just a bit cheesy...

Most Pop Songs Have a *Verse-Chorus Structure*

After the intro, the structure of a pop song basically goes verse-chorus-verse-chorus...

- All the verses usually have the same tune, but the lyrics change for each verse.
- The chorus has a different tune from the verses, usually quite a catchy one.
  The lyrics and tune of the chorus don't change.
- In a lot of songs the verse and chorus are both 8 or 16 bars long.

Songs usually finish with a coda or outro — a bit that finishes it off nicely.

The old verse-chorus thing can get repetitive. To avoid this most songs have a middle 8, or bridge, that sounds different. It's an 8-bar section in the middle of the song with new chords, new lyrics and a whole new feel. Some pop ballads have an uplifting modulation (key change) towards the end. It's quite easy to recognise — e.g. in a Westlife song, it's the bit where they stand up.

Singers Can Do All Sorts of *Fancy Stuff*

There's more than one way to sing a song.
Make sure you can describe exactly what you're hearing. Listen out for...

1) **A CAPELLA** — singing with no instrumental backing. See p.175 for more about a capella.
2) **VIBRATO** — when singers quiver up and down slightly in pitch. It makes the voice sound warmer and more expressive.
3) **FALSETTO** — when men make their voices go really high, like Justin Timberlake or The BeeGees.
4) **PORTAMENTO** — when a singer slides from one note to another.
5) **RIFFING** — when singers decorate and add bits to the tune. They often go up and down a scale before coming to rest on one note. Riffing usually comes at the end of a phrase, between sections or to finish the song. You'll have heard Whitney Houston, Mariah Carey and Celine Dion riffing.

The *Lead Singer* Sings the *Main Tune*

The lead singer (or vocalist) sings the main tune of a song. They're the soloist, and often the most famous member of the band. If you get a pop song in the Listening Test, say something about the lead vocalist's style. It's even worth mentioning dead obvious stuff like whether the singer's male or female.

Backing Singers Sing the *Harmonies*

The backing vocalists are the ones who sing the harmonies.
These are the main ways backing singers do their thing:

IN HARMONY	IN UNISON	DESCANT	CALL AND RESPONSE
all singing different notes	all singing the same notes	singing a higher part in time with the main tune	repeating whatever the lead vocalist sings or answering the lead with another tune

I'm singing in the shower, just singing in the shower...

I'm guessing you're familiar with pop songs from life outside of the classroom — but now you've learnt a bit more about them, you can think about the different features the next time you listen to them.

Warm-up and Exam Questions

Warm-up Questions

1) When did rock music first start to appear?
2) What instruments were in the first rock bands?
3) What are power chords?
4) What are pop ballads?
5) Give the names of **three** famous singer-songwriters.
6) What is *a capella* singing?
7) Name **four** types of backing singing.

Exam Question

Make sure you know your rock and pop before sorting out your exam technique with this question.

This extract is from *Grace* by Jeff Buckley.
Play the extract **four** times, leaving a short pause between each playing.

(Track 37)

a)   i)   What is the rhythm played by the guitar accompaniment at the start of the extract?
Tick the correct box.

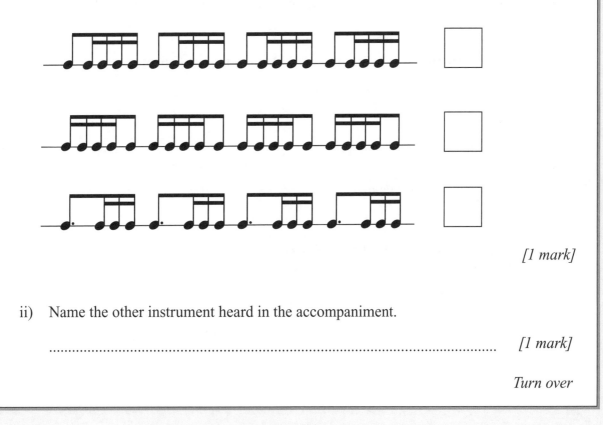

[1 mark]

   ii)   Name the other instrument heard in the accompaniment.

.... *[1 mark]*

Turn over

Exam Questions

b) What is the time signature of this extract?

.... *[1 mark]*

c) In which decade was this track released?

.... *[1 mark]*

d) Name and describe **one** vocal technique used by the lead singer in the extract.

Name of vocal technique

....

Description

....

.... *[2 marks]*

e) Which word best describes the role of the backing singers in the extract.
Circle your answer.

Harmony   **A capella**   **Descant**   **Unison**   *[1 mark]*

f) Describe the tonality the extract.

.... *[1 mark]*

g) Do you like or dislike this piece of music?
Give two musical reasons for your answer.

....

....

.... *[2 marks]*

Dance/Electronic Music

Electronic music is any music that uses electrical devices or instruments to produce and alter the sounds used in the music (see pages 68-69 for more on this). Most club dance music has electronic influences.

Lots of *Twentieth Century Music* Uses Electronic Instruments

Electronic devices and instruments were used by composers in the 20th century and are still used today.

In the 1920s, the idea of 'futuristic music' really took off. Darius Milhaud was the first composer to use sampling (see p.136) in his work. He experimented with changing the speeds of vocal recordings. A composer called Ottorino Respighi used a recording of a nightingale in his orchestral composition *Pini di Roma* (*Pines of Rome*). Another composer, George Antheil, composed a piece for pianos, xylophones, pianola (a self-playing piano), doorbells and an aeroplane propeller.

In the 1940s, music that used non-musical or man-made sounds (like car doors slamming, car horns, hitting car bonnets, bird songs, etc.) was known as 'Musique Concrète'. The sounds were recorded onto tapes then manipulated in different ways, for example:

* Playing them at different speeds.
* Cutting up the tape and putting it back together in a different order.
* Looping (recording a short section on to a tape, then making a loop of the tape to play it over and over again).

Electronic Dance Music is Played in *Clubs*

1) Most dance music today is created by electronic devices. There are lots of different types of electronic dance music and they're all slightly different.

2) The different types can be hard to define — there are so many sub-groups, and bands can play more than one type. The name 'club dance music' covers things like house, techno, trance and ambient.

Synthesizers and *Sequencers* are Used to *Create* Music

1) The main development in electronic music happened in the 1960s, when Robert Moog and Herbert Deutsch produced the voltage-controlled synthesizer. A synthesizer is an electronic device used to produce sounds.

2) Synthesizers are usually controlled by a keyboard (a piano keyboard rather than a computer keyboard), with buttons and slides to create different effects.

3) Lots of music can be produced just using a laptop — you can even download a virtual synthesizer.

4) A sequencer is a piece of computer software. It's a MIDI recording and playback device (MIDI stands for Musical Instrument Digital Interface — every note, instrument sound, key signature, tempo and any other musical direction is given a computer code. This means that different types of computers and recording equipment can 'talk' to each other). The sequencer tells a MIDI instrument to play notes in a certain way or particular order.

5) A sequencer doesn't actually record sound — it just uses MIDI information. This makes it easy to correct mistakes or change volume or timing.

6) A sequencer lets you make loops of short sections of sounds, which can be repeated and recorded to produce backing tracks. You can make loops of drumbeats, chords and even tunes. They're used a lot in electronic club dance music.

7) Cubase, Pro-Tools® and Logic Pro are sequencer programs that are widely used.

It was the nightingale — no, it was Ottorino Respighi...
Plenty of 'tech' terms for you to learn on this page. Cover up the page, and get writing a mini essay.

Dance/Electronic Music

All the technology used in electronic music can get a bit confusing — you've got synthesizers and sequencers (covered on the previous page) and samplers too. You also need to know the different ways these electronic devices can change sounds and music.

Samplers are a Bit Like Synthesizers

1) Samplers are another type of electronic equipment used to produce and alter music. They're a bit like synthesizers but they don't create the sounds themselves — they just play music back. The first digital sampler was invented in 1975.

> Stevie Wonder used a digital sampler on his album 'The Secret Life of Plants'.

2) Samples are short bits of recorded music. You can use samples of anything from live instruments to vinyl records. Samples can also be taken from a CD or MIDI track.

3) Samplers are told which samples to play by a sequencer or keyboard controller — the samples are assigned to a note on a keyboard and can be played, looped or recorded straight onto a track.

4) Samplers, synthesizers and sequencers mean that you don't have to be able to play any of the instruments you want to use in your recording, you can just use a computer program to get the sounds you want.

You Can Change Samples

You can use a virtual recording studio on your computer to alter and manipulate your samples. These are some of the main ways that samples can be altered:

LOOPING	Uses a computer to loop music rather than doing it by hand — see p.135.
PITCH SHIFTER	Plays the sample at different pitches.
PANNING	Changes which speaker the music comes out of.
CHORUS	Creates several layers of the sample — it sounds like there is more than one copy playing.
ECHO/DELAY	Adds echoes to the music — and even makes them in time with the beat.
REVERB	Changes the sample to make it sound as if it's being played in a large concert hall. (It can also take away all sound of reverb and make it feel flat.)
PHASER	Makes a 'whooshing' sound using the sample.
EQ	Short for equalization. It amplifies or removes frequencies (like bass or treble) — it can filter out frequencies above/below a certain level. Low-pass and high-pass filters are both types of EQ.
LOW-PASS FILTER	Gets rid of 'noise' (like hissing or other background noises).
HIGH-PASS FILTER	'Cleans' the sample — it can get rid of low-pitched rumblings in the background.
DISTORTION	Changes the sound of a sample (it distorts it). Used as a guitar effect as well.

Some Musicians use Samples in Live Performances

There are some musicians who use and manipulate samples live, using effects units like:

1) **KAOSS** — a DJ program that's connected to the decks and a laptop. You use your fingers on a touch screen to pull, bend and distort the music as it's playing.

2) **SERATO (or SCRATCH LIVE)** — a program that takes digital audio files and lets you create the DJ effect of scratching a vinyl record on a turntable. DJs like Fatboy Slim and Mark Ronson use it.

I'd like a sample of that cake please...

Don't be scared by all the technical stuff here — you don't need an in-depth understanding of how each bit works, you just need to know what they can do. Remember, lots of dance music uses this equipment.

Electronica

Not to be confused with electronic music in general, Electronica is in a sub-category all of its own.

The Definition of Electronica has Changed Over Time

1) In the early 1990s, Electronica was used to describe all electronic music that used electronic instruments and sequencers or manipulated sounds electronically.

2) Towards the end of the 90s, it was used for bands and artists who made it really obvious that they were using electronic instruments and samples in their music, as by this point, most non-classical groups were using some electronic equipment in their music. This form of Electronica included artists like Björk, Goldfrapp and Moby.

3) Most Electronica groups use instruments like drum machines, synthesizers and sub bass. Sub bass is a bass line that's lower than a normal electric bass guitar. It makes the speakers shake when it's played loud enough — you can really feel the music.

4) Lots of Electronica music has breakbeats — syncopated rhythms or polyrhythms (see p.174) used in electronic music.

5) Electronica groups often use influences from other types of music like folk and world music. This makes even more sub-genres of Electronica — e.g. Folktronica uses elements of Electronica and folk music.

There are No Rules of Composition

Electronica artists vary a lot in terms of the style of music, the electronic instruments they use, their typical audience and their performance style.

1) Live performances often use more than one laptop so that the artists can use different effects on different programs at the same time.

2) They're composing and sequencing live, so every performance is different.

3) They use techniques and ideas from 'Musique Concrète' (see p.135). They can turn samples of almost anything into music.

4) Performers use as many effects (like looping or pitch shifting — see p.136) as they want.

5) Sounds are manipulated in different ways, so they often can't be copied exactly by other artists.

6) Just about all the sounds of the instruments are altered in some way.

7) A lot of Electronica is polyphonic (different lines weaving in and out of each other).

Moby Uses Other Influences

Some Electronica artists (like Moby) use ideas from lots of other types of music — his music has ambient, hip-hop and techno influences.

1) Ambient music is also known as 'chill-out music'. It's very slow and calm — it's often used in clubs to create a more relaxing atmosphere for the clubbers that want a break from dancing.

2) Hip-hop music is the music of the hip-hop culture that appeared in the Bronx, New York in the 1970s. It has Jamaican and African-American influences (like the drumbeats) and includes a lot of rapping (or 'toasting').

3) Techno is a type of club dance music that has a very fast beat. It sounds very mechanical and electronic.

Stressed about exams — listen to some ambient music...

Beatboxing came from hip-hop music — it's where you make percussion noises using only your voice. It's not just used in hip-hop music — there are even beatboxing world championships.

Moby — Why Does My Heart Feel So Bad?

Moby's *Why Does My Heart Feel So Bad?* is from his album 'Play'. Make sure you're familiar with the electronic equipment in this type of music — check the last few pages if you're not.

Moby's Real Name is *Richard Melville Hall*

1) Richard Melville Hall was born in America in 1965. Moby was a nickname his parents gave him.

2) When he was young, he learnt guitar, piano and drums.

3) His music covers a range of genres from punk to rock to Electronica. He's also remixed music by The Prodigy and Michael Jackson, and written songs for Sophie Ellis-Bextor and Britney Spears.

4) Lots of his music has been used in films, like Tomorrow Never Dies and The Bourne Identity.

5) Moby uses a lot of samples in his music (see p.136).

'Play' was Released in 1999

1) Moby's album 'Play' was released in 1999. It reached number 1 in the UK album charts in 2000.

2) It was his first real mainstream pop success — before 'Play', most of his music was only popular as electronic dance music (though lots of the tracks on 'Play' are dance tracks too).

3) All the songs on the album have been used in films, TV programmes and adverts.

4) He uses samples of Gospel, folk and rock music.

5) Some of the tracks are completely electronic, while others have more of a rock influence.

Why Does My Heart Feel So Bad? is from 'Play'

1) The track *Why Does My Heart Feel So Bad?* is the fourth track on the album 'Play'. It was released in November 1999 and got to number 16 in the UK charts.

2) It was used in the trailer for the film *Black Hawk Down*, and also in an advert for Portuguese beer.

3) Most of the piece is made up of samples — Moby uses samples of a Gospel choir and a hip-hop drumbeat (see p.137). The drumbeat sample has been adjusted to fit to the tempo of the piece.

4) He also uses synthesized strings, a sub bass (see p.137) and a keyboard.

The Vocal Samples Haven't Been Altered

1) Moby uses two different vocal samples from a 1953 recording of The Shining Light Gospel Choir.

2) He didn't change the recordings — any background noise has been left in.

3) He uses the sample 'Why does my heart feel so bad? Why does my soul feel so bad?' as the verse, and 'These open doors' as a chorus. He also makes a loop of 'These open doors'.

This 8-bar vocal sample makes up the verse...

... and this sample is repeated to form the chorus

It's also played on loop in the chorus

Lots of the other tracks on 'Play' have been used in films and TV programmes — Honey was used in the film Holes, Porcelain was used in The Beach, Bodyrock was used in Ali and Veronica's Closet was used in the TV series Buffy the Vampire Slayer. You'll probably recognize some of the tracks from these.

Moby — Why Does My Heart Feel So Bad?

The structure of this piece is quite straightforward, but make sure you can follow it and understand it.

The Texture Builds Up as Instruments are Added

1) *Why Does My Heart Feel So Bad?* is divided up into 8-bar sections (except for a 1-bar bridge about three-quarters of the way through the piece). It has a fairly standard pop structure (it goes intro, verse, chorus, verse, bridge, chorus, verse, outro).

2) The instrumentation's built up — more instruments are added in each section.

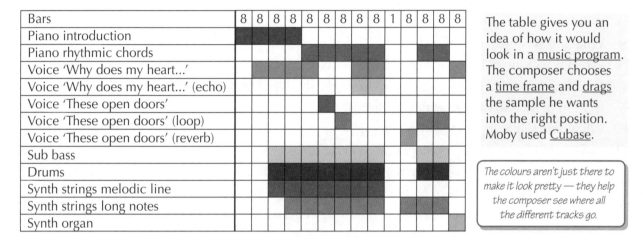

Bars	8	8	8	8	8	8	8	8	8	1	8	8	8	8
Piano introduction														
Piano rhythmic chords														
Voice 'Why does my heart...'														
Voice 'Why does my heart...' (echo)														
Voice 'These open doors'														
Voice 'These open doors' (loop)														
Voice 'These open doors' (reverb)														
Sub bass														
Drums														
Synth strings melodic line														
Synth strings long notes														
Synth organ														

The table gives you an idea of how it would look in a music program. The composer chooses a time frame and drags the sample he wants into the right position. Moby used Cubase.

The colours aren't just there to make it look pretty — they help the composer see where all the different tracks go.

3) It starts off with an 8-bar piano intro, then the verse starts. The 'Why does my heart feel so bad? Why does my soul feel so bad?' vocal sample's played 4 times. At first, there's just the piano playing in the background, then the hip-hop drumbeat, the sub bass and synthesized strings come in. The strings add melodic interest during the rests in the vocal line. On the third time through, more synthesized strings are added, playing long notes. The piano part then changes to rhythmic chords.

4) The chorus section uses the 'These open doors' vocal sample. It's played twice — once with rests in between the phrases, and once on loop. The backing in the chorus is both synth strings parts, the drumbeat, the sub bass and the rhythmic piano chords.

5) It goes back to the verse, using the same backing. The vocal sample is played twice, but with an echo part.

6) In the 1-bar bridge, the music seems to stop for a bar, but if you listen carefully, you can hear a pedal point (held on low note).

7) After the bridge, 'These open doors' is heard again — this time with a reverb effect. It's accompanied just by the long notes on the synthesized strings.

8) The 8-bar 'These open doors' loop is then played twice, over the rhythmic piano chords, sub bass, drums and long synth strings notes.

9) The piece finishes with one last 'Why does my heart feel so bad? Why does my soul feel so bad?', over the top of synthesized organ notes (the only time we hear the synth organ in the whole piece).

You Need to Know the Chords Moby Uses

1) The 8-bar verse uses 4 chords, each lasting for two bars. These are A minor, E minor, G major and D major.

2) The first time 'These open doors' is played, it uses C major and A minor chords (the chord pattern goes C, C, Am, Am, C, C, Am, Am). When the sample's looped, an F major chord comes in — the chord pattern is F, F, C, C, F, F, C, C.

3) Both vocal samples are in A minor, but they're harmonised differently — the 'Why does my heart feel so bad? Why does my soul feel so bad?' sample sounds minor, as it's harmonised with mainly minor chords, but the 'These open doors' sample sounds major because of the chords used.

Revision Summary for Section Seven

You'll probably be familiar with all kinds of popular music already but that doesn't mean you can listen to the radio for half an hour and call it revision. Go through these questions until you can answer them without looking back — it's the only way you'll learn.

1) Write down the seven notes of the blues scale starting on C.

2) Write down the chord pattern of the 12-bar blues (using I, II, III, IV etc).

3) Describe the call and response pattern in the 12-bar blues.

4) When and where did jazz music develop?

5) What is swing music?

6) What are syncopated rhythms?

7) When was 'Kind of Blue' by Miles Davis released?

8) Give four ways that Miles Davis' solos changed the way jazz music was played.

9) Is 'Kind of Blue' based on scales or chords?

10) What time signature is used in *All Blues*?

11) How does Davis create a mellow timbre in *All Blues*?

12) When and how does Davis change the traditional 12-bar blues chord pattern (it happens twice)?

13) Which six instruments make up the band which plays *All Blues*?

14) Four instruments take turns to play in the improvised section of *All Blues*. Which instruments are they and what order do they play in?

15) Name three well-known singer-songwriters and a ballad they've composed.

16) What's the posh name for verse-chorus-verse structure?

17) Explain what these words mean when you're talking about singing:
   a) a capella   b) vibrato   c) falsetto   d) portamento   e) riffing

18) Write down three different ways backing singers perform.

19) In 1990s rock music, which two notes are used in 'power chords'?

20) When did Jeff Buckley release the album 'Grace'?

21) What is the song *Grace* about?

22) What is falsetto?

23) What time signature is used in *Grace*? What time signature are rock songs usually in?

24) Describe the basic structure of *Grace*.

25) Name and explain two of the electronic effects used in *Grace*.

26) What key is used for the main section of *Grace*?

27) Explain the function of the following electronic equipment:
   a) synthesizer   b) sequencer   c) sampler.

28) What is sub bass?

29) What is meant by ambient music and where might you hear it played?

30) Give a definition of techno music.

31) When did Moby release *Why Does My Heart Feel So Bad?*

32) Give two types of music which Moby samples in *Why Does My Heart Feel So Bad?*

33) Name three instruments which play in *Why Does My Heart Feel So Bad?*

34) Describe the structure of *Why Does My Heart Feel So Bad?*

35) Which sequencer program does Moby use in *Why Does My Heart Feel So Bad?*

36) The 8-bar verse of *Why Does My Heart Feel So Bad?* features 4 chords which last for 2 bars each. What are the four chords?

37) Describe the two sets of chords used to accompany the 'These open doors' vocal sample in *Why Does My Heart Feel So Bad?*

Dance Music — The Basics

Metre, tempo, rhythm and phrasing are the absolute basics in dance — they're the bits
in the music that tell the dancers when and how to move. Here's how they work...

The **Pattern of Beats** is Called the **Metre**

The beats in a piece of music make
different patterns of strong and
weak beats, depending on the
time signature. The pattern they make
is called the metre.

Nearly all dance music has a regular
metre. The strong beats make the
same pattern throughout the music.

> **THE MAIN METRES USED IN DANCE ARE...**
>
> **DUPLE METRE**
> 2 beats per bar. It goes 'TUM tum, TUM tum'.
>
> **TRIPLE METRE**
> 3 beats per bar. It goes 'TUM tum tum, TUM tum tum'.
>
> **QUADRUPLE METRE**
> 4 beats per bar. It goes 'TUM tum TUM tum, TUM tum TUM tum'.

The **Tempo** Tells Dancers **How Fast to Move**

1) The movements in a dance normally fit the speed of the beat — the tempo.

2) The speed of a dance does a lot to set the mood. An Irish jig, with a lot of
   leaping about, has a zippy tempo to match the carefree mood of the dance.

3) In dance music the tempo usually stays the same all the way through a
   piece to make it easier for the dancers to follow the beat.

*See p.12 for words
to describe mood
and tempo.*

Dance Moves Usually Follow the **Rhythm**

Some dances have a set rhythm that goes with
set movements. E.g. in tango, the 'arm out,
strut across the floor and throw your partner back'
move fits a repeated rhythm in the music.

In formal dances the set movements often match regular phrases in the music. The phrases
are usually 4 bars long. When a new phrase begins the set movements are repeated.

There are **Different Types** of Dance

There are loads of types of dance:

1) PAIRED DANCES — these can be stately ballroom dances like the waltz, or some of the more
   lively dances that came out of Latin America like salsa or the tango from Argentina.

2) GROUP DANCES — dances that are popular with big groups of people, like American line
   dancing, the Irish jig and reel and Bhangra, a folk dance originally from India and Pakistan.

3) IMPROVISED DANCES — you just make up the dance on the spot to fit the music you're
   listening to, usually to dance music in discos or clubs.

4) DANCES THAT TELL STORIES — like classical ballet, which is usually set to orchestral music.

5) INSTRUMENTAL DANCE MUSIC — music that's written in the style of a dance, but meant for
   listening, not for actual dancing, e.g. some of the waltzes and minuets written by Chopin.

Show the examiners you know all the moves...

Examiners often like to test you on dance music in the Listening exam. To help you there's lots of
jargon for talking about dance music on this page, so make sure that you learn it all — no excuses.

Waltz

The **Waltz Craze** Started in **Vienna**

1) People first started writing and dancing waltzes in Austria — mostly in the ballrooms of Vienna.

2) The first waltzes were written in the 1790s.

3) The waltz ended up being one of the most popular dances of the nineteenth century — not just in Vienna, but all over Europe and in North America too.

4) People thought the waltz was really saucy at first — it was the first dance ever where people held each other so closely. They sometimes got head-rushes from spinning so fast.

The Rhythm Goes '**Oom Cha Cha, Oom Cha Cha**'

1) A waltz is always in triple metre. The time signature's usually 3/4.

2) Viennese waltzes go pretty fast — their tempo markings can be as quick as $\text{\textdotaccent}$ = 70, which means 70 dotted minim beats (or bars) a minute (a bit faster than one bar a second).

3) The 'oom' is stronger than the 'cha cha', so the rhythm feels more like one beat in a bar than three.

4) The 'oom cha cha' rhythm is emphasised in the accompanying chords.

OOM cha cha   OOM cha cha   OOM cha cha   OOM cha cha

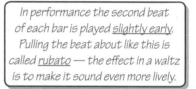

In performance the second beat of each bar is played slightly early. Pulling the beat about like this is called rubato — the effect in a waltz is to make it sound even more lively.

The **Chords** are **Simple** and **Don't Change Much**

A waltz has a strong clear tune, closely backed by the chords.
It's called a homophonic texture — see p.39 for more on texture.

1) The chords are pretty simple — mostly they're the primary chords I, IV and V.

2) The same chord's used for at least one bar, and sometimes two or four bars.

3) One note of the chord's played on the 'oom'. On the 'cha cha' the rest of the notes are played together, or the whole chord's played.

4) The speed of chord changes is called the harmonic rhythm.
Waltz chords change slowly, so waltzes have slow harmonic rhythm.

5) This slow, simple chord pattern can get a bit repetitive, so composers use appoggiaturas (see p.83) and chromatic notes to spice up their tunes.

The **Dance Steps** Match the '**Oom Cha Cha**' Rhythm

1) The waltz is danced in the ballroom hold. This is also sometimes called the closed position because the partners dance facing each other, holding each other closely.

2) One of the dancers faces forwards whilst their partner moves back and does the steps backwards.

3) Waltz steps match the 3/4 time signature of the music.

4) The feet move in different directions on the first two beats but they meet on the final beat of the bar.

5) The first step is longer to mark the start of a new bar.

6) The long step matches the 'oom' and the two shorter steps match the 'cha cha' rhythm of the music.

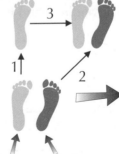

left foot   right foot

Here's how the feet move on each beat of every other bar for the basic waltz step. In the next bar, the right foot would do steps 1 and 3 and the left foot would do step 2.

Waltz

In the nineteenth century waltzing was simply everywhere — it seemed a really exciting craze.

Waltzes Started Simple and Ended up Complex

The first waltzes were written in <u>binary</u> <u>form</u> with two 8-bar repeated sections.

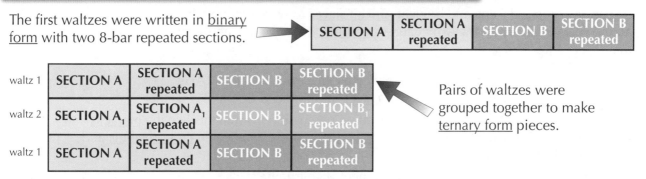

SECTION A	SECTION A repeated	SECTION B	SECTION B repeated

waltz 1	**SECTION A**	**SECTION A repeated**	**SECTION B**	**SECTION B repeated**
waltz 2	**SECTION A$_1$**	**SECTION A$_1$ repeated**	**SECTION B$_1$**	**SECTION B$_1$ repeated**
waltz 1	**SECTION A**	**SECTION A repeated**	**SECTION B**	**SECTION B repeated**

Pairs of waltzes were grouped together to make <u>ternary form</u> pieces.

Two Viennese composers — <u>Joseph Lanner</u> and <u>Johann Strauss the Elder</u> added various things to make waltzes <u>longer</u> and more <u>complex</u>. A later waltz has...

1) **A SLOW INTRODUCTION** In the introduction you hear stuff like wavering strings (posh word = <u>tremolo</u>), <u>arpeggios</u> (probably on the harp) and little <u>tasters</u> of the main tunes on the woodwind instruments.

2) **FIVE OR MORE WALTZ TUNES** Each waltz includes several different tunes, all in <u>related keys</u>. Each tune lasts between <u>16</u> and <u>32 bars</u> and is in <u>binary</u> or <u>ternary</u> form.

3) **A CODA** This is a <u>final section</u> that rounds off the waltz by pulling together bits from all the tunes.

> *There were lots of waltzing Strausses:*
> *The dad was <u>Johann Strauss the Elder</u>, and he had three sons who all composed waltzes — <u>Johann</u>, <u>Josef</u> and <u>Eduard</u>.*
> *Johann Strauss the Younger composed two of these longer-style waltzes — <u>Tales from the Vienna Woods</u> and*
> *<u>The Blue Danube</u>. Each one lasts about <u>ten minutes</u>.*

Viennese Waltzes Were Played by Big Orchestras

Viennese waltzes were played by the <u>large orchestras</u> that were standard in the <u>Romantic period</u>. There's a lot of <u>brass</u> and <u>woodwind</u>, including more unusual instruments like piccolos. The percussion sections have a big <u>variety</u> of instruments, e.g. timpani, tambourines, triangles and snare drums.

Waltzes Spread Beyond the Ballrooms

Waltzes got to be so popular during the nineteenth century that they spread into other types of music.

1) Waltzes crop up as <u>dances</u> and <u>songs</u> in <u>operettas</u>. Some of the more famous ones are by <u>Johann Strauss the Younger</u> (e.g. *Die Fledermaus*) and <u>Gilbert and Sullivan</u> (e.g. *Pirates of Penzance*).

2) Waltzes were so popular in the nineteenth century that people liked to play them <u>at home</u> on the piano. <u>Chopin</u>, <u>Schumann</u>, <u>Brahms</u> and <u>Weber</u> all wrote tons of waltzes for playing at home, and some harder virtuoso waltzes for concert pianists, like Chopin's *Minute Waltz*.

3) Some nineteenth century composers included waltzes in their <u>orchestral works</u>, e.g. <u>Berlioz's</u> *Symphonie Fantastique*, <u>Tchaikovsky's</u> *4th* and *5th Symphony*, and <u>Ravel's</u> *La Valse*.

4) Tchaikovsky put waltzes in his <u>ballets</u> too — *Swan Lake* and *Sleeping Beauty* both include waltzes.

5) In the twentieth century the waltz was used in a few <u>musicals</u>. There are waltzes in <u>Cole Porter's</u> *High Society* and <u>Rodgers and Hammerstein's</u> *The Sound of Music*.

Remember the waltz is not just a dance...

A waltz is pretty easy to spot — if you can say '<u>oom cha cha</u>' in time to the music, it's probably a waltz.

Salsa

Salsa is <u>Latin American dance music</u> which blends the <u>son style</u> from Cuba with elements of <u>jazz</u>.

Salsa Grew Out of **Son**...

The <u>Spanish</u> colonised Cuba and brought <u>African slaves</u> to work there on the sugar plantations.
Over the years, music from the two cultures <u>combined</u> to make a dance style called <u>son</u>.
Traditional son music has:

1) A basic repeated rhythm pattern called a <u>clave</u> (pronounced *CLAH-VEY*)
   played by hitting two sticks called <u>claves</u> (pronounced *CLAYVES*) together.

2) <u>More</u> repeated rhythm patterns played on percussion instruments like the <u>maracas</u> and
   <u>bongos</u>. These parts are often <u>syncopated</u> and form complicated <u>cross-rhythms</u> and
   <u>polyrhythms</u> against the clave part.

3) The melody is played by <u>brass instruments</u> like trumpets.

4) <u>Call and response</u> between the lead singer (called the <u>sonero</u>) and the chorus (the <u>choro</u>)
   — in salsa music call and response is called <u>pregón and choro</u>.

5) Son music is meant for people to <u>dance</u> to. Most lyrics are <u>simple</u> or about the dancers but
   when the singers get a chance to <u>improvise</u>, they can sing about anything they feel like.

...and **Big-Band Jazz**

1) Salsa grew up in the <u>1960s</u> and <u>1970s</u> in <u>New York</u>, in the city's Latin American community.
   Salsa means <u>sauce</u> in Spanish — it's meant to be <u>spicy music</u>.

2) Taking the basic structure of son, salsa bands added the harsher,
   brass-based arrangements of <u>big band jazz</u>. The <u>trombone</u> was a big focus.

3) Salsa also took inspiration from <u>Puerto Rican</u>, <u>Brazilian</u> and <u>African</u> music.

4) Big names in the rise of salsa music include the Puerto Rican-American trombonist,
   singer and producer <u>Willie Colon</u>, and the Cuban-American singer <u>Celia Cruz</u>.

5) Salsa soon became popular throughout <u>Latin America</u> and <u>beyond</u>.

The **Clave** is the **Key** to Any Salsa Tune

The clave is the <u>basic rhythm</u> of a piece of salsa music. The most common salsa rhythm is the <u>son clave</u>.
The son clave rhythm has a group of <u>three</u> notes and a group of <u>two</u>.

It goes like this...   ...or like this...

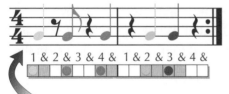   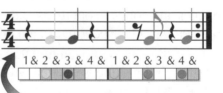

Have a go at <u>clapping</u> out the rhythm. <u>Count out loud</u> as you clap to make sure you're getting it right. Don't be surprised if you find it fairly <u>tricky</u> at first.

This one's called a <u>3-2 son clave</u>.   *This one's called a <u>2-3 son clave</u>.*

1) A piece of salsa music doesn't use the same clave all the time —
   it might switch to a different clave half way through.

2) The piece always stays in a <u>4/4</u> time signature.

3) All the other parts <u>fit round</u> the instruments playing the clave.

You say clave — I say clave...

Listen to some salsa and make sure you recognise the rhythms — see if you can pick out the son clave.

Salsa

Get yourself a <u>salsa</u> tunè on the stereo, and see if you can pick these features out...

The **Salsa Band** Combines Son and Big-Band **Instruments**

A traditional son band has six instruments: <u>guitar</u>, <u>string bass</u>, <u>bongos</u>, <u>maracas</u>, <u>claves</u> and the <u>tres</u>, which is a bit like a guitar but with three sets of two strings. These instruments are combined with <u>big band brass</u> instruments like <u>trombones</u> and <u>trumpets</u> to form the salsa band.

These are the main sections in a <u>modern salsa band</u>:

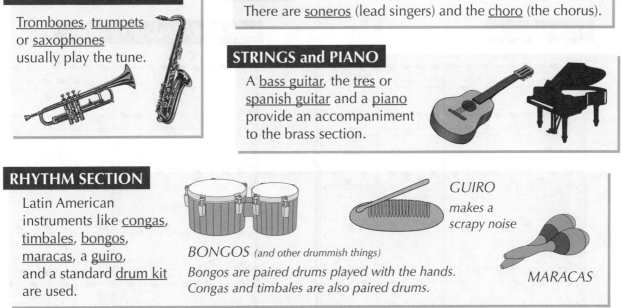

FRONT LINE or HORNS

<u>Trombones</u>, <u>trumpets</u> or <u>saxophones</u> usually play the tune.

VOCALS

There are <u>soneros</u> (lead singers) and the <u>choro</u> (the chorus).

STRINGS and PIANO

A <u>bass guitar</u>, the <u>tres</u> or <u>spanish guitar</u> and a <u>piano</u> provide an accompaniment to the brass section.

RHYTHM SECTION

Latin American instruments like <u>congas</u>, <u>timbales</u>, <u>bongos</u>, <u>maracas</u>, a <u>guiro</u>, and a standard <u>drum kit</u> are used.

BONGOS (and other drummish things)
Bongos are paired drums played with the hands.
Congas and timbales are also paired drums.

GUIRO
makes a scrapy noise

MARACAS

Some musicians use rapping, <u>samplers</u> and <u>synthesizers</u> to transform traditional salsa music into club music. This modern interpretation of salsa music is called <u>salsaton</u>.

A Salsa Tune has **Three Main Sections**

There are <u>three main chunks</u> in a salsa tune. The three different chunks can appear in <u>any order</u>, and they can all be used <u>more than once</u>.

1) In the <u>verse</u> you hear the main tune, usually sung by the <u>sonero</u> or played by an instrumentalist.

2) The <u>montuno</u> is a kind of chorus where the sonero or lead instrumentalist <u>improvises</u> and the choro or other instrumentalists <u>answer</u>.

3) You'll also hear a break between choruses, called the <u>mambo</u>, with new musical material, e.g. different chords or a different tune. It's often played by the <u>horn section</u>.

4) You're also likely to hear an <u>introduction</u> and <u>ending</u>.

5) There could also be a 'break' — a bit where the main tune <u>stops</u> and just the rhythm section plays.

Here's a fairly <u>typical</u> salsa structure:

| INTRO | VERSE | BREAK | MONTUNO | MAMBO | MONTUNO | ENDING |

> *The <u>timbale</u> player plays a <u>drum roll</u> called an <u>abanico</u> at the <u>start</u> of each new section. Listen out for it — it'll help you work out when the sections are <u>changing</u>.*

Intro, verse, break, montuno, mambo, montuno, ending...

There are plenty of instruments found in a salsa band. Make sure you can recognise them all. Also, make sure you learn the three main sections of a salsa, and how the sections might fit together.

Salsa

Half a billion Latin Americans can't be wrong — salsa is gorgeous, fantastic and back for a <u>third page</u>.

The **Rhythms Change** in Each Section

The <u>conga</u>, <u>bongo</u> and <u>timbale</u> parts all change between a verse and montuno or mambo.

1) The <u>conga</u> player uses <u>two drums</u> in the <u>montuno</u> and <u>mambo</u>, but just <u>one</u> in the <u>verse</u>.

2) The <u>bongo</u> player switches to a <u>cowbell</u> and a different <u>rhythm</u> in the montuno and mambo.

3) The <u>timbale</u> player plays the <u>mambo bell</u> as well as the timbale in the <u>montuno</u> and <u>mambo</u>.

Have a look at these percussion parts. Take it <u>one line at a time</u> or it could get confusing...

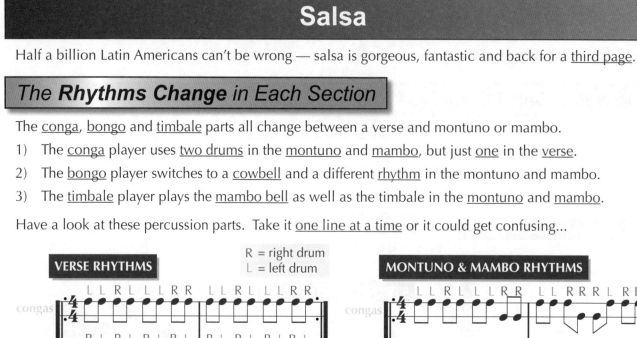

Salsa Dance Steps **Match** the **Rhythm**

1) The partners dance facing each other in the <u>closed position</u>. There's sometimes a chance for the pair to break apart and <u>improvise</u> — like the instruments and singers in the <u>montuno</u>.

2) Partners dance <u>on the spot</u> rather than moving round the room.

3) It takes <u>8 beats</u> for one complete cycle of the dance moves. That's <u>two bars</u> of 4/4 music or <u>one clave</u>.

4) <u>Two quick steps</u> on the first 2 beats of the bar are followed by a <u>longer step</u> on the third beat and then a tap or pause.

5) The leader steps <u>forward</u> on the first beat of the cycle whilst his partner steps <u>backwards</u>, then they return to their original places.

6) The pattern is then <u>repeated</u> as the leader steps backwards.

7) The main thing is that the dancers move <u>in time</u> with each other and the music — so they don't stand on each other's feet.

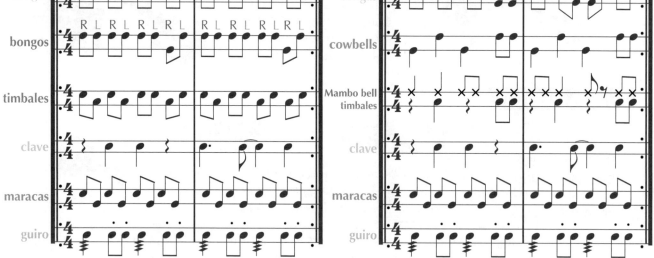

These are the man's steps in a salsa dance — the woman's are a mirror image of this.

If you were Cuban you'd have to learn all this in Spanish...

It's no good just reading about salsa. You've got to <u>listen to it</u>, <u>have a go at playing it</u> and <u>try writing some</u> so you can get your head round all those tricky clave rhythms. Trust me, it'll help...

Tango

Here's another style of music and dancing from Latin America...

Tango Has Roots in **Europe** and **Africa**

1) Early tangos first appeared in the 1850s in Argentina and Uruguay.

2) Argentina's a country with a lot of immigrants from different European countries, and many Africans were brought over as slaves. Tango is a mix of the music of all these different cultures.

3) Immigrants from Italy, Spain and Eastern Europe added their influences to the music of Latin America. Tango melodies often have an Italian origin.

4) One of tango's ancestors was milonga — a type of Argentinian and Uruguayan music in a syncopated style. Many famous tango musicians have also written and played milongas.

5) Another influence was candombe, a style of music created by the Afro-Uruguayan community in Montevideo. Candombe's rhythms were brought over by African slaves, and were used in tango.

Tango Moved From the **Bars** and into the **Concert Halls**

1) The tango was first found in the bars and brothels in the port areas of Buenos Aires in Argentina and Montevideo in Uruguay.

2) It soon moved into more respectable surroundings of cabarets and dance halls, directed by band leaders. Early tango orchestras included flute, violin and guitar, but tangos were also played on solo piano.

3) The double bass, the bandoneon (a type of accordion made in Germany) and percussion instruments were soon added. Larger bands contained up to 4 bandoneons.

4) Singers accompanying themselves on guitar and even brass bands were soon playing tangos. One classic tango lineup is the sextet of two bandoneons, two violins, a piano and a double bass.

5) In about 1950, orchestras started performing tangos without dancers in concert halls.

6) After the 1950s tango wasn't so popular — the large tango orchestras gradually disappeared when the dance halls and concert halls fell into decline. Currently, small tango groups of between three and six musicians are the most common in Argentina. They play in smaller venues.

Tango has Branched Out into **Different Varieties**

1) The tango song (tango-canción) was seen during the Golden Age during the 1920s-30s.

2) Ballroom tango developed as a dance for competitions in Europe and the US — it's based on the original Argentine tango, which is more improvised (and less competitive) than ballroom tango.

3) Tango Nuevo combined elements of tango, classical and jazz music. It used complex rhythms and harmonies that dancers weren't used to — it became music to listen to rather than dance to.

4) Astor Piazzolla, a famous bandoneon player and composer, moved to Buenos Aires as a young man. He used his experience of studying and composing classical music in Paris to turn the tango into concert music rather than dance music. This fusion angered the traditional tango audience in Argentina, but brought him success in North America and Europe.

5) Tango rock (tango-rokéro) replaced the bandoneon and double bass with a rock band rhythm section, electric guitars and keyboards. Tango has also moved into mainstream jazz — with some groups using saxophones and clarinets.

6) Electro tango uses electronic elements like sampling (see p.159) mixed with traditional tango music.

7) The tango scene is now a very broad one with musicians of all styles of music playing together.

Tango originated in Argentina and Uruguay...
To get a real feel for tango, the best thing to do is to listen to as many of the different styles as possible.

Tango

Have a listen to some tango music and see if you can spot the rhythms described on this page.

The **Tango** is a Powerful **Paired Dance**

1) The tango is a <u>paired dance</u>. Partners 'parade' around the room with <u>cheek-to-cheek</u> contact, with their legs often becoming <u>entwined</u>. It's a very <u>passionate</u>, <u>sensual</u> dance.

2) There isn't the same focus on one main step as you find in some other dances — the dance is usually <u>improvised</u> around a range of basic steps.

3) Originally men would dance together while waiting for women in the sleazy bars. They would rehearse new steps in a <u>showy</u> and <u>threatening style</u> that often reflected a struggle for one woman between two men.

4) The dancers' movements are <u>provocative</u> yet <u>controlled</u> — the music reflects this by having <u>beautiful melodies</u> and strong <u>rhythmic energy</u>.

5) <u>Deliberate</u> and <u>exaggerated</u> dance movements are supported by <u>precise performance details</u> in the music — such as <u>staccato marks</u>.

6) In <u>restricted</u> spaces (like <u>crowded bars</u>), tango steps are <u>small</u> and the dancers hold each other <u>close</u>. Other types of tango (done in <u>larger</u> dance halls) have <u>bigger</u> steps and dancers can <u>let go</u> of each other to perform some of the <u>fancier</u> steps.

Rhythm is an Important Feature of **Tango Music**

1) Tangos have <u>2</u> or <u>4</u> beats in the bar. These are some of the <u>basic rhythms</u>:

2) The main melody often uses a <u>slow rhythmic pace</u> with <u>triplets</u> (three equal notes in one beat) and <u>syncopation</u> (stressing normally unstressed beats or offbeats). <u>Staccato</u> notes (played abruptly with clear gaps between them) give the music <u>precision</u> and its deliberate nature. <u>Simple harmonies</u>, usually in a <u>minor key</u>, based on the <u>tonic</u> and <u>dominant</u> chords (e.g. A minor and E major).

3) Prominent and repeating <u>dotted rhythms</u> in the bass often move between the <u>tonic</u> (root) and the <u>dominant</u> (fifth) chord notes:

> This is a <u>habanera</u> rhythm used in early tango music. It comes from 19th century <u>Cuban</u> dance music.

Tango has **Influenced Composers** All Over the World

1) The tango _El Choclo_ was written by <u>Angel Villoldo</u> in 1905 was one of the first big tango hits.

2) <u>Carlos Gardel</u> spread the popularity of the tango across the world during the <u>1920s</u> and <u>1930s</u>. He was a singer and songwriter who <u>broadened the appeal</u> of the tango among <u>different social classes</u>. He became <u>internationally famous</u>. He often sang to a <u>guitar accompaniment</u> and recorded hundreds of songs.

3) Piazzolla's works include _Libertango_ for accordion and strings and _Adiós Nonino_ for solo guitar. He also wrote a concerto for bandoneon and orchestra that includes a tango — it pays tribute to Bach.

4) In his ballet _The Soldier's Tale_ (1918), the Russian composer <u>Igor Stravinsky</u> included a tango. One of the 21 pieces in British composer William Walton's _Façade_ (1922) is a tango.

Tan-going, going, gone...

Make sure you learn the main features of tango music, as well as the main rhythms used by composers. It's also worth remembering that tango music has influenced composers the world over.

Warm-up and Exam Questions

Questions on dance music are popular in the Listening Exam — so get the practice while you can.

Warm-up Questions

1) Name **two** paired dances.
2) In which city did the waltz craze begin?
3) Write down **three** characteristic features of a waltz.
4) What's the basic rhythm of son music called?
5) Which **two** styles of music combined to create salsa?
6) Give **three** instruments that are in the rhythm section of a salsa band.
7) Give **three** rhythmic features of tango music.

Exam Question

Here's another exam-style question to get you in the swing ready for the real thing.

Play the extract **five** times, leaving a short pause between each playing.

(Track 38)

a) What is this style of music called? Put a ring around your answer.

        pavan   **salsa**   **sarabande**   *[1 mark]*

b) In which country did this style of music originate?

.... *[1 mark]*

c) Name **three** percussion instruments that play in this extract.

....

.... *[3 marks]*

d) At the beginning of this extract the piano plays some off-beat jazz chords. Which of the following rhythms is it playing? Put a ring round your answer.

[1 mark]

Turn over

Exam Question

e)   Which other instrument plays the same rhythm as the piano at the
beginning of this extract?

....   *[1 mark]*

f)   About 13 seconds into the extract, the music stops. What is this called?

....   *[1 mark]*

g)   When the main theme starts again, what is the piano doing to accompany
the tune?

....   *[1 mark]*

h)   Give the names of **two** different instruments that are added immediately
after the music stops (when the main theme begins).

....   *[2 marks]*

i)   When the main theme comes in, how are the instruments playing together?
Circle **one** answer only.

   call and response   **chords in harmony**   **walking bass line**   *[1 mark]*

j)   Circle **two** of these words, which you think best describe the rhythmic
accompaniment throughout the extract.

   tuneful   syncopated   slow   cross-rhythms   simple   octave   *[2 marks]*

Line Dance — American

Line Dancing has its Roots in European Folk Dancing

1) American line dancing is a type of group dancing with choreographed steps. It was influenced by European immigrants to the USA — it has lots of similarities to European folk dancing.

2) The first popular American dances to be danced in lines were 1920s dances like the Charleston and the Cha Cha — modern line dancing grew from these.

3) The Madison and the Stroll were crazes in the 1950s and 60s — as well as being danced in lines these had called steps and a regular back-and-forth pattern. The Madison was a jazz piece, and the Stroll was done to slow swing or rhythm and blues. Some dances were done to rock and roll.

4) Modern line dancing didn't really appear until the 1970s. Disco dances like the Bus Stop and the Hustle (which was made popular by the film *Saturday Night Fever)* were similar to modern line dances, and were danced to disco music.

5) The term 'line-dancing' wasn't really used until the 1980s — the Tush Push (choreographed in 1980) was one of the first dances to be called a 'line dance'.

6) In 1992, Billy Ray Cyrus released *Achy Breaky Heart*. It was a massive hit — it made line dancing really popular. Cyrus was a country and western star, so that style of music became associated with line dancing. The Grid's *Swamp Thang* (1994) and Steps' *5, 6, 7, 8* (1998) had a techno influence — synthesized sounds and a modern drumbeat.

7) In America today, country and western is the most popular type of music for line dancing — some people think it should only be danced to country and western, with dancers wearing stetsons and cowboy boots. Most line dancing in the UK is done to pop music, though.

Lots of Line Dance Music is Played by a Folk Band

1) In America, line dance music is often played by a folk band (as country and western has its roots in folk music). The band might include a fiddle, a banjo or mandolin, accordion, harmonica and double bass. Sometimes there's a guitar too.

2) Advances in technology like the electric guitar, MIDI (Musical Instrument Digital Interface), sampling and drum machines have moved line dancing music into a more modern style. Older country and western music is still popular though.

3) Line dance music has clear sections and lots of repetition, so it's easy to choreograph dances to it.

4) The music normally has a moderate tempo with a strong beat and memorable tunes. Most line dances have 4 beats in a bar. The State Line Waltz is one of the few with 3 beats in a bar.

5) The harmonies are fairly static — the chords don't change very often.

Sets of Steps in Line Dancing Have Different Names

1) Each beat in a line dance is called a count. The more counts, the trickier the line dance (a 48-count dance might not have 48 different dance steps though — a step can be held for more than one beat).

2) A basic is the set of steps from the first count to the last count, without tags or bridges.

3) Tags (2 or 4 steps) or bridges (8 or 16 steps) are extra sets of steps added to a basic to make the dance fit to the music.

4) A restart is when the basic dance sequence is interrupted and started again. Restarts are another way of making the dance fit to the music.

5) The most common step is the grapevine. Others include the shuffle step, the lock step and the sailor step.

6) Each dance has a number of walls — a wall is just the direction the dancers face. Most dances are 4-wall dances — they're done facing the front, back and sides of the room.

7) Most line dances are done as solo dances, but some are done in pairs or groups. Group line dances aren't always done in lines — barn dances are done in circles.

152

Irish Jig and Reel

Next on the dancefloor — the Irish jig and reel...

Irish Dance Music Has a **Strong**, **Regular Beat**

1) Traditional Irish music is played on instruments like a violin (fiddle), Irish open-holed wooden flute, tin whistle, concertina or accordion, guitar, Uilleann pipes (the Irish version of bagpipes) and percussion such as the bodhrán (a framed drum) and the spoons. The instruments usually play the tune in unison.

2) It has a strong regular beat with the emphasis on the first beat, so it's easy to dance to. It's quite fast.

3) The melody has clear phrases in a question and answer pattern. Melodies are often made up of two 8-bar sections, each played twice (once for the left foot and once for the right) to make a 32-bar melody. The regular phrases make it easy to fit steps to and to keep in time with.

4) The music has simple harmonies. Some are in a major key, often D major or G major, and some are in minor modes (see p.21).

5) Traditional Irish music wasn't written down — it was passed down over hundreds of years.

Irish Dances Can be **Social Dances** or **Performance Dances**

1) Social dances are ones where everyone joins in — they're either céilí dances or set dances. A céilí involves couples dancing in a square, circle or line. In a set dance, four couples dance in a square.

2) Social dances take place at celebrations like fairs and weddings.

3) Performance dances are dances that the audience watch, rather than join in.

4) Most performance dances are a form of step dancing. In step dancing, the complicated footwork is the most important part of the dance — dancers often keep the top half of their body still.

5) Performance dances are either hard shoe dances (the noise the dancers' feet make is important) or soft shoe dances (they're more about moving around the dance floor).

Reels, Jigs and Hornpipes are all **Performance Dances**

REELS
- Reels were first taught by travelling dance teachers in the 1700s.
- Reels are in 4/4 (sometimes 2/4 or 2/2), with accents on the first and third beats of the bar.
- The tunes are often made up of straight (not dotted) quavers. They're quite quick.
- For women, a reel is a soft shoe dance — it's light, with lots of leaps. Men wear hard shoes.

HORNPIPES
- The hornpipe was originally an English dance — it spread to Ireland in the 18th century. It comes from the music of sailors.
- Hornpipes are in 4/4.
- They often have dotted rhythms, though the musicians can choose to play them straight.
- They're a bit slower than a reel.
- They're hard shoe dances.

JIGS
- Some people think jigs started out as the marches of ancient Irish clans.
- Jigs are lively and fast. They often start on an anacrusis (upbeat).
- Single, double, light and heavy jigs are in 6/8.
- Most jigs are soft shoe dances, except for the heavy jig (also called a hard jig or triple jig), which is a hard shoe dance.
- Slip jigs are in 9/8, and are graceful with hops and skips.

Some Irish **Pop** has Dance **Influences**

1) Modern Irish dance music combines folk rhythms with contemporary beats. It uses both live instruments and MIDI sequencers. A good example of this is the music from Riverdance.

2) Irish pop groups like The Corrs, Westlife and Van Morrison sometimes use elements of Irish music — for example, the Corrs use traditional Irish instruments in some of their songs.

Bhangra

Bhangra mixes traditional dance rhythms and tunes from India and Pakistan with club dance music.

Bhangra was Originally a Folk Dance

1) Traditional bhangra is a type of folk music from the Punjab — an area in northern India and Pakistan.

2) It's played at harvest time when people dance and sing to celebrate the end of the harvest.

3) The key instrument is the dhol, a double-headed, barrel-shaped drum.
Each drumhead has a different sound. One is much lower than the other.

4) This is one of the traditional rhythms in bhangra:

| CHAAL | The most popular rhythm for traditional and modern bhangra is the chaal. It's an eight-note repeated pattern. The quavers are swung like in the blues. | DHA NA NA NA NA DHA DHA NA |

The words that go with the beats are called bols. They help players remember the drum strokes for the rhythm...

NA = play the small drumhead.
GE = play the large drumhead.
DHA = play both drumheads.

5) Bhangra tunes are often based around intervals of a minor third and you'll hear lots of repeated notes.

There are Lots of Different Bhangra Dances

1) The Jhumar is a flowing, slow dance. Dancers move in a circle around the drummer and dance in time to the beat. They sing a quiet chorus to accompany the rhythm of the drum.

2) Only women dance the Giddha which uses dance to tell stories or act out events.
The dancers control the beat of the music by clapping their hands.

3) The Daankara is danced at weddings. Men dance in pairs and beat the rhythm using coloured sticks.

4) Bhangra dances often include ambitious stunts like human pyramids and spinning jumps.

Modern Bhangra Developed in the UK

1) The modern bhangra style developed in the UK in the 1970s and 1980s.

2) Asian musicians fused the chaal rhythm with Western styles like hip-hop, disco, drum'n'bass, rap and reggae, creating a whole new sound and making bhangra much more popular with mainstream audiences.

3) They also used Western instruments like the electric guitar and synthesizers.

The band Alaap took bhangra to mainstream audiences with the song Bhabiye Ni Bhabiye in the 1980s. Other well-known bhangra performers are Malkit Singh, Sahotas, Sangeeta and Panjabi MC.

Modern Bhangra Uses Lots of Music Technology

Music technology plays a big part in modern bhangra. Listen out for...

1) Remixes — tracks with lots of different layers mixed together in new ways. A remix normally sounds very different from a live performance because so much has been changed in the studio.

2) Samples from other music, e.g. bass lines, drum parts, words or other sounds mixed in with the new track.

3) Drum machines instead of the dhol.

4) DJ techniques like scratching (see p.159).

Warm-up and Exam Questions

American line dancing, Irish jigs and reels, and Bhangra — you need to know about them all.
Have a go at the warm-up questions below and then test yourself with the Exam question.

Warm-up Questions

1) Where does American line dancing have its roots?
2) Name **three** instruments that are traditionally used to play Irish dance music on.
3) Name **three** types of Irish performance dance.
4) What's the name of the most popular rhythm used in bhangra?
5) Where and when did modern bhangra develop?
6) Give **two** examples of modern music technology used in bhangra.

Exam Question

This is a long question — take a deep breath and dive in.

Play the extract **four** times, leaving a short pause for writing time between each playing.

Track 39

a) (i) Which of these words best describes the style of the music?

boogie-woogie   bhangra   baroque   *[1 mark]*

(ii) Give two reasons for your choice above.

....

....   *[2 marks]*

b) Which of these examples most closely matches the rhythm played at the beginning of the extract? Tick the box next to the rhythm of your choice.

[1 mark]

Exam Question

c) Ten seconds into the extract the texture changes and you hear a melody being played with percussion accompaniment.
Which traditional Indian instrument plays this melody?

.... *[1 mark]*

d) Name two different percussion instruments you can hear in this extract.

....

.... *[2 marks]*

e) (i) About two-thirds of the way through the extract there is a break in the music.
What Western string instrument features in the music immediately after this?

.... *[1 mark]*

(ii) When this instrument does enter, it changes the feel of the music.
Which of these phrases best describes the change that takes place?
Put a ring around your choice.

major to minor   **minor to major**   **sharp to flat** *[1 mark]*

f) Name **two** other Western instruments that you can hear in this extract.

....

.... *[2 marks]*

Disco

The dancing was embarrassing. The clothes were awful. The make-up was unspeakable. But the examiners think disco is important so you've <u>got</u> to learn about it.

Disco was the Dance Music of the 1970s

Disco first reared its groovy head in nightclubs in <u>New York</u>. The roots of disco were in <u>soul</u>, <u>jazz</u> and <u>funk</u>. Disco was played in clubs and it <u>totally changed them</u>...

1) Until about the 1960s <u>audio equipment</u> was pretty ropey — you couldn't play a recording loud enough to dance to, so most clubs had live bands.

2) In the 1970s, <u>amplifiers</u>, <u>turntables</u> and <u>loudspeakers</u> got loads better. Suddenly you could play records loud enough to fill a club with sound. <u>DJs</u> took over from band leaders as the important people in a club.

3) People danced <u>on their own</u> rather than in pairs and they really enjoyed <u>showing off</u> their groovy dance moves and flashy outfits.

4) <u>Lighting technology</u> got more exciting too — <u>flashing lights</u> and <u>effects</u> became part and parcel of the experience of a night out in a club.

The Strong Beat and Catchy Tunes Made Disco Easy to Like

1) Disco tunes are almost always in <u>4/4</u>. They're played at around <u>120 beats per minute</u>.

2) The simple beat makes disco tunes really <u>easy to dance</u> to because just about any dance move will fit. People loved this because it gave them the freedom to make up their <u>own moves</u>.

3) People also liked the <u>catchy tunes</u>. Every disco tune has a <u>hook</u> — a short stab of <u>tune</u>, a <u>word</u> or a <u>phrase</u> that sticks in people's minds so they remember (and buy) the record.

Disco Songs have a Verse-Chorus Structure

A disco tune will almost always start with an <u>intro</u>.
The introduction does two jobs — it grabs people's <u>attention</u> and <u>sets the mood</u>.
Intros often use the best bit from the rest of the song to make people <u>sit up and listen</u>.

After the intro, the structure of a disco song basically goes <u>verse-chorus-verse-chorus</u>...
All the verses usually have the <u>same tune</u>, but the <u>lyrics change</u> for each one.
The chorus has a <u>different tune</u> from the verses, usually quite a catchy one.
The lyrics and tune of the chorus <u>don't change</u>.
In a lot of songs the verse and chorus are both <u>8 bars long</u>.

The verse-chorus structure can get repetitive. To avoid this most songs have a <u>middle 8</u>, or bridge, that sounds different. It's an <u>8-bar section</u> in the <u>middle</u> of the song with <u>new chords</u>, <u>new lyrics</u> and a whole <u>new feel</u>.

One verse, or the middle 8, can be switched for an <u>instrumental section</u>.

The song ends with a <u>coda</u> or <u>outro</u> that's <u>different</u> to the verse and the chorus. In disco it usually <u>fades out gradually</u> so the DJ can <u>mix</u> the end of one song with the beginning of another.

Disco

One of your coursework compositions can be a disco tune. To get that full-blown disco sound you need to use a good mixture of <u>acoustic</u> and <u>electric</u> instruments. These are the main ones...

Electric Guitars Play Lead and Rhythm Parts

The guitar sound in disco is pretty distinctive.

1) As with most pop music up to the 1980s, the <u>main instruments</u> in a disco line-up are the <u>electric guitars</u>.

2) The <u>lead guitar</u> plays the <u>solo tunes</u>.

3) The <u>rhythm guitar</u> strums <u>chords</u> along with the beat.

4) The strings on the rhythm guitar are often <u>muted</u> by pressing down with the side of the hand. This stops the chords from ringing on and makes them sound more <u>percussive</u>.

An electric guitar has six strings tuned to E, A, D, G, B and E. It has to be plugged in to an amplifier and loudspeaker.

Bass Guitars Play Short Riffs

Most disco music has <u>short</u>, <u>rhythmic</u>, <u>heavy-sounding</u> bass riffs.

There's more on guitars on p.61

The bass guitar works in the same way as the electric guitar, except it usually has four strings, tuned to E, A, D and G. Bass guitarists pick out the individual notes of a bass line — they don't play chords.

Brass and Strings Fill Out the Sound

1) <u>Sweeping string sounds</u> fill the gaps between the other sounds and make the music feel really solid.

2) Brass instruments are used to add in an occasional '<u>parp parp</u>'. They're called <u>stabs</u> and they almost always fall on an <u>offbeat</u>.

Disco Uses Drum Kits, Drum Machines and Sequencers

You hear acoustic <u>and</u> electronic drum kits playing alongside each other on many disco tracks.

1) The low <u>bass drum</u> plays every crotchet beat.

2) The <u>snare drum</u> mostly plays on beats <u>2</u> and <u>4</u>. The <u>hi-hat</u> plays <u>offbeat quavers</u>.

3) This basic drum rhythm plays <u>all the way through</u> the song.

4) The little circle means the hi-hat's played <u>open</u> — so it <u>rings on</u>.

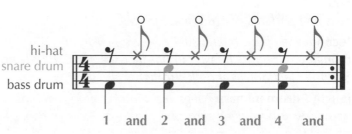

Extra percussive sounds like <u>hand claps</u> are often added by <u>drum machines</u>. Disco also creates backing <u>loops</u> using <u>sequencers</u>. Short snippets of music, e.g. bass lines, tunes, chords and rhythms, are recorded on sequencers. They're <u>played repeatedly</u> through the recording. Loops are usually made so they'll <u>fit together</u> in different combinations.

Learn to love it, love to learn it...

Disco's not a particularly complicated style. Concentrate on learning the <u>details</u> of the disco sound and the way disco tracks are produced so you have <u>something to say</u> if it comes up in the exam.

Club Dance

Put dub, disco, hip-hop and electronic music together, and you get... club dance.

It all Started in **Chicago...**

Chicago's one of the music capitals of the world. One of the many music genres that started there was house music, one of the earliest forms of club dance music.

In the early 1980s, producers took disco and made the 4/4 beat deeper and stronger. Dub, jazz and synthpop motifs were layered over the bass using the technologies developed by bands like Kraftwerk.

> The style was popularised by a DJ called Frank Knuckles who worked at a Chicago club called the Warehouse, affectionately known as 'the house'.

The basic house sound set the pattern for all the later variations of dance music. Around the same time, a similar music style called techno was developing in Detroit.

Club Dance Really Took Off in the **1980s** and **1990s**

1) In the 1980s and 1990s club dance music became more and more popular.

2) All-night raves were organised in big deserted buildings like warehouses (mostly illegally). Dance music developed its own culture separate from the pop and rock scene.

3) As the recording and mixing technology developed, new styles of dance music appeared. A lot of the new techniques people came up with are still used today.

4) In recent years, the technology has become cheaper and more widely available. Just about anyone can make their own music and distribute it via the internet. Because there's so much new music around, new styles are popping up all the time.

5) Dancing at raves and clubs is improvised. There are some moves that crop up involving dramatic arm movements in time to the beat, such as the ever-so-cool "big fish, little fish, cardboard box". People also wave glowsticks around and jump in time to the fast beat of the music.

Club Dance Comes in **Many Styles**

Styles and names in club dance change all the time — they vary so they can be a bit tricky to define. Here are a few basic definitions to get you started:

house *Four-four beat (like all club dance). Lots of repetition, especially in the bass line and lots of drum machine sounds.*

techno *Fast, hard beat, usually between 130 and 150 bpm (beats per minute), though can be much faster in hardcore techno. Rarely any voices or live sounds. Sounds mechanical and electronic.*

jungle / drum 'n' bass *Mega-fast tempo, often reaching 170 bpm. Drum-based with very strong, deep bass line. There are lots of short, fast notes called 'breakbeats' played between the main beats, giving it a disjointed feel.*

UK garage *Dance music that uses ideas from jungle, drum'n'bass and modern rhythm'n'blues. Vocal sounds are used like percussion.*

trance *A very repetitive sound. Uses echoey and electronic sounds and lots of effects. Slow chord changes over a fast beat are meant to make you feel like you're in a trance.*

ambient *Slow, sometimes jazzy. Usually sounds chilled and 'out of this world'.*

rave *Fast, electronic dance music using samples from different songs.*

Club Dance

Take away technology and you basically <u>can't have</u> club dance...

All Club Dance Uses **Music Technology**

1) Club dance music uses music <u>technology</u> rather than live <u>instruments</u>.

2) At a <u>live performance</u> in a club, the DJ or MC plays <u>backing tracks</u> and adds in <u>extra sounds</u> with samples, keyboards or a drum machine to build the piece up. They might do a bit of live rap too.

3) In a <u>studio</u> a <u>producer</u> basically does the same thing — laying down a backing track then adding other sounds over it.

4) <u>Fatboy Slim</u> and <u>Calvin Harris</u> are famous DJs. Their music isn't just popular in clubs — it's made it into the <u>charts</u> as well. Fatboy Slim's 'Praise You' got to <u>Number 1</u> in 1999.

DJs Use **Different Techniques** to Make **Dance Tracks**

1) *MIXING* DJs work with <u>twin record decks</u> and <u>vinyl records</u>. Records with a <u>similar</u> number of <u>beats per minute</u> and in the <u>same key</u> are mixed together to create continuous dance music.

2) *SCRATCHING* DJs turn records backwards and forwards by hand. The stylus makes a <u>scratchy</u> noise in the groove of the vinyl.

3) *SAMPLING* This is using snippets of other people's <u>tunes</u>, <u>rhythms</u> or <u>voices</u> in your own music, e.g. Audio Bullys featured a sample of Nancy Sinatra in *Shot You Down*. <u>Distortion</u> changes the sound of a sample (it <u>distorts</u> it).

4) *LOOPING* Recordings of short patterns of notes or rhythms, usually four bars long, are constantly <u>repeated</u> (looped) to make longer patterns.

5) *DIGITAL EFFECTS* Special effects are used to create interesting sounds like <u>reverb</u> and <u>echo</u>. Another popular one is a <u>vocoder</u> which makes human voices sound like synthesised sounds. Digital effects can also be used to change the <u>attack</u> on certain sounds.

6) *QUANTISING* Computers can shift notes backwards and forwards to the nearest semiquaver, giving a track that's in <u>perfect time</u>. Lots of club dance tracks are quantised to make them sound <u>robotic</u>. <u>Groove quantising</u> is the opposite — it makes computer-generated tracks sound more human.

7) *SEQUENCING* This is a way of building up a song by recording <u>lots of tracks</u> one over another. It's usually done on a computer. The tracks could be electronic sounds, samples, real instruments and voices, synthesised instruments, or a mixture of all these. This is sometimes called <u>multitracking</u>.

Club Dance Remix Uses Lots of **Samples**

A lot of record companies release a <u>club dance remix</u> of a pop or rock tune to get it better known on the club scene. Basically it'll be <u>faster</u>, <u>snappier</u> and a lot <u>easier to dance to</u> than the original. This is the kind of thing that <u>DJs</u> and <u>producers</u> do to create a remix:

1) They <u>MIX IN SAMPLES</u> from other songs, e.g. a <u>chorus hook line</u> or <u>bass riff</u>, to create a <u>collage</u> of sound. The collage is often laid over the top of a repeating <u>drum and bass loop</u>.

2) They <u>CHANGE THE TEXTURE</u> to keep the music <u>interesting</u>. Texture changes are often created by <u>stopping</u> the drum and bass for a few beats — when they <u>kick back in</u>, the deep thumping makes a big impression.

3) They <u>INTRODUCE BREAKS</u> — sections where there's just one or more solo instrument. This changes the texture too.

I want to see Strictly Club Dancing...

Club Dance is everywhere now — listen to some, bearing in mind the different features described above.

Warm-up and Exam Questions

Last set of questions for this section — don't rush through them though, they're all important.

Warm-up Questions

1) Give **two** reasons why disco music became so popular.
2) What's the usual time signature for disco tunes?
3) Name **three** items commonly used to create the rhythm and accompaniment in disco music.
4) What **two** important elements do all dance styles from the 1970s onward have in common?
5) Name **four** styles of club dance music.

Exam Question

Make sure you've learnt all about disco and dance by trying the question below.

Play the track **three** times, leaving a short pause between each playing.

Track 40

a) This bass line is taken from the first bar of the extract.
Add ties or change note values at points **X** and **Y** to make the rhythm correct.

[2 marks]

b) What is the technical term for the type of repetition used in this extract?

.... *[1 mark]*

c) Which of these is the rhythm played by the drums when they come in
for the second time? Tick the box next to the one you think is correct.

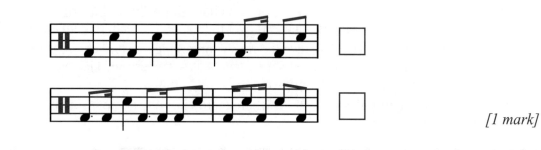

[1 mark]

Exam Question

d) What is the main method used in this track to create variety?

.... *[1 mark]*

Now play Track 40 again, followed by Track 41.
Then play both extracts **again**.

(Track 40)　(Track 41)

e) What one word links both types of music?

.... *[1 mark]*

f) Name three instruments used in the first extract but not in the second.

....

....

.... *[3 marks]*

g) Describe four ways (apart from the instruments used) in which Extract A differs from Extract B.

....

....

....

.... *[4 marks]*

Revision Summary for Section Eight

There are a lot of different types of dance music in this section. Luckily, here's a revision summary for you to test what you've learnt. Don't turn the page to the next section just yet — remember, you only <u>really know</u> your stuff when you can answer all the questions without looking back through the book.

1) Write a definition of metre.
2) Why don't you get lots of tempo changes in dance music?
3) Where did the waltz start its rise to fame?
4) Describe the rhythm of a waltz.
5) Name the three main chords used in waltzes.
6) What was the structure of a typical early waltz?
7) Describe the structure of later waltzes.
8) Name three composers who wrote piano pieces inspired by the Viennese waltz.
9) What are the two main elements of salsa?
10) Where does son come from?
11) What's the basic repeated rhythm pattern in salsa called?
12) Describe the four sections of a modern salsa band.
13) What are the three main sections of a salsa tune?
14) Name four different percussion instruments used in salsa.
15) How many beats are there in one complete cycle of the salsa dance moves?
16) Where does the tango come from?
17) Name two types of music that influenced the tango.
18) How many players are there in a typical small tango group in Argentina today?
19) Name three elements of Tango Nuevo.
20) How many beats per bar are there in a tango?
21) What type of music is line dancing often done to?
22) Name two popular line dances from the 1970s.
23) Why does line dance music have lots of repetition?
24) What sort of events would Irish social dancing take place at?
25) Are hornpipes hard shoe dances or soft shoe dances?
26) What is the main difference between single jigs and slip jigs?
27) Where does traditional bhangra music come from?
28) When did modern bhangra start to develop?
29) Give three different types of music technology used in modern bhangra music.
30) Where did disco start up?
31) What's the usual structure for a disco song?
32) What's the difference between the lead guitar part and the rhythm guitar part in disco music?
33) Write out a standard percussion line for a disco track.
34) When did club dance music become popular?
35) Describe each of these types of dance music:
    a) house b) drum 'n' bass c) trance d) rave.
36) Describe each of these techniques DJs use to make dance tracks:
    a) mixing b) sampling c) looping d) sequencing.
37) What are the three main ways to create a remix?

British Folk Music

Folk's the original British pop music — the music that was most popular with most people at least until the beginning of the twentieth century. It's still pretty popular nowadays too.

Folk Music was Played by **Ordinary People**

1) Folk music's still around nowadays but it used to be much more popular. In olden times, before radios and record players, the only music ordinary people had was music they played themselves.

2) The tunes tend to be quite simple and work with just a few instruments or voices. This made them easier for people in the pub, or field, or factory, to learn and play.

3) Folk music was hardly ever written down. It survived through the oral tradition — people heard a song or tune they liked and memorised it.

4) Folk music changes over time as people add new ideas. Sometimes they're being deliberately creative, sometimes they can't remember exactly what they've heard and make up a new bit.

5) The instruments used to play along with folk songs and dances tend to be small and easy to carry. The most popular ones are the pipe and tabor (a three-holed recorder and a drum, played together for a one-man band effect), the fiddle, the hurdy-gurdy, the bagpipes, the accordion and the concertina.

These are the **Main Types** of Folk Music...

WORK SONGS

- British work songs were made up by people like farm workers, builders, sailors and miners.
- They sang to take their minds off the grind of hard labour, and to help them work as a team.
- The songs are unaccompanied — the workers didn't have spare hands for playing instruments.
- Lots of songs were in call-and-response style. The 'shantyman' sang the story and the other men joined in the chorus.

SHORT SONGS

- There are many shorter songs with romantic or comic lyrics.

BALLADS

- Ballads tell stories.
- Some stories are made up — they tell stories from legends or about love affairs.
- Other ballads are about real events like shipwrecks or battles. Before radios and television when many people couldn't read, ballads were a way of passing on the news.

DANCE MUSIC

- At events like weddings and parties people danced to live music.
- Lots of these dances are still around today — you still see people doing Morris dances, sword dances, Scottish country dancing and Irish dancing.

Folk Tunes are Fairly **Simple**

1) A lot of folk melodies are based on pentatonic scales (see p.21). They've only got five notes, which makes writing tunes with them lots easier.

2) A major pentatonic scale uses notes 1, 2, 3, 5 and 6 of an ordinary major scale.

3) A minor pentatonic scale uses notes 1, 3, 4, 5 and 7 of a natural minor scale.

4) There are no semitone intervals in pentatonic scales. It makes it much easier to add a harmony because the notes don't clash. It also makes them easy to sing.

The structure in folk tunes tends to be pretty simple too. Songs are often strophic — the tune stays the same for each verse. Strophic songs can either be a number of musically identical verses (with different words), or can have a chorus that's just a slight variation on the verse (so the structure's A A' A A' A...). Phrases have even numbers of bars — usually four. Often each phrase begins with an anacrusis (upbeat).

Folk songs were often just passed from person to person...

'Scarborough Fair', 'Danny Boy', 'Cockles and Mussels' are all folk songs you might have heard before.

Capercaillie — Skye Waulking Song

Every <u>country</u> in the world has its own type of <u>folk music</u>. The music uses <u>local languages</u>, <u>dialects</u> and <u>instruments</u>, so it's <u>different</u> in different places — sometimes even from <u>village</u> to <u>village</u>.

Lots of **Celtic Folk Music** Comes From **Scotland** and **Ireland**

1) Lots of places in <u>Western Europe</u> have traditional Celtic folk music — like <u>Wales</u>, <u>Cornwall</u> and <u>Brittany</u> in France.

2) Celtic folk music also includes <u>traditional Scottish</u> and <u>Irish</u> music.

3) The songs are often sung in <u>Gaelic</u>, traditional Celtic languages spoken in Scotland and Ireland. The two most common forms are <u>Scots Gaelic</u> and <u>Irish Gaelic</u> — some people in Scotland and Ireland <u>still</u> speak Scots and Irish Gaelic.

4) Traditional Celtic instruments include <u>fiddles</u>, <u>bagpipes</u>, <u>tin whistles</u> and <u>accordions</u>. An Irish framed drum called the <u>bodhrán</u> is also used.

5) Some bands turn folk music into a more <u>modern</u> style by adding a <u>bass line</u> and <u>drum kit</u> — bands like <u>Capercaillie</u> and <u>Runrig</u> have made Celtic folk music really popular.

Capercaillie is a **Celtic Folk Band**

1) Capercaillie is a <u>modern folk band</u>. It's made up of <u>eight</u> musicians mainly from <u>Scotland</u> and <u>Ireland</u> (though one's from <u>Manchester</u>). It was formed in <u>Oban</u> in Scotland in <u>1984</u>, and has become famous <u>worldwide</u>.

2) They play <u>traditional</u> folk instruments — <u>Uilleann pipes</u>, <u>flute</u>, <u>fiddle</u>, <u>accordion</u> and <u>bouzouki</u> (a string instrument a bit like a <u>mandolin</u>) over the top of more <u>modern</u> instruments like <u>drums</u>, <u>piano/keyboard</u> and <u>bass guitar</u>.

3) Their <u>singer's</u> called <u>Karen Matheson</u> — she mainly sings in <u>Scots Gaelic</u>.

4) Their music is a <u>mix</u> of <u>traditional Celtic</u> songs and more <u>contemporary</u> ideas — they blend <u>traditional instruments</u> and <u>ideas</u> with <u>modern drumbeats</u>.

5) They've sold over <u>1 million</u> albums and are popular all over the world. They also appeared in and wrote some music for the film <u>*Rob Roy*</u>.

Waulking is a Part of **Clothmaking**

1) '<u>Waulking</u>' is a name for a stage in traditional <u>clothmaking</u> — woollen cloth or tweed was <u>cleaned</u>, <u>thickened</u> and <u>softened</u> by this process. Women <u>pounded</u> the cloth against a table or <u>trampled</u> on it.

2) The women would <u>sing songs</u> to <u>pass the time</u> and <u>keep the rhythm</u> of the pounding. They needed to move the cloth <u>in time</u> with each other, and singing helped them do this — the songs have a strong <u>rhythm</u>. It also <u>lifted their spirits</u> — waulking was hard work.

3) Songs could last for well over an hour. One woman would sing the <u>verses</u>, and the rest would join in on the <u>choruses</u>.

Skye Waulking Song is From the Album **'Nàdurra'**

1) Capercaillie released their album '<u>Nàdurra</u>' in <u>2000</u>. 'Nàdurra' is Gaelic for '<u>naturally</u>'.

2) The full title of the piece is <u>*Chuir M'Athair Mise Dhan Taigh Charraideach (Skye Waulking Song)*</u>, which translates as '<u>My Father Sent Me to a House of Sorrow</u>'.

Skye's the limit...

The band was named after the capercaillie (or wood grouse), a large bird. It's found all over Northern Europe, but in the British Isles it's only found in Scotland. Capercaillies are under threat though — there are less than 2,000 left in Scotland and they're at risk of extinction. Save the capercaillie.

Capercaillie — Skye Waulking Song

Skye Waulking Song brings together <u>traditional folk music</u> with elements of <u>pop music</u>.

The Song is in **Two Sections**

1) *Skye Waulking Song* is divided into <u>two</u> main sections.

2) The melody is based on a <u>pentatonic scale</u> (see p.163).

3) It's in <u>12/8</u>, with <u>4</u> beats in a bar. The <u>strong rhythm</u> helped the workers <u>keep in time</u>.

4) It's played on a mix of <u>traditional</u> and <u>modern</u> instruments. The <u>fiddle</u>, <u>pipes</u>, <u>whistle</u>, <u>accordion</u> and <u>bouzouki</u> are all traditional, while the <u>guitar</u>, <u>bass guitar</u>, <u>drum kit</u> and <u>keyboard</u> are more modern. They all play in their <u>middle range</u> — there are <u>no</u> high-pitched screeching notes.

5) It has a <u>polyrhythmic</u> texture — lots of <u>different rhythms</u> are being played at the <u>same time</u>. The singer's part has a <u>different rhythm</u> to the rest of the band. At some points, the <u>singer's</u> part is in <u>12/8</u>, while the <u>hi-hat's</u> playing <u>3 beats</u> in a bar, making it feel like <u>3/4</u>.

6) It has a <u>fade-out</u> ending.

Some of the features are different in the two different sections:

SECTION ONE

- The first section feels very <u>traditional</u>, with just a <u>simple beat</u>.
- It's in <u>E minor</u> — the chords change between <u>Em</u> and <u>G</u>.
- It's quite <u>quiet</u>, <u>calm</u> and <u>peaceful</u> — it sounds almost <u>subdued</u>.
- None of the instruments really <u>stand out</u> in this section — the focus is on the <u>singer</u>.

SECTION TWO

- The <u>full rhythm section</u> (drums and bass part) play in the second section and <u>drive it forward</u>.
- It's in <u>G major</u> (the <u>relative major</u> of E minor).
- It's generally much <u>louder</u>, though there's a quieter bit when the drums and bass guitar <u>stop</u>.
- There's a <u>pipe solo</u> that uses some of the vocal melody line in its <u>improvisation</u>.
- There are <u>harmonised backing vocals</u> too.

The **Lyrics** are in **Scots Gaelic**

1) The lyrics to *<u>Skye Waulking Song</u>* are in Scots Gaelic. It has <u>two</u> main <u>verses</u> and two '<u>inserts</u>' (called '<u>seisd 1</u>' and '<u>seisd 2</u>'). 'Seisd' is pronounced 'shesht'. Seisd 1 is '<u>Hi ri huraibhi o ho</u>' and seisd 2 is '<u>O hi a bho ro hu o ho</u>'. After <u>each line</u> of the verse, one of the <u>inserts</u> is sung (though the introductory vocal part starts with seisd 1) — so the first part of verse 1 (after a few introductory lines) goes:

> Chuir m'athair mise dha'n taigh charraideach
> Hi ri huraibhi o ho   **SEISD 1**
> 'N oidhche sin a rinn e bhanais dhomh
> O hi a bho ro hu o ho   **SEISD 2**

The inserts are an example of <u>vocables</u> — <u>nonsense syllables</u> like 'Hey nonny nonny' and 'Fa la la'. Vocables are an <u>important part</u> of traditional folk music — they're lines that everyone can <u>join in</u>.

2) The lines of the verses are taken directly from a 13th century <u>lament</u> called *<u>Seathan, Mac Righ Eireann</u>* ('<u>Seathan, Son of the King of Ireland</u>'). It's about a girl who's <u>unhappy</u> with the <u>marriage</u> her father's <u>arranged</u> for her.

3) The two verses are divided up by the <u>pipe solo</u>.

4) The structure's a bit <u>different</u> to <u>traditional waulking songs</u> — they would have a <u>verse-chorus</u> structure, where one woman would sing the <u>verses</u> and the rest would join in with the <u>choruses</u>. As *Skye Waulking Song* is a <u>modern</u> version of a waulking song, Capercaillie didn't stick to the <u>traditional form</u> — they have the two <u>verses</u> and two <u>inserts</u> but no chorus. *Skye Waulking Song* has a <u>strophic structure</u> — the melody is the <u>same</u> for both verses.

It's all Gaelic to me...

You need to make sure you know the <u>key features</u> of this piece, and which bits are <u>typical</u> of <u>folk music</u>.

Warm-up and Exam Questions

Warm-up Questions

1) How were folk songs traditionally passed on?
2) Name **four** instruments traditionally used to play folk music.
3) Give **three** types of folk music.
4) What notes are used in the two types of pentatonic scales:
   a) major pentatonic   b) minor pentatonic

Exam Question

Make sure you're familiar with folk music and then try the exam question below.

Play Track 42 **three** times, leaving a short pause for writing time between each playing.

Track 42

a) What type of music is heard in this extract?

.... *[1 mark]*

b) The song in this extract has a strophic structure. Explain what this means.

.... *[1 mark]*

c) Is the music in this extract in simple or compound time?

.... *[1 mark]*

d) Which word best describes the tonality of the melody heard in this extract?

          chromatic   **pentatonic**   **minor**   *[1 mark]*

e) i)   Which instrument plays the solo towards the end of the extract?

      .... *[1 mark]*

    ii) Name two instruments that play the accompaniment during this solo.

      ....

      .... *[2 marks]*

Indian Classical Music — Raga

This is the section where you look at music from other parts of the world. The music's great, but make sure you can <u>spell all the words</u> so you can write about them in the exam.

Indian Classical Music is Based on Ragas

1) A <u>raga</u> is a <u>set of notes</u> (usually between 5 and 8) which are combined to create a particular <u>mood</u>.

2) Raga performances are <u>improvised</u>, but based on traditional tunes and rhythms. These are <u>never written down</u> — they're passed on from generation to generation <u>aurally</u>.

3) Ragas use a scale similar to the Western 12-note scale. But while the Western scale is <u>tempered</u> (there's the same distance between neighbouring notes), the raga scale is not — the intervals can vary.

4) In Northern India, raga students join a school of players called a <u>gharana</u>. Each gharana is run by a teacher or 'master' and each gharana has its own traditions and theories about how to play.

5) <u>Spirituality</u> is an important part of almost all Indian Classical Music. In Southern India, there is a long tradition of the <u>Karnatic kriti</u>. This is a raga set to words in praise of a particular <u>Hindu deity</u>.

The Traditional Instruments are Sitar, Tambura and Tabla

Sitar

1) A <u>sitar</u> is a large, long-necked <u>string</u> instrument.

2) On a seven-stringed sitar, five of the strings are plucked for the <u>melody</u> and the other two create <u>drone</u> notes.

3) Sitars also have '<u>sympathetic</u>' strings <u>underneath</u> the main strings. The sympathetic strings <u>vibrate</u> when the main strings are played, creating a thick, shimmery sound.

4) The <u>frets</u> on a sitar can be moved — they're <u>adjusted</u> to different positions for different pieces.

5) Sitar players can pull strings to make notes '<u>bend</u>' or distort.

6) Sliding a finger along a string as it's plucked gives a sliding glissando sound called <u>mind</u>.

Tambura

The tambura's a similar shape to the sitar. It usually has <u>four</u> metal strings, but can have up to <u>six</u>. It's used as more of a <u>backing</u> instrument.

Tabla

Tabla is a <u>pair</u> of drums. The smaller, right-hand drum is called the <u>tabla</u> or <u>dayan</u>. The larger, lower-sounding drum is called the <u>baya</u>.

Other instruments are used too...

1) The <u>sarod</u> — a <u>mini-sitar</u> with a <u>fretless</u> fingerboard.

2) The <u>sarangi</u> — a small, <u>bowed</u> stringed instrument with <u>no frets</u>.

3) The <u>bansuri</u> — a <u>flute</u> made of <u>bamboo</u>.

4) The <u>shenhai</u> — an instrument with a <u>double reed</u>, like an oboe.

5) The <u>harmonium</u> — a <u>keyboard instrument</u> powered with air pumped by hand bellows.

6) <u>Singers</u> sometimes perform with the instruments as well.

Indian Classical Music — Raga

Each instrument in raga has a different job. The <u>sitar</u> plays the <u>melody</u>. The <u>tabla</u> play the <u>rhythm</u>. The tambura creates the harmony — it's covered on the next page.

The **Melody** is **Improvised** on the **Sitar**

1) In a classical Indian group the sitar plays the <u>melody</u>.

2) The sitar player <u>improvises</u> the melody. He or she chooses a scale called a <u>raga</u>, and makes up the melody using notes from that scale.

3) There are <u>hundreds</u> of different raga scales. Each one is named after a different <u>time of day</u> or <u>season</u>. Each raga's supposed to create an <u>atmosphere</u> like the time or season it's named after.

4) Each raga scale is a set of <u>ascending</u> and <u>descending</u> notes. The notes on the way up can be different from the ones on the way down.

5) Some ragas have rules for individual notes in the scale. There could be notes that are always played <u>quickly</u>, notes that have to be <u>decorated</u>, or notes have to be played <u>tivra</u> (slightly sharp) or <u>komal</u> (slightly flat).

6) The notes of a raga scale are called <u>sa</u>, <u>ri</u>, <u>ga</u>, <u>ma</u>, <u>pa</u>, <u>dha</u> and <u>ni</u>. Unlike Western scales, ragas don't always have the full set of notes.

7) Sometimes the melody part's taken by a <u>singer</u> instead of the sitar.

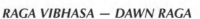

RAGA VIBHASA — DAWN RAGA

SA   RI   GA   MA DHA NI   DHA   MA   GA   RI   SA

The **Tabla** is the **Rhythm** Section

1) The main rhythm is played on the <u>tabla</u>.

2) The tabla player plays a rhythm called a <u>tala</u> with a set number of beats (called <u>matras</u>). There are hundreds of talas, just like there are hundreds of ragas.

3) The <u>first beat</u> of a tala is called the <u>sam</u>. <u>All</u> the performers in a group <u>play together</u> on each sam and the whole piece always <u>ends</u> on a sam.

4) Each tala is split into groups called <u>vibhags</u>. A vibhag is a bit like a <u>bar</u> in Western music, except that you can have different numbers of beats in each vibhag.

5) One, or sometimes two, vibhags in a tala have a <u>different sound</u> from the others — this section's called the <u>vibhag khali</u>. For contrast, the vibhag khali is played on the <u>smaller</u> tabla drum.

6) As well as playing the tala, tabla players improvise <u>more complicated rhythms</u> over the top. They can vary their sound with different <u>finger positions</u>, and by <u>speaking</u> the beat (with syllables like <u>dhin</u> or <u>ta</u>) as they play.

7) Sometimes the <u>audience</u> joins in, and claps along with the tala. They clap at the beginning of each vibhag. In the vibhag khali they do a quiet clap, called a <u>wave</u>, tapping the back of the right hand into the left.

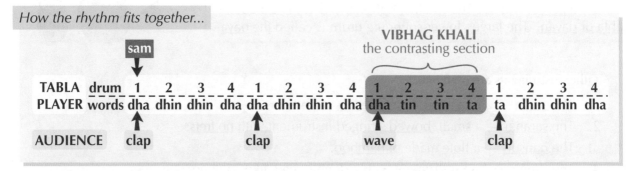

How the rhythm fits together...

Just take it one vibhag at a time...

Some people find it tricky to get to grips with raga because it's so different from the music they're used to. The fact that it's different is the whole point — that's <u>why</u> they make you study it.

Indian Classical Music — Raga

To complete the sound of raga you add the <u>tambura</u> to the sitar and tabla.

The **Tambura** Creates the **Harmony**

1) The <u>tambura's</u> job in a raga performance is to create the <u>harmony</u>. The sitar part is a bit like the right-hand part in a piano piece, and the tambura's like the left.

2) The tambura's part is often described as a <u>drone</u>. It's not quite as boring as the name suggests, but it is quite <u>repetitive</u>. The tambura player plays a <u>simple rhythmic pattern</u> based on just <u>two notes</u> from the raga all the way through the performance.

3) The sitar player works his or her improvisations <u>around</u> the tambura part — and it's the combination of the two that gives the raga harmony.

Usually the drone uses the 'sa' and 'pa' notes, but the one for the Raga Vibhasa uses 'sa' and 'dha'.

SA DHA DHA SA

A Typical Raga has **Four Sections**

The tradition is for a raga performance to have <u>four phases</u>.
There are <u>no gaps</u> between the different phases — each one flows into the next.

 The Alap

The <u>sitar</u> player introduces the notes of the chosen <u>raga scale</u>, improvising freely. There's <u>no beat</u> or pulse to the melody at this point — it just flows along. The only accompaniment at this point is the <u>tambura drone</u>.

 The Jhor

In this second section, the music <u>speeds up</u> a bit. It's still just the tambura player and sitar player, but the music gets more rhythmic, and the melody improvised by the sitar player takes on a <u>steady beat</u>.

 The Jhala

This section is <u>loads faster</u> than the alap and jhor, and feels a lot more exciting than the bits that came before. The players <u>improvise</u> around the melody.

4 **The Gat or Bandish**

In the gat, the raga really takes off.

- The <u>tabla player</u> comes in — at last.
- The group plays a <u>pre-composed</u> piece. It's called a 'gat' if it's for instruments only, and a 'bandish' if there's a song.
- The players also add improvisations to the gat or bandish, and pass their musical ideas around in a sort of musical <u>question and answer</u>.

Make sure you know the four sections of a raga...

I reckon the trickiest bit here isn't <u>understanding</u> it — it's remembering all the new words. But they are just words — like <u>egg</u> and <u>car park</u>. Close the book and scribble down what they mean from memory. And keep at it till you've got them all off by heart. They won't get in your brain unless you do.

Rag Desh

The Rag Desh is an example of how one raga can be used to create lots of different pieces.

Rag Desh is the Rainy Season Raga

1) Each raga is meant to be played at a <u>specific time of day</u> during a <u>specific season</u>. They're supposed to <u>create certain moods</u>. The <u>Rag Desh</u> is supposed to be played at <u>night</u> during the <u>rainy season</u>. It's meant to give the feeling of <u>romance</u> and <u>devotion</u>.

2) <u>Different</u> versions of the Rag Desh sound very different but they're all based on this <u>raga</u>:

SA RI MA PA NI SA <u>NI</u> DHA PA MA GA RI SA

N.B. The ascending pattern is <u>different</u> to the descending one — there are <u>more notes</u> on the way down and <u>ni</u> is <u>flattened</u>.

'Priyagitah' was Recorded in a Studio

1) Steve Gorn and Benjy Wertheimer's version of Rag Desh was <u>improvised</u> in a <u>recording studio</u>. It's based around the <u>traditional raga structure</u> (see p.169), but there are a few <u>differences</u> — some <u>modern</u> ragas <u>miss out</u> some sections to keep the audience's <u>attention</u>.

2) This version is divided up into <u>three</u> tracks on the CD — the first is the <u>alap</u>, then the second two are both <u>gats</u>. Each gat's based on a different <u>tala</u> (see p.168).

3) At the beginning of the <u>alap</u>, you can hear the <u>tambura drone</u>. Then the <u>bansuri</u> and <u>esraj</u> (an instrument that's quite like a <u>sarangi</u> but with frets) come in. They <u>improvise</u> using the notes of the Rag Desh. This section is quite <u>slow</u> and <u>flowing</u> — there's <u>no pulse</u> to drive it along.

The melodic instruments in this Rag Desh are the <u>bansuri</u> (a bamboo flute) and the <u>esraj</u> (a bowed string instrument with frets). Make sure you can identify them.

4) In the next section, the <u>tabla</u> comes in, playing a <u>steady rhythm</u>. The bansuri plays another improvised melody. It's a bit <u>faster</u> than the alap. This gat is based on the *rupak* tala, which has <u>7 beats</u>.

5) In the final track (the second gat), the raga is a lot <u>faster</u>. The <u>tabla</u> plays a <u>fast complicated rhythm</u> using the <u>12-beat</u> *ektal* tala. The bansuri plays over the top of it, but the melody is much more <u>structured</u>. It's now playing a <u>pre-composed</u> melody with lots of <u>runs</u>. It's still based on the Rag Desh.

The rainy season in the UK — that'll be April to March...

There's a chance you'll be asked what <u>notes</u> are in the Rag Desh, so make sure you <u>learn</u> what they are. Remember that the notes on the way down are <u>different</u> to the ones on the way up. Practise writing the raga out from <u>memory</u>. It'd be useful to know <u>when</u> the Rag Desh is meant to be played as well.

Rag Desh

No two performances of a raga are the same. The improvised nature of the music means there can be lots of different interpretations of it.

Anoushka Shankar Plays the Sitar

1) Anoushka Shankar is a classically-trained pianist, conductor and sitar player. She's the daughter of Ravi Shankar, an Indian musician who's famous all over the world. He taught her to play the sitar.

2) Her version of Rag Desh was recorded live at the Carnegie Hall in New York. It was composed by Ravi Shankar, and Anoushka's accompanied by two tabla players — Bikram Ghosh and Tanmoy Bose. There's also a tambura drone.

3) It's made up of an alap and two different gats.

4) In the alap, when there's just the sitar and tambura playing, you can hear the different techniques Anoushka Shankar uses — she strums, plucks and bends notes. Bent notes are made by pulling the string to change the sound.

5) The first gat uses a 10-beat tala called the *jhaptal*. The second gat is a bit faster and uses the 16-beat *tintal* tala. In both, Anoushka Shankar is playing a pre-composed melody.

6) This rag desh is all on one track — there are no gaps between the different sections. You have to listen out for the changes in tempo and the tabla coming in.

'Mewar Re Mira' Has a Singer

1) The version of Rag Desh on the album 'Mewar Re Mira' uses a voice to sing the raga. It's performed by S. D. Dhandhada and H. Dhandhada. It was recorded in a studio. The Chiranji Lal Tanwar version also has a male singer.

2) In the alap, the sitar improvises using the notes of the raga over a tambura drone. It's joined by a sarangi, then the voice comes in. The singer is male, and uses a lot of vibrato. He also scoops notes — starts on a different note then slides to the right one (also called a portamento). It's quite a short alap.

3) The tempo increases in the next section, and the tabla comes in.

> This might be slightly different to the piece your teacher has shown you — but don't worry, you can still use these points in the exam.

4) In the final section (the bandish — like a gat but with a singer), the vocal part becomes more elaborate. There are lots of trills and portamentos. Hand cymbals are also used towards the end.

You Need to Identify the Instruments

1) It's important that you can spot which instruments are being played in the different versions of the Rag Desh. Each one has a different instrument playing the main melody — the bansuri in 'Priyagitah: The Nightingale', the sitar in 'Live at Carnegie Hall' and a male singer in 'Mewar Re Mira'.

2) You'll also need to be able to identify the different sections of the music — see p.169 for a detailed description of each bit.

3) Make sure you can describe the differences between the extracts too — mention the instruments, the tempos and even whether the melody is improvised or pre-composed.

There are lots of tricky names to learn here...

...but make sure you know them all — you'll be throwing away easy marks if you haven't learnt the names of the different sections of a raga, or don't know which instruments are used.

African Music

The next few pages are called 'African Music', but you don't have to learn about every type of African music. You just have to learn about the sub-Saharan bits. That means the massive area south of the Sahara — the rainforest and savannah bits.

Drums Play a Big Part in **African Culture**

1) Drums are probably the most widely played instrument in Africa. In African tribal society, drums get a lot of respect — they're thought of as one of the best instruments.

2) Drums are used to play an accompaniment for singing, dancing and even working.

3) Drums are also used to call people together for important community events like weddings and funerals — a bit like church bells in Europe. There are different drumbeats for different events, so people from neighbouring villages can tell what's going on just by listening out for the drumbeats.

4) Most African drum music is passed on through oral tradition — it's not written down.

These are the **Main Types of Drum**...

1) The djembe is played in Guinea and Mali in West Africa. It has a single head and is shaped a bit like a goblet. It's played with the hands. The overall size of the drum affects its pitch — smaller drums are higher-pitched.

2) The dundun is played in Guinea and Mali too. Dunduns are cylindrical drums played with sticks. There's a drum skin at each end, so they're played horizontally.

   There are three types:

   kenkeni — a high-pitched drum that keeps the pulse going,

   sangban — a mid-pitched drum,

   doundoun — a large, low-pitched drum.

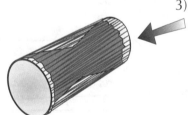

3) The donno from Ghana is also known as the hourglass or talking drum. The player holds it under one arm, and with the other arm hits the drumhead with a thin curved stick.

   The strings round the sides attach to the drumhead. The player can squeeze and release the strings as they play to change the pitch of the drum.

4) The kagan (a small barrel-shaped drum) and the kidi (a medium-sized barrel drum) are both from Ghana.

The Drums have Lots of **Different Names**

1) Not only do the materials and playing styles vary from area to area — the names for similar designs of drums vary too.

2) For example, Burkina Faso, a country in western Africa that is bordered by six countries, including Mali and Ghana. It's also quite close to Guinea as well — so the drums played in Burkina Faso have similar names to the ones played in these countries.

Drums are very important in African music...

Ok, let me guess — you probably skipped learning the names of the drums. Unless you've got a photographic memory, or are otherwise brilliantly gifted with superhuman powers you need to learn them. Learn how to spell them. Learn the facts about them. Learn it all now. It'll be worth the effort.

African Music

There are more African drums than you can shake a <u>stick</u> at (unless it's a drumstick of course). You don't just need to learn the names — read on and find out how you <u>play them</u>.

Talking Drums are Used to Send Messages

Skilled drummers can make drums '<u>talk</u>'. They <u>change the pitch</u> to imitate changing pitch levels in ordinary <u>speech</u>. The drum sounds carry over long distances, so they can be used to <u>send messages</u>.

There are literally <u>thousands</u> of different languages and dialects in Africa. Each drummer imitates his own language to send messages. Drummers like to play on instruments made with <u>local materials</u>. They believe that this <u>helps</u> the instrument 'speak' the local language.

What with local languages and materials being so varied, you get very <u>different instruments</u> and <u>different playing styles</u> from area to area.

There's a Big Variety of Playing Techniques

There's a bit more to African drumming than hitting a drum with a stick or a brush — there are several different <u>playing techniques</u>.

1) There are no prizes for guessing that one technique is hitting the drum with a <u>stick</u>.

2) A lot of African drummers also play using their <u>hands</u>. There are three basic strokes:

- <u>slap</u> — hit the edge of the drum with the fingers splayed open
- <u>tone</u> — hit the edge of the drum with the fingers held together
- <u>bass</u> — hit the centre of the main drum skin with a flat hand.

3) <u>Dampening</u> is <u>resting</u> one <u>hand</u> or <u>stick</u> on the drum skin whilst playing with the other.

4) On some styles of drum you can <u>change pitch</u> as you're playing, by tightening the skin.

5) To get a <u>contrasting</u> sound you can <u>strike the wood</u> instead of the skin.

The Master Drummer Leads the Group

1) In most African drum ensembles there is a <u>master drummer</u>. He's accompanied by any number of other drums and percussion.

2) A system of <u>call</u> and <u>response</u> is used to <u>structure</u> the music:

The master drummer plays a <u>rhythmic signal</u> which sets the <u>tempo</u> and <u>rhythm</u> for the other players. After this call the other players join in with the response. This call and response pattern is usually repeated <u>many times</u> during a performance.

Call and response is used in singing too, especially for church music.

3) The master drummer also <u>controls</u> the build-up and release of <u>tension</u>. He leads the other players in changes of <u>dynamics</u>, <u>tempo</u>, <u>pitch</u> and <u>rhythm</u>. In general the drum beats are quite <u>repetitive</u> — these <u>changes</u> are what keep the audience hooked.

Keep going till you've learnt it all...

Learn those techniques inside out — commit every detail to memory. When it comes to the exam they want <u>detailed</u> answers. "The drummers hit the drums" isn't enough. You have to give detail.

African Music

Drums have a special place in African music but the voice and other instruments are important too.

The **Thumb Piano**, **Balophon** and **Kora** are Popular

These are some of the most popular instruments apart from drums.

A balafon is a wooden xylophone. The lumpy things hanging under the keys are dried gourds. They create a warm, mellow sound.

The kora is made and played by the Mandingo people. It's got 21 strings and you play it by plucking — a bit like a harp.

The mbira or thumb piano is really popular — partly because it's pocket-sized. It makes a liquid, twangy sound.

These two are mostly played in West Africa.

The thumb piano is played all over Africa.

The Rhythms are **Complex**

1) African music is based on rhythmic cycles of varying lengths.

2) Drummers accent particular beats in a rhythmic cycle.

3) Sometimes different rhythmic cycles, with the accents in different places, are played together — this effect is called polyrhythm.

4) Sometimes you'll get two or more rhythms that don't fit easily together. They kind of fight against one another, creating tension in the music. The technical term for this effect is cross-rhythm.

5) Notes that don't fall on a strong beat can be emphasised, giving a syncopated effect.

6) Even though the music is based on repeated cycles, individual players introduce minor variations. These gradually develop the basic patterns throughout the performance.

Performances are **Long** and **Involve the Audience**

Performances can last for several hours and involve an audience response — shouting and cheering or repeating a phrase sung by the main performers is an integral part of the performance. It's often a capella (unaccompanied singing) — see next page.

African music often uses call and response. Call and response is a spontaneous, often improvised style of music where someone sings or plays a musical 'question' and another responds.

Listen out for call and response in *Ladysmith Black Mambazo*'s work. They became world-famous when they featured on *Paul Simon*'s album *Graceland*.

Polyrhythms — learn them parrot fashion...

This might not sound very exciting on paper. You've really got to hear a recording to "get it".

African A Capella Singing

'A capella' literally means 'in the style of the chapel' — Gregorian monks used to sing chants in churches. This page looks at African a capella singing — in particular the music of the Zulu people.

A Capella is Just Singing Without Accompaniment

1) A lot of religious music was sung unaccompanied.

2) In the Renaissance period (just before Baroque), the Catholic mass would often be sung unaccompanied. A lot of Jewish and Islamic music is also traditionally sung without accompaniment.

3) Gradually, the term a capella came to just mean 'without accompaniment', whether it was performed in the chapel or not.

4) Some all-male groups sing a capella, like barbershop quartets.

5) South African all-male choirs sing a capella. Their music has been made famous by the group Ladysmith Black Mambazo.

Mbube and Isicathamiya are Types of African Singing

MBUBE

1) 'Mbube' is a Zulu word meaning 'lion'.

2) It's a type of South African a capella singing.

3) Mbube music is loud and powerful.

4) It's usually sung by all-male choirs, though some groups have a female singer too.

5) It has one or two high-pitched lead vocals over a four-part harmony bass line.

6) Mbube music can be homophonic (parts moving in harmony at the same time) or polyphonic (many different parts moving at different times).

7) It goes back to when Zulu men used to leave home to work in the mines.

8) They formed Mbube choirs to sing songs after work — it helped to reinforce their identity.

ISICATHAMIYA

1) 'Isicathamiya' means 'to tip-toe' — it's the other main type of Zulu a capella singing.

2) It's much softer and more gentle than Mbube.

3) Isicathamiya groups are usually all male.

4) It focuses on blending the voices together in harmony.

5) It uses four-part harmonies in call and response (call and response is also called antiphony).

6) Isicathamiya has dance moves — stamps and tip-toeing to keep the singers in time.

> Disney's The Lion King has lots of examples of isicathamiya singing.

Ladysmith Black Mambazo Sing A Capella

1) Ladysmith Black Mambazo is an all-male choir from South Africa.

2) They sing both Mbube and Isicathamiya music.

3) The choir was formed by Joseph Shabalala in the 1960s. He converted to Christianity in 1975, and since then they have released albums featuring lots of Methodist hymns.

4) They sang on Paul Simon's album Graceland — this made them famous all over the world.

5) Since then, they have recorded with artists like Stevie Wonder and Dolly Parton, and performed for the Pope, Nelson Mandela and the Royal Family.

6) The song 'Freedom Has Arrived' celebrates Nelson Mandela's release from prison, and the end of the apartheid in South Africa.

Koko — Yiri

There's <u>more</u> to African music than just <u>drumming</u>. You need to know about <u>singing</u> too.

Singing is Important in Sub-Saharan African Music

1) <u>Singing</u> is an essential part of <u>everyday life</u> in sub-Saharan Africa. Like traditional <u>folk music</u> from England, Ireland, Scotland and Wales, it's sung by <u>ordinary people</u>. It plays an important part in the <u>community</u>.

2) It's also a big part of <u>celebrations</u> and events like <u>birthdays</u>, <u>weddings</u>, <u>funerals</u>, <u>harvests</u> and <u>rituals</u>.

3) As well as singing, instruments like the <u>balafon</u>, <u>kora</u> and <u>mbira</u> are used to play <u>tunes</u> and create <u>harmony</u>. There's more about these instruments on p.174.

4) Music is <u>passed down</u> from generation to generation, and <u>isn't</u> usually <u>written down</u>.

5) <u>Key features</u> of this type of music are:

- <u>Cross-rhythms</u> and <u>polyrhythms</u> (see p.174)
- <u>Polyphony</u> (lots of parts weaving in and out of each other)
- <u>Repetition</u>
- <u>Call and response</u> (see p.173-174)
- <u>Heterophony</u> (all parts play different versions of the same tune at the same time, often at different pitches)
- <u>Improvised melodies</u> (can sound a bit like theme and variation form — see p.81)

Koko are From Burkina Faso

1) The group <u>Koko</u> come from <u>Burkina Faso</u> in Western Africa.

2) It's led by <u>Madou Koné</u>, who <u>sings</u> and plays the <u>balafon</u>. He was born in <u>Bobo Dioulasso</u>, a city in Burkina Faso that's famous for its music.

3) There are <u>five</u> other members of the group. They play other percussion instruments like the <u>dundun</u>, the <u>djembe</u> and the <u>donno</u> (see p.172). Some of them also <u>sing</u>.

4) The <u>themes</u> of their songs are:

- The <u>struggle to survive</u> in day-to-day life.
- The importance of the <u>environment</u> and how it should be <u>protected</u>.
- <u>Creation</u> and the <u>celebration of life</u>.
- The importance of <u>friendship</u>.
- The importance of their <u>surroundings</u> and the <u>earth</u>.

5) Koko's music is <u>typical</u> of Burkina Faso — it includes a lot of <u>drumming</u> and <u>balafon playing</u>, as well as <u>singing</u>.

6) The track <i>Yiri</i> comes from their album '<u>Burkina Faso — Balafons et tambours d'Afrique</u>', which translates as 'Burkina Faso — Balafons and African drums' (the main language of the country is <u>French</u>, though the lyrics of <i>Yiri</i> are in an <u>African dialect</u> native to Burkina Faso).

Learn the key features of African music...

...then have a <u>listen</u> to Koko, and try and <u>spot</u> them in that. You'll need to be able to <u>recognise</u> them if you want to talk about them in your exam.

Koko — Yiri

Listen out for call and response in this piece — it's a key feature of sub-Saharan African music.

Yiri Starts With a Solo Balafon

1) The opening of Yiri has just one balafon playing. When the keys of the balafon are hit, they produce a very short note. To get the longer notes you hear in this piece, the player has to hit the same notes over and over again very quickly (a bit like the way steel drums are played, almost a roll).

2) The second balafon joins in after the introduction. It's pitched a bit lower than the first.

3) The two balafons play throughout the rest of the piece. They're playing polyrhythms (see p.174), and are independent of each other for most of the piece. Lots of what they play is improvised around the original theme.

4) They sometimes play in heterophony (see p.176) — they're playing the same melody but at different pitches, e.g. bars 10-13.

5) The balafons either complement the vocal line or boost the drum part.

The Drums all Play the Same Rhythm

1) When the drums come in, they all play the same rhythm. It's repeated all the way through the piece — it's an ostinato.

2) The drums are at different pitches (the smaller drums are higher than the bigger ones). The drummers can get different sounds from the drums by changing the way they hit them — they can hit them with beaters or with their hands.

3) The rhythm changes very slightly at the end of the piece and there are moments of silence — this signals to the others that the piece is about to finish.

4) At the end of Yiri, all the other instruments stop, except for the bell, which plays a final 'ting'.

The Vocal Parts Change

1) The first time you hear the singers, they're singing in unison. The tune is quite repetitive.

2) Later in the piece, they use call and response. A soloist sings a phrase (the call) and the other singers sing the response in unison.

3) The call is fairly long — much longer than the response. The soloist holds some of the notes on for quite a few bars.

4) Towards the end of the piece, the voices sing in unison again.

The Timbre and Texture Build Up During the Piece

1) The timbre (tone colour) is developed throughout the piece. It starts off with a single balafon, then changes slightly when the second is added. The drums change it a bit more, then the two different types of vocals (unison and call and response) produce two new timbres.

2) The texture is very simple to begin with, but it builds up too.

3) Yiri is polyphonic — the different parts weave in and out of each other. There are at least four distinct parts — two balafons, the drums and the singers, and they're all independent of each other.

A nice cup of Koko before bed...

The easiest way to learn about this piece is to look at each section of the group separately. Concentrate on the balafon parts, then listen to the drums, then finally focus on the vocal parts.

Gamelan

Gamelan music is very different from most European and American music traditions.
The main instruments are gongs, metallophones and drums — not your average orchestra.

Gamelan is an Important Part of Indonesian Culture

Gamelan music comes from the islands of Java and Bali in Indonesia. Gamelan is played at celebrations, religious events and entertainments like shadow puppet plays and dance performances. Most villages have a special area, a bit like a park bandstand, where the gamelan plays. In Java and Bali it's traditional for people to keep their emotions hidden in public. The music gives them a different way to express themselves.

1) Gamelan music is played by a kind of percussion orchestra, also called a gamelan. There can be between 4 and 40 instruments in a Balinese gamelan and between 15 and 20 in a gamelan from Java.

2) The big difference from a European-style orchestra is that Indonesians think of a gamelan as one single instrument — all the performers are jointly playing the same instrument. All players and the parts they play are equally important — all the parts should merge to make one sound.

3) Gamelan instruments are made in sets with lots of carved and painted decoration. All the instruments in a set are decorated and tuned in the same way. You couldn't borrow one instrument and play it on its own or play it with another gamelan — it would look wrong and sound wrong.

4) The gamelan is thought to be magical and spiritual. People in Java and Bali believe the instruments have a tie to heaven. They never step over an instrument in case they damage this connection.

5) People don't play the gamelan just because they think it looks like fun — players are chosen by their community. It's supposed to be a big honour to play the gamelan.

6) Gamelan music isn't written down. Players learn their parts by listening, watching and copying their teachers. Players don't just learn one part either — they're expected to learn all the parts in a piece so they can understand how the whole thing fits together.

Gamelan Music is Based on Two Types of Scale...

There are two scales used in gamelan music. All the notes have numbers.
These are never written down, but they are used to help players memorise their parts.

1) THE FIVE-NOTE GAMELAN SCALE IS CALLED SLENDRO

Gamelan notes don't exactly match Western scales — the five notes are spread evenly throughout an octave. A slendro is roughly equivalent to a pentatonic scale. Different gamelans are tuned to different scales.

2) THE SEVEN-NOTE GAMELAN SCALE IS CALLED PELOG

Gamelan music often only uses 5 notes of the seven-note pelog scale. Again, different gamelans are tuned to different scales, so the music sounds different depending on which gamelan it's played on.

Most sets of gamelan are tuned either to the slendro or to the pelog scale.
Others are tuned to both — these are called double gamelan.

The only way is to listen to some Gamelan music...

Unless you're lucky and have a full-blown gamelan in the music store cupboard at school, you're not going to be able to play this music, so it's extra important that you listen to some before the exam.

Gamelan

There are <u>four main parts</u> in a gamelan piece, each played by different instruments...

The **Main Tune** is Called the **Balungan** or **Pokok**

1) All the parts work around a <u>core melody</u>. In Java this melody is called the <u>balungan</u>.
In Bali it's called the <u>pokok</u>.

2) The tune is repeated over and over again, creating a rhythmic cycle. It's played by the <u>metallophone</u>.

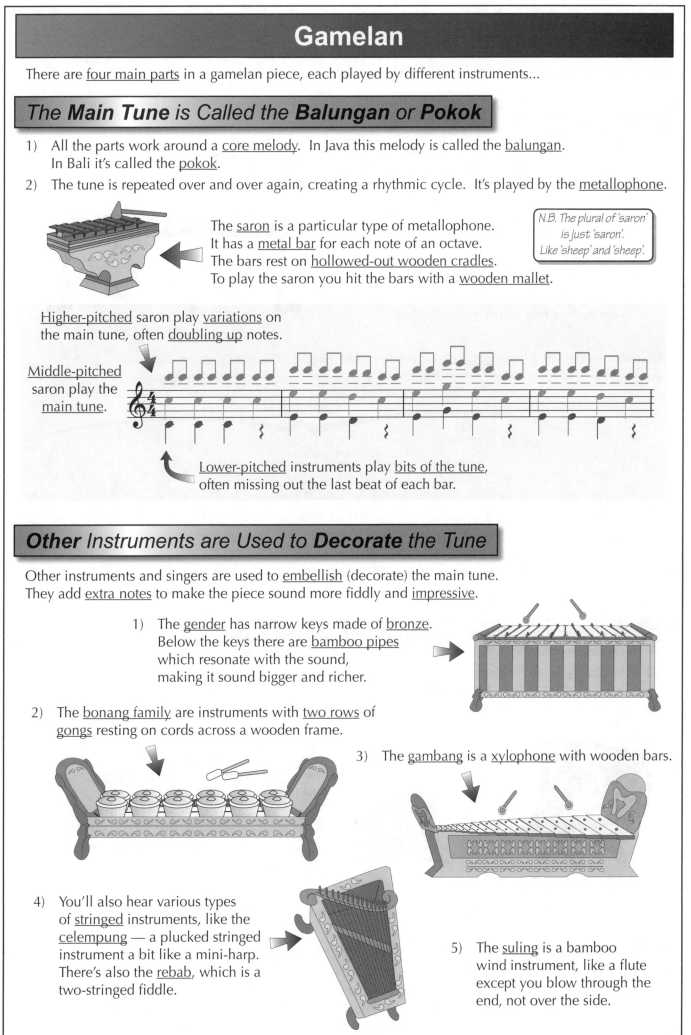

The <u>saron</u> is a particular type of metallophone.
It has a <u>metal bar</u> for each note of an octave.
The bars rest on <u>hollowed-out wooden cradles</u>.
To play the saron you hit the bars with a <u>wooden mallet</u>.

> N.B. The plural of 'saron'
> is just 'saron'.
> Like 'sheep' and 'sheep'.

<u>Higher-pitched</u> saron play <u>variations</u> on
the main tune, often <u>doubling up</u> notes.

<u>Middle-pitched</u>
saron play the
<u>main tune</u>.

<u>Lower-pitched</u> instruments play <u>bits of the tune</u>,
often missing out the last beat of each bar.

Other Instruments are Used to **Decorate** the Tune

Other instruments and singers are used to <u>embellish</u> (decorate) the main tune.
They add <u>extra notes</u> to make the piece sound more fiddly and <u>impressive</u>.

1) The <u>gender</u> has narrow keys made of <u>bronze</u>.
Below the keys there are <u>bamboo pipes</u>
which resonate with the sound,
making it sound bigger and richer.

2) The <u>bonang family</u> are instruments with <u>two rows</u> of
<u>gongs</u> resting on cords across a wooden frame.

3) The <u>gambang</u> is a <u>xylophone</u> with wooden bars.

4) You'll also hear various types
of <u>stringed</u> instruments, like the
<u>celempung</u> — a plucked stringed
instrument a bit like a mini-harp.
There's also the <u>rebab</u>, which is a
two-stringed fiddle.

5) The <u>suling</u> is a bamboo
wind instrument, like a flute
except you blow through the
end, not over the side.

Gamelan

Here are some more instruments you'll find in the gamelan orchestra.

*Gongs Mark the **Rhythm***

On p.179, we said the tune repeats over and over again in a <u>rhythmic cycle</u>.
This cycle is called a <u>gongan</u>. <u>Gongs</u> mark time so the performers and
audience know where they are in the gongan.

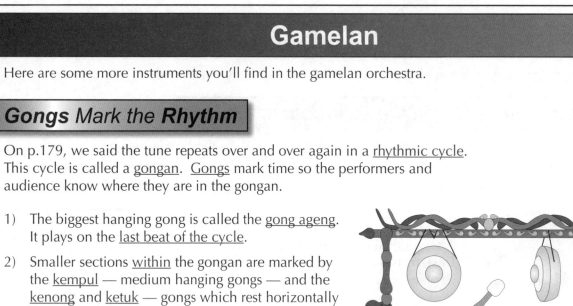

1) The biggest hanging gong is called the <u>gong ageng</u>.
   It plays on the <u>last beat of the cycle</u>.

2) Smaller sections <u>within</u> the gongan are marked by
   the <u>kempul</u> — medium hanging gongs — and the
   <u>kenong</u> and <u>ketuk</u> — gongs which rest horizontally
   on cords stretched across a wooden box.

Gamelan music has <u>4 beats per bar</u> — a bar is called a <u>keteg</u>. The gongs accent the
<u>last beat</u> of each keteg. Here's an example of the gong patterns in an <u>8-bar gongan</u>.

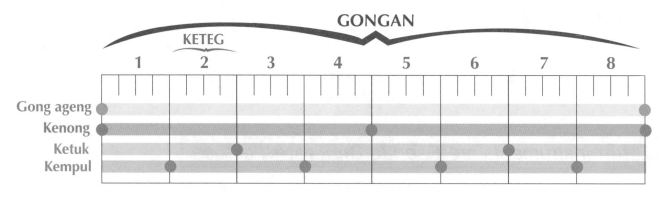

Drummers Cue Performers and Keep Tempo

1) The <u>main job</u> of the drummers in the gamelan is to <u>keep the tempo</u> — but they also act like
   the <u>conductors</u> of the gamelan, cueing in the other players so they know when to play.

2) The drummers sometimes accent the rhythm to follow the movement of <u>puppets</u> or <u>dancers</u>.

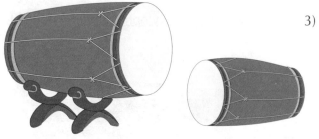

3) There are <u>two main types of drum</u>.
   The bigger one is called the <u>kendang gending</u>
   and the smaller one is called the <u>ketipung</u>.
   They're <u>cone-shaped</u> with two drum skins, one
   larger and one smaller. They're played resting
   <u>sideways</u>, so the drummer can play <u>one skin</u>
   with <u>each hand</u>.

4) Other percussion includes <u>wood blocks</u>, <u>metal plates</u> and <u>small cymbals</u>.

Oh now what's its name...It'll come...wait...no...no...it's gong ageng.
Gamelan is basically lots of versions of the same tune all being played at the same time.
The 100% bona fide, genuine, real McCoy technical term for this musical texture is <u>heterophony</u>.
If you get the chance in the exams, go ahead and use the word <u>heterophony</u>. The examiners will love it.

Warm-up and Exam Questions

Warm-up Questions

1) List **four** types of drums used in African music.
2) Name **two** other instruments used in African music.
3) What is a master drummer?
4) Name **two** types of African singing and describe their features.
5) What are the names of the two types of scale used in Gamelan music?
6) What is the main tune in Gamelan music called?

Exam Question

Try the exam question below and see what you've learnt.

Play Track 43 **three** times, leaving a short pause for writing time between each playing.

Track 43

a) i) Where is the music in this extract from?

.... *[1 mark]*

ii) Give **three** key features of music from this country.

....

....

.... *[3 marks]*

b) Name the instrument playing the melody in this extract.

.... *[1 mark]*

c) Describe the rhythmic features of the extract.
Use musical terminology where appropriate.

....

....

.... *[2 marks]*

d) Which word describes the singing at the beginning of the extract?
Circle your answer.

descant   **solo**   **unison**   *[1 mark]*

Exam Questions

Play Track 44 **two** times, leaving a short pause for writing time between each playing.

Track 44

This extract comes from a piece of Gamelan music.

a)   Which country is this music from?

   .... *[1 mark]*

b)   Gongs are often used in Gamelan music.
     Describe what function they have in the music.

   .... *[1 mark]*

c)   Name and describe one other instrument found in a Gamelan orchestra.

   Name

   ....

   Description

   ....

   .... *[2 marks]*

d)   How many beats per bar does the music in this extract have?

   .... *[1 mark]*

e)   Give one feature of this extract that is typical of this style of music.

   .... *[1 mark]*

Revision Summary for Section Nine

This section really isn't all that long but there's plenty of information packed between the pages. Don't try and learn the whole section at once — you could end up muddling all the new names. Tackle it one page at a time. And don't even think about turning the page without having a go at this revision summary. Answer all the questions, then answer them again and again. And keep answering them until all the answers are securely and permanently lodged in your memory. No excuses.

1) Name four popular instruments used in British folk music.
2) Name the four main types of British folk music.
3) What type of scales do folk tunes tend to use?
4) Where does Celtic music come from?
5) Name five traditional instruments and three more modern instruments played by Capercaillie.
6) What time signature is *Skye Waulking Song* in?
7) Describe three differences between the two sections of *Skye Waulking Song*.
8) What are vocables?
9) What is a raga?
10) Name five instruments used in Indian Classical Music.
11) What do *tivra* and *komal* mean?
12) What instrument plays the rhythm in Indian Classical Music? What's the rhythm called?
13) Describe the four different sections of a raga.
14) When is the Rag Desh supposed to be played?
15) Write out the raga used for the Rag Desh.
16) Which sections of a raga do you hear in 'Priyagitah'?
17) Name the two melodic instruments played in 'Priyagitah'.
18) How many beats are there in a *rupak* tala? How many are there in an *ektal* tala?
19) What instrument does Anoushka Shankar play in Rag Desh?
20) Describe the structure of the Rag Desh from 'Live at the Carnegie Hall'.
21) Which two talas are used in this Rag Desh? How many beats do they have?
22) Name two different vocal techniques the singer uses in 'Mewar Re Mira'.
23) Name three different types of African drum.
24) Name three different ways that drums can be played.
25) Describe the master drummer's job.
26) Name three other African instruments (not drums).
27) What are polyrhythms? What are cross-rhythms?
28) Name four key features of sub-Saharan African music.
29) Describe the main differences between Mbube and Isicathamiya singing.
30) What is heterophony?
31) Describe the two different ways the singers perform in *Yiri*.
32) Give three themes of Koko's music.
33) Describe the texture of *Yiri*.
34) In a gamelan piece, what's the balungan?
35) Name and describe five instruments that have the job of embellishing the tune in gamelan.
36) What do the gongs do in gamelan?
37) Describe the texture of a gamelan piece.

Section Nine — World Music

Programme Music — From 1820 onwards

When you listen to music, it sometimes <u>reminds</u> you of places or objects. Some composers want you to think of a <u>specific place</u> or <u>idea</u>, so they try and make their music <u>describe</u> them.

Programme Music *Tells a Story* or *Sets a Scene*

1) <u>Programme music</u> is a type of music that <u>describes</u> an <u>item</u> or <u>person</u>, <u>tells a story</u> or <u>sets a scene</u>. It's <u>descriptive</u> music.

2) The name was first used in the <u>19th century</u> — it was very popular in the <u>Romantic period</u> (from about 1820 to 1900). There are <u>earlier</u> examples of programme music though — <u>Vivaldi</u>'s *Four Seasons* (written in the <u>1720s</u>) portray <u>spring</u>, <u>summer</u>, <u>autumn</u> and <u>winter</u>.

3) Programme music is <u>instrumental</u> — it <u>doesn't</u> have <u>words</u>. All the imagery comes from the <u>music</u>.

4) <u>Symphonic poems</u> (also called <u>tone poems</u>) are examples of programme music. They're <u>single-movement</u> works that tell <u>stories</u> — like <u>myths</u> and <u>fairy tales</u>.

5) <u>Beethoven</u>, <u>Liszt</u>, <u>Debussy</u> and <u>Richard Strauss</u> all composed programme music.

Composers Use Music to Represent *Moods*, *Places* or *Objects*

1) Composers use music to <u>set the mood</u> (like using a <u>minor</u> key to make it sound <u>sad</u>) or <u>set the scene</u> (the <u>instruments</u> used in Beethoven's *Pastoral Symphony* make it sound like it is in the <u>countryside</u> — e.g. he uses <u>flutes</u>, <u>oboes</u> and <u>clarinets</u> to imitate <u>birds</u>).

2) Composers often <u>imitate</u> real-life sounds — for example, a composer might use <u>flowing notes</u> to represent a <u>brook</u>. In <u>Mendelssohn</u>'s *Spinner's Song* (from *Songs Without Words*), the <u>fast</u>, <u>trundling rhythm</u> sounds like someone working at a <u>spinning wheel</u>.

3) When the programme music is telling a <u>story</u>, different <u>characters</u> are sometimes <u>represented</u> by different <u>themes</u>. Every time the character appears, their theme will be played. The composer can <u>vary</u> the theme depending on what is happening — e.g. if the character has just <u>won</u> a <u>fight</u>, it'll sound <u>triumphant</u> and <u>majestic</u>.

Danse Macabre is an Example of a *Symphonic Poem*

1) *Danse Macabre* was written by a <u>French</u> composer called <u>Camille Saint-Saëns</u>. You'll probably recognise it — it's used as the theme tune to the TV series *Jonathan Creek*.

2) It's based on a <u>poem</u> by Henri Cazalis and illustrates <u>Death</u> calling <u>skeletons</u> from their graves to <u>dance</u>. Death plays the <u>fiddle</u> and the skeletons dance to his tunes.

3) <u>Death</u> is represented by a <u>solo violin melody</u>. The <u>E-string</u> is tuned to an E♭ to make it sound <u>creepy</u>. When the violin plays an <u>A</u> against the E♭ (both on open strings), it produces a <u>tritone</u> (or <u>augmented fourth</u> — two notes with an interval of three whole tones, like F and B). The tritone's often used to make things sound <u>weird</u> and <u>scary</u>.

4) The <u>skeletons</u> are represented by a <u>xylophone</u> — it sounds like the <u>bones knocking together</u>.

5) He also uses a melody from the *Dies Irae* (which means '<u>day of wrath</u>') from a <u>Requiem Mass</u> by <u>Thomas of Celano</u>. A requiem mass is a <u>mass for the dead</u> — so it's quite appropriate in this piece.

Death, skeletons — it all sounds a bit grave to me...

The most important bit to remember about programme music is that it <u>describes</u> things. It'll be good if you can come up with <u>reasons</u> why a particular bit of music could <u>represent</u> a particular thing.

Programme Music — From 1820 onwards

Some programme music is used for <u>different purposes</u> than it was written for.
It's often used in <u>adverts</u>, <u>TV programmes</u> and <u>films</u> because it's very <u>expressive</u>.

Peer Gynt is an Example of **Programme Music**

1) *Peer Gynt* is a piece of programme music by <u>Edvard Grieg</u>. It was originally written to accompany a <u>play</u> by <u>Henrik Ibsen</u> about the adventures of a boy called Peer.

2) Grieg later took out <u>8 movements</u> and made them into <u>two suites</u>.

3) The first suite includes the well-known pieces '<u>Morning Mood</u>' (often just called 'Morning') and '<u>In the Hall of the Mountain King</u>'. The other two pieces are '<u>Ase's Death</u>' and '<u>Anitra's Dance</u>'.

4) 'Morning Mood' describes the <u>sun rising</u> over the <u>Sahara desert</u>. It's very <u>calm</u> and <u>peaceful</u>.

5) The second suite isn't as well known. It includes movements called '<u>Homecoming (Stormy Evening on the Sea)</u>' and '<u>Arabic Dance</u>'.

'In the Hall of the Mountain King' is About **Trolls**

1) In the play, Peer Gynt <u>sneaks</u> into the castle of the <u>King of the Trolls</u>. 'In the Hall of the Mountain King' is about him <u>sneaking in</u> then trying to <u>escape</u>.

2) You might recognise the theme — it's used in the adverts for <u>Alton Towers</u> (and played around the park).

3) At first, the theme is played <u>slowly</u> by <u>bassoons</u> with <u>quiet</u>, <u>staccato</u> quavers imitating his <u>careful footsteps</u>. Occasional <u>accented notes</u> give it a <u>nervous</u>, <u>edgy</u> mood. ➡

4) It's then repeated at a <u>higher pitch</u> on the <u>strings</u> and <u>higher woodwind</u> — this represents the <u>trolls</u> moving around the castle.

5) The instruments play in <u>different octaves</u> until the trolls notice Peer, then they all play at the <u>same pitch</u>.

6) It gradually gets <u>faster</u> and <u>faster</u> as the <u>chase</u> gets more <u>exciting</u>.

7) There are <u>sudden pauses</u> towards the end of the piece — this is the <u>King</u> searching for Peer. When Peer's spotted, the music is very <u>loud</u> and very <u>fast</u> — it's really <u>dramatic</u>.

8) The piece ends with <u>cymbal crashes</u> and <u>timpani rolls</u> — this is where the mountain <u>collapses</u> around the trolls and Peer <u>escapes</u> to safety.

'Billy the Kid' is a More Modern Piece of Programme Music

1) '<u>Billy the Kid</u>' is a <u>ballet</u> written by <u>Aaron Copland</u> in 1938. It tells the story of <u>William Bonney</u> (who became known as Billy the Kid), an <u>American outlaw</u>. It's set in <u>America's Wild West</u>.

2) Copland used <u>folk melodies</u> and <u>cowboy tunes</u> to create the <u>sound</u> of the Wild West. The tunes are played on a <u>piccolo</u> or <u>tin whistle</u>.

3) He used <u>percussion</u> to mimic the sound of a <u>gun battle</u>.

4) <u>Quick, jaunty rhythms</u> are used for the <u>cowboys</u>, while <u>slow</u> passages tell a <u>love story</u>.

5) This piece of programme music really <u>sets the scene</u> for the ballet. The <u>instruments</u> give it the <u>feel</u> of being in the Wild West.

Programme music tells a story...

Pay attention to the music on TV next time you're watching it. If you see a show or advert that uses a piece of classical music have a think about why the makers chose the particular piece of music.

Programme Music — From 1820 onwards

Programme music is used for <u>story-telling</u> — anything from a <u>walk in the woods</u> to a complete <u>Shakespeare play</u>. Composers need to be able to describe lots of <u>characters</u>, <u>emotions</u> and <u>action</u> in their music.

Tchaikovsky's *Romeo and Juliet* is Based on the **Play**

1) *Romeo and Juliet* is a <u>symphonic poem</u> (see p.184) by <u>Tchaikovsky</u>. It's based on <u>Shakespeare's play</u>. You probably know the story — it's about <u>Romeo Montague</u> and <u>Juliet Capulet</u> who fall in <u>love</u>, despite being from <u>feuding families</u>. It ends <u>tragically</u>, with the lovers <u>killing themselves</u>.

2) Tchaikovsky uses the <u>music</u> to <u>tell the story</u> — there are <u>no words</u>. There's a lot of stuff for him to <u>describe</u> — from the <u>street fighting</u> of the <u>rival families</u> to the <u>young couple falling in love</u>.

3) It has <u>four</u> main <u>themes</u> — two for the <u>lovers</u>, one for the <u>warring families</u> and one for <u>Friar Lawrence</u> (Romeo's friend and advisor). The themes are <u>repeated</u> throughout the piece, but they're <u>altered</u> to <u>reflect</u> what happens in the story.

The **Themes** Represent the **Characters**

1) The two themes for <u>Romeo and Juliet</u> are <u>slow</u> and <u>lyrical</u>. The first part is originally played as a <u>duet</u> between the <u>cor anglais</u> (a double-reeded instrument a bit lower than an oboe) and <u>viola</u> — the two <u>instruments</u> represent the two <u>lovers</u>. There are <u>big jumps</u> in pitch in these two themes — this could represent the <u>obstacles</u> keeping Romeo and Juliet apart.

The two love themes

2) The <u>Montagues and Capulets</u> theme is <u>fast</u> and <u>aggressive</u>. It represents the <u>hatred</u> and <u>rivalry</u> between the two families. It's used for the <u>battles</u> and the <u>sword fight</u>. Tchaikovsky uses <u>dialogue</u> (question and answer) between the <u>strings</u> and the <u>woodwind</u> to show the <u>opposing sides</u>.

The Montagues and Capulets theme

3) <u>Friar Lawrence's</u> theme sounds <u>religious</u> — like a <u>hymn</u>. It's <u>homophonic</u> (the parts move together in chords). It's quite <u>solemn</u>, and the low strings sound a bit <u>sinister</u>. This represents the friar's part in the tragedy — he <u>marries</u> Romeo and Juliet, then gives a <u>potion</u> to Juliet so she can <u>fake her own death</u>.

Friar Lawrence's theme

The Music is Very **Dramatic**

1) Tchaikovsky uses a lot of <u>percussion</u> to make the piece <u>dramatic</u>. <u>Timpani</u> and <u>cymbals</u> are really important — there's a big <u>cymbal crash</u> that represents Romeo and Juliet's <u>deaths</u>.

2) The <u>contrasts</u> between the different themes help to show the different <u>emotions</u> of the story.

3) The <u>rhythms</u> are really important too — the <u>irregular rhythms</u> in the <u>fight sections</u> are very different to the <u>smooth crotchets</u> (<u>legato</u>) in the <u>love theme</u>.

Two orchestras, both alike in dignity...

You might recognise this piece — it's used in films like *Clueless* and *Moonraker*, and TV programmes like *Scrubs*. The love theme is well known — it's often used when stuff is supposed to be romantic.

Film Music

Composers who write film music use similar techniques to composers of programme music, but have to write music to fit to actions already set by the film makers.

Look Out for the **Leitmotif** in Most Film Music

N.B. 'Leitmotif' can also be spelt 'leitmotiv'.

1) The leitmotif is the main tune in the film.

2) It represents a particular object, idea or character in the story, and often returns in the background or in an altered form.

3) For example, the leitmotif in the *Harry Potter* films is called 'Hedwig's Theme' — it's repeated by different instruments throughout the films.

4) Sometimes the leitmotifs give you a hint as to what will happen later in the film — if a character turns out to be a bad guy, their theme might have menacing chords being played in the background.

- A good example of this occurs in *Star Wars*® Episode I — *The Phantom Menace*™ (1999).
- In the final few bars of 'Anakin's Theme', you can hear echoes of 'Darth Vader's Theme' from the later films (all by John Williams). This is a subtle hint that Anakin (who was good in this film) will become Darth Vader.

Composers Use Lots of **Repetition** in Film Music

1) Repeated sections of music can be used to link different parts of the film together — it can remind you of something that happened earlier in the film.

2) A leitmotif can be repeated throughout the film, but might be transformed to reflect what's going on. The instrumentation can be changed, or it can be repeated in a different key. Sometimes just the rhythm of the leitmotif is played in the background — it might be so quiet it's hardly noticeable, but it all adds to the drama.

3) Often at the end of the film there's a triumphant modulation of the main theme (as long as the film has a happy ending). It ends in a happy, uplifting key with a drawn-out cadence (see p.36-37), to show that the story of the film has been resolved.

4) Of course, if the film doesn't have a happy ending (or if there's going to be a sequel), the theme may be left unresolved, giving the film a more open or darker ending.

5) Repetition can be used to create tension and suspense — a repeated sequence that's getting louder and louder can really have you on the edge of your seat.

Some Films Use **Pop Songs** to Get **Publicity**

1) Lots of films have pop songs over the opening or closing credits. These songs aren't always in the same style of music as the rest of the film, but they're released in the charts to generate publicity. They're often performed by famous pop stars — like Take That's song 'Rule The World' for the film *Stardust* (2007).

2) A song might be used as the title track but can return in the background later — like a leitmotif. For example, the song 'My Heart Will Go On' by Celine Dion pops up many times in the film *Titanic* (1997).

3) Sometimes the pop song doesn't appear anywhere else in the film though (e.g. 'Rule The World' is only heard over the closing credits).

A good excuse to watch some films...

Film music is written to create a certain atmosphere. Composers use it to set a scene, create a mood or describe a character. It should help the overall effect of the film and add to the drama of the story.

Film Music

Film composers use music to <u>set the scene</u> — it helps you believe it's in a <u>different country</u> or <u>time</u>.

Traditional Instruments Give You a Feel for Time and Place

1) Music can be used to create the mood of a different <u>time</u> or <u>place</u>.

2) <u>Westerns</u> are set in 19th century North America. They generally tell a simple story and they can often be very <u>dramatic</u> and <u>violent</u>.

3) Some westerns use music <u>from the time</u> to <u>set the scene</u>. For example, guitarist <u>Ry Cooder</u> composed music for *The Long Riders* (1980). He used <u>traditional music</u> and <u>instruments</u> like the Spanish guitar, banjo, honky-tonk piano, tin flute, trombone and percussion.

4) John Barry's score for *Out of Africa* (1985) combines <u>original compositions</u> with <u>traditional African music</u> to help the audience imagine the film's setting — the track 'Karen's Journey' is based on 'Siyawe', a traditional African song.

5) It's not just films set hundreds of years ago that use music from the time. Films set in the <u>70s</u> or <u>80s</u> might use <u>pop songs</u> from the time to set the scene. People will <u>recognise</u> the songs and it'll <u>remind</u> them of that decade.

The Music in War Films Creates the Atmosphere

1) The music in war films needs to create an <u>atmosphere</u> for the <u>time</u> and <u>place</u> of the war, as well as showing the <u>action</u> and <u>emotion</u> of the plot. For example, the battle scenes of *Gladiator* (2000) are accompanied by <u>threatening music</u> (by <u>Hans Zimmer</u>) which creates tension.

2) <u>Sound effects</u> (like <u>explosions</u> and <u>gunfire</u>) can be incorporated into the music to create a feeling of <u>war</u>.

3) *633 Squadron* (1964) is set in the <u>Second World War</u>. The theme music (by <u>Ron Goodwin</u>) is very <u>heroic</u>. It's <u>fast</u> with <u>strong accents</u> — it matches the <u>action</u> of the <u>battle scenes</u>. The <u>soaring brass melodies</u> represent the <u>soaring planes</u>.

Unnatural Sounds Make Strange Places Seem Even Stranger

<u>Horror</u> or <u>science fiction</u> films are often set in <u>strange places</u> — maybe even another <u>planet</u>. Wherever they're set, composers need to <u>transport</u> the audience to a <u>weird reality</u>, where nothing is quite what you'd expect.

1) <u>Unusual harmonies</u> and <u>time signatures</u> are used when things are a bit <u>weird</u> — they're not what you're expecting, so they sound odd.

2) <u>Synthesizers</u> and <u>samples</u> of bizarre <u>sounds</u> often have no relation to what's happening on-screen, but make the audience wonder what's going on and set their imagination racing.

3) <u>Instruments</u> or <u>voices</u> can be <u>distorted</u> using <u>computers</u>.

4) There's often no clear <u>structure</u> so it's hard to predict what's going to happen.

5) <u>Discords</u> and <u>diminished</u> chords make it difficult to listen to.

6) <u>Rapid scalic patterns</u> (going up and down scales) and <u>interrupted cadences</u> (see p.36-37) can make <u>pulse-raising</u> scenes feel more frantic.

7) In *Psycho* (1960), for every <u>stab</u> of the <u>knife</u> the <u>violins</u> also <u>stab</u> out a <u>high-pitched tritone</u> (p.184). Each chord goes right through you, and makes what you're seeing on-screen feel much more real.

Music revision can be used to put you in a mood...

There are loads of little tricks that composers of film music can use to create an atmosphere and make the viewer more engrossed in a film. Have a stab at writing a mini essay on this page.

Film Music

Sometimes, film music helps you <u>understand</u> what's happening. It's used to help <u>communicate</u> what's going on, instead of just relying on the action and dialogue <u>on-screen</u>.

The *Style* of Music *Changes* With the *Mood* of the Scene

1) The soundtrack for the film *Pirates of the Caribbean: The Curse of the Black Pearl* (2003) was written by Klaus Badelt.

2) There's a simple <u>love theme</u> to accompany the growing romance between Will and Elizabeth, using <u>string</u> and <u>woodwind</u> instruments playing <u>quietly</u>.

3) In the <u>humorous</u> scenes involving Captain Jack Sparrow, the music is <u>playful</u> to create a <u>light-hearted mood</u> and provides a <u>contrast</u> with the <u>fight scenes</u>.

4) During <u>battle scenes</u>, the mood is <u>tense</u> and <u>dramatic</u> — it's played by <u>low brass</u> instruments.

The Music *Shows* What's *Not On Screen*

It's often the composer's job to create a <u>feeling</u> of something <u>being there</u> that's <u>not seen</u>.

1) <u>Minor</u> and more <u>dissonant chords</u> make you feel <u>uneasy</u>.

2) <u>Low pitches</u> in <u>brass</u> and <u>strings</u> sound <u>dark</u> as if you're <u>underground</u>.

3) <u>Percussive, metallic</u> sounds with <u>reverb effects</u> make you imagine someone <u>lurking</u> about on <u>lonely backstreets</u>.

4) <u>Suspensions</u> that don't <u>resolve</u> (see p.35) build <u>tension</u> and make you think <u>danger</u> is near.

5) <u>Dynamics swell</u> from <u>quiet</u> to <u>loud</u> to <u>quiet</u> as if someone's coming in and out of the <u>shadows</u>.

Music Has to be *Structured* and *Timed* to *Fit* the Film

1) <u>Film directors</u> need music to be <u>synchronised</u> with the <u>action</u> to the <u>split second</u>.

2) The different <u>sections</u> of a <u>film</u> show different <u>moods</u>, e.g. from <u>fighting</u> to <u>romance</u>. The music can easily be <u>chopped up</u> and <u>moved</u> around using <u>samplers</u> and computer programs such as <u>Cubase</u> and <u>Pro-Tools</u>®.

3) Music is used during action scenes to <u>imitate</u> the movements of the actors — like in the fight scenes in the *Pirates of the Caribbean* films.

Diegetic Music is Music the Characters Can *Hear*

1) In most films, the music is <u>extra-diegetic</u> — it's <u>not</u> actually <u>part of the story</u>. It's put '<u>over the top</u>' of the action to increase the <u>effect</u> of the film. It's for the <u>audience</u>'s benefit only.

2) Sometimes film-makers want to <u>include</u> music in the story for the <u>characters</u> (as well as the <u>audience</u>) to <u>hear</u> — this is <u>diegetic</u> music.

3) In *Atonement* (2007), the sound of Briony using a typewriter <u>combines</u> with the piano music so that the two play in time with each other, giving the impression that she can <u>hear</u> the music.

4) Throughout *Brief Encounter* (1945), <u>Rachmaninov</u>'s *Second Piano Concerto* is used <u>extra-diegetically</u>. It represents the main character's <u>changing emotions</u> as she has an extra-marital <u>affair</u>.

5) At one point in the film, she turns on the <u>radio</u>, and what should be playing but Rachmaninov's *Second Piano Concerto*. The music has <u>become diegetic</u>.

6) Her husband later asks her to <u>turn the music down</u> — this could be seen as him <u>suppressing</u> his wife's emotional needs.

Film Music

Music for horror and fantasy often makes you feel like you're in <u>another world</u> or a kind of <u>nightmare reality</u>. The music can also help to <u>build tension</u> and to <u>make you jump</u>.

You Are **Lulled** Into a **False Sense of Security**

1) When music's in a calm <u>major key</u>, you don't feel like anything bad's going to happen. For example, in *Gladiator*, the music that plays when Maximus thinks of his home is a <u>simple</u>, gentle melody composed by Hans Zimmer and Lisa Gerrard. In *The Lord of the Rings* (2001-3), <u>Howard Shore</u> composed a happy piece of music to reflect the comfort and safety of the Shire.

2) <u>Beware</u> — sometimes the same <u>theme</u> comes back in an <u>altered form</u> — like in a <u>minor key</u> — to show that things have started to <u>go wrong</u>.

Composers Can Keep You on the **Edge** of Your Seat

1) <u>Ostinati</u> keep the <u>audience</u> on <u>edge</u> for a long time. For example, in *Halloween* (1978), there's an ostinato played in a <u>minor key</u> — it's then played on a <u>different note</u> to keep the audience wondering where the scary person is going next.

2) In some sci-fi films there's background music with just drums and bass, generated on <u>computers</u>, that's played under the <u>dialogue</u> throughout the film. This lets the audience know that the danger is always there.

3) <u>Sustained</u> notes create <u>suspense</u> (e.g. tremolo strings).

4) Composers know how to build the <u>tension</u> and make you feel like <u>something bad</u> is going to happen:

> - <u>Dynamics</u> get <u>louder</u>.
> - <u>Tempo</u> gets <u>faster</u>.
> - <u>Pitch</u> gets <u>higher</u>.
> - A <u>tune</u> played earlier in a <u>scary bit</u> sometimes <u>comes back</u> to remind you.
> - Sometimes they use <u>silence</u> before a <u>loud</u> bit just to make you <u>jump</u>.

Thrillers Have Lots of **Tension** and **Action**

1) Thrillers and spy movies are often <u>serious</u> and <u>tense</u> — the music has to create the right atmosphere. It has to set the scene for <u>conspiracies</u> and people dealing with <u>shadowy figures</u> and <u>underground organisations</u>.

2) There are often lots of <u>layers</u> to the story. A composer uses lots of <u>techniques</u> to show that there's more than one thing going on. E.g. in *The Usual Suspects* (1995), the composer <u>John Ottman</u> creates <u>tension</u> and <u>drama</u> by using:

> - <u>Long notes</u> in the <u>foreground</u> with <u>ostinato</u> patterns in the <u>background</u>.
> - A <u>repeated pattern</u> on the <u>woodblock</u> sounds like someone's <u>on the move</u> while <u>percussive bursts</u> and <u>brass motifs</u> played on top suggest someone's trying to catch them.

Silence — something bad's about to happen...
Turn the volume down when you're watching a scary film and it's <u>nowhere near as nail-biting</u>. Perhaps more than in any other film genre, the music in horror is <u>crucial</u> to setting the atmosphere.

Warm-up and Exam Questions

Warm-up Questions

1) What is programme music?
2) Why do composers often use tritones in programme music?
3) What is a leitmotif?
4) How is repetition used in film music?
5) Why are instruments from a particular time or place sometimes used in film music?

Exam Question

Skim reading isn't enough — write the answers out properly to really test yourself.

Track 45 is from Vivaldi's *The Four Seasons*.
Play Track 45 **three** times, leaving a short pause for writing time between each playing.

Track 45

a) Name the instrument playing the melody in this extract.

.... *[1 mark]*

b) This extract is said to represent resting by a fire in winter,
whilst the rain falls outside.
How does Vivaldi represent the rain?

.... *[1 mark]*

The score below shows the first **two** bars of the melody.

c) Fill in the missing notes. The rhythm is given above the stave. *[6 marks]*

Exam Questions

Track 46 is taken from the film *Gladiator*.
Play Track 46 **four** times, leaving a short pause for writing time between each playing.

(Track 46)

The music in the extract has two contrasting sections.

a) Which word describes the texture at the start of the extract?

Polyphonic   **Homophonic**   **Monophonic**   *[1 mark]*

b) Give a suitable word for the tempo at the beginning of the extract.

....   *[1 mark]*

c) The second section of the piece represents the atmosphere and
   threat of a battle. Explain how the composer uses the following
   musical features to create the mood.

- Instrumentation
- Texture
- Rhythm
- Dynamics
- Tempo

....

....

....

....

....

....

....

....

....

....

....   *[10 marks]*

Revision Summary for Section Ten

It's the final page of the final section at last. But that doesn't mean you can skip these questions. You know the drill by now. Look back through the section to help yourself answer them the first time round. The next time try doing it without looking. And keep answering them, looking as little as possible until finally you can answer them all without any trouble at all.

1) When was programme music most popular?
2) What is a symphonic poem?
3) Name three composers of programme music.
4) Name the instrument used to represent Death in *Danse Macabre*.
5) Name the instrument used to represent the skeletons in *Danse Macabre*.
6) Who wrote the *Peer Gynt* suite?
7) How are Peer's footprints represented in *In the Hall of the Mountain King*?
8) How does Aaron Copland create the sound of the Wild West in *Billy the Kid*?
9) Name the section of the orchestra he uses to represent the gun battle in the ballet.
10) Describe the four main themes of Tchaikovsky's *Romeo and Juliet*.
11) Give two ways that Tchaikovsky makes *Romeo and Juliet* dramatic.
12) What's a leitmotif (in film music)?
13) How do composers use repetition in film music?
14) Why do some films use pop songs?
15) What's an ostinato?
16) Name three traditional instruments used in film music for Westerns.
17) How does John Barry create the African setting of *Out of Africa*?
18) Describe how Ron Goodwin's music in *633 Squadron* represents the battle scenes.
19) What type of films would use unusual harmonies or weird time signatures?
20) Describe how the music in *Pirates of the Caribbean: Curse of the Black Pearl* illustrates the romantic scenes, the humorous scenes and the battle scenes.
21) Give three techniques that composers use to create a feeling of something that isn't on screen.
22) Name two computer programs that are used to synchronise the music to the action.
23) What is diegetic music?
24) Describe how Rachmaninov's *Second Piano Concerto* is used both extra-diegetically and diegetically in the film *Brief Encounter*.
25) How can a composer show that things have started to go wrong?
26) How do composers create suspense?
27) Give three ways composers build tension.
28) Describe two ways John Ottman creates tension and drama in *The Usual Suspects*.

Practice Exam

Once you've been through all the questions in this book, you should feel pretty confident about the exam. As final preparation, here's a **practice exam** to prepare you for the real thing. It's designed to give you the best exam practice possible for the listening exam, whichever syllabus you're following.

General Certificate of Secondary Education

GCSE
Music

CGP Practice Exam Paper GCSE Music

Centre name				
Centre number				
Candidate number				

Listening & Appraising

Surname
Other names
Candidate signature

Time allowed: up to 90 minutes

Instructions
- Write in black or blue ink or ballpoint pen.
- Before the CD is started, you will be allowed **2** minutes during which you may read through the questions.
- Answer **all** questions in the spaces provided.
- Give all the information you are asked for, and **write neatly**.
- Do all rough work in this book. Cross through any work you do not want marked.

Information
- The marks are shown by each question.
- The maximum mark for this paper is 100.
- You will have one minute to read through each question before a new extract is played.
- There will be pauses between repeated playings of the extracts.
- You may write at any time.
- After the final playing of each extract there will be one minute for you to write your answers.
- You do not need to write in full sentences.
  You may respond using phrases and key words.

Instructions for playing the CD:
- There are 8 questions, covered on the CD by tracks 47-54.

Question No.	1	2	3	4	5	6	7	8
CD Track No.	47	48	49	50	51	52	53	54

- Leave 2 minutes at the start to read through the exam.
- Play the CD, one track at a time, stopping the CD after each track.
- Each question will tell you how many times the track should be repeated.
- Allow a short pause between each playing for writing time.
  After the final playing of each track allow 1 minute for writing time.

Answer ALL questions

1   You will hear a version of a tune called *Ain't Misbehavin'*.
     Play the track **three** times.

(Track 47)

a)   Name the style of music in this extract. Circle your answer.

         soul   jazz   reggae   blues   ragtime   *(1 mark)*

b)   Which **two** of the features or devices listed below can you hear in this excerpt?
     Circle your answers.

             pedal   riff   improvisation   chromatic notes   *(2 marks)*

c)   Tick one box to indicate which structure best represents the extract.

Introduction	Verse	Chorus	Verse	Chorus
Introduction	A	A	B	A
Introduction	A	B	B	A

(1 mark)

d)   Describe **two** ways in which the left **and** right hands of the piano parts vary in
     texture in the three main contrasting sections.

     ....

     ....

     ....

     ....   *(4 marks)*

e)   Circle the word that best describes the tonality of this extract.

             major   minor   pentatonic   atonal   modal   *(1 mark)*

Turn over

2   Play the track **four** times.

Track 48

a)   Fill in the missing notes of the opening melody of the vocal part in bars 7 to 8
     using the given rhythm. Write your answer on the score.

(5 marks)

b)   Identify **four** of the following devices or features you can hear in this extract.
     Circle your answers.

accelerando   broken chords   vibrato   crescendo

descant   sequence   ritardando   *(4 marks)*

c)   What type of voice is singing in the extract?
     Circle your answer.

contralto   soprano   tenor   treble   bass   *(1 mark)*

d)   What kind of song is this?
     Circle your answer.

   recitative   chorus   aria   anthem   lied   *(1 mark)*

e)   The original version of this piece was written in the Baroque period.
     The extract you have heard is from an adaptation of the original Baroque piece.

   (i)   In which period was this version composed? Circle your answer.

   classical   1800-1830   1830-1900   twentieth century   *(1 mark)*

   (ii) Give one reason for your choice.

         ....   *(1 mark)*

f)   What instrument plays the accompaniment in the opening bars?
     Circle your answer.

   piano   celesta   harp   harpsichord   electronic keyboard   *(1 mark)*

Turn over

198

g)   Describe the tempo of the extract. Circle your answer.

allegro   **vivace**   **andante**   **largo**   **presto**   *(1 mark)*

h)   What section of the orchestra is heard towards the end of this extract?

....   *(1 mark)*

i)   Describe the texture, instrumentation/voice, phrasing and rhythm of the extract.

....

....

....

....   *(4 marks)*

There are four marks up for grabs and they've suggested
four things to write about — instruments, voice, phrasing
and rhythm — so make sure you mention them all.

3   You will hear an extract of solo piano music.
On the next page is a skeleton score of the music.
The answers for parts (d) and (f) should be written on this score.
Play the extract **six** times.

(Track 49)

a)   What musical device is heard during the playing of the first six bars?
Circle the correct answer.

   sequence   **drone**   **imitation**   **ostinato**   *(1 mark)*

b)   Name the ornament heard towards the end of bar 13.

   ....   *(1 mark)*

c)   What is the time signature of this extract? Circle your answer.

   $\dfrac{2}{4}$ $\dfrac{3}{4}$ $\dfrac{4}{4}$ $\dfrac{6}{8}$ *(1 mark)*

d)   Fill in the notes in bar 8 to show the note values and the correct rhythm.   *(7 marks)*

e)   (i)   Name the key at the end of this extract.

      ....   *(2 marks)*

   (ii) Describe the cadence at the end of the extract.

      ....   *(2 marks)*

f)   Write in the pitches of the bass notes in bars 10–11 using the note values indicated
below the score.   *(8 marks)*

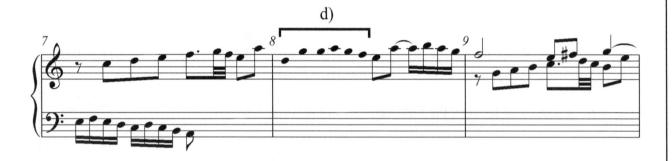

4 Play this extract of film music **four** times.

(Track 50)

a) How would you describe the style of the music?
Circle your answer.

                electronic   **orchestral**   **acoustic**   *(1 mark)*

b) At the beginning of the extract you can hear the deep rumbling of thunder.
What instrument is used to create this sound?

....   *(1 mark)*

c) In what **two** ways are the brass instruments used to create drama in this section?

....

....   *(2 marks)*

d) The second section of the extract starts as the first section dies out.
Describe **three** differences between the two sections.

....

....

....   *(3 marks)*

*Lea
bla.*

e) (i) What instrument plays the theme in the second half of the extract?

.... *(1 mark)*

(ii) Name one musical device used to create a mood change at the start of the second section.

.... *(1 mark)*

(iii) What instrument is used in this section to imitate the sound of sleigh bells?

.... *(1 mark)*

f) (i) Near the end of the extract the music gets very quiet.
What group of instruments is playing on its own at this point?

.... *(1 mark)*

(ii) This group of instruments is being played in two different ways.
Name these **two** different ways of playing.

....

.... *(2 marks)*

5   Play this extract of guitar music **three** times.

(Track 51)

a)   How many beats are in each bar?

   ....   *(1 mark)*

b)   What **two** techniques are used by the solo guitarist?
     Circle your answers.

   finger picking   **tremolo**

   vibrato   **glissando**

   rubato   **strumming chords**   *(2 marks)*

c)   What is the most frequently used rhythmic feature used in this music?

   ....   *(1 mark)*

d)   This music is constructed by the repetition of short phrases.
     What is the name given to this technique?

   ....   *(1 mark)*

e)   Underline the word that best describes the texture created by this music.

   monophonic   **polyphonic**   **homophonic**   *(1 mark)*

f)   Describe the dynamics in this extract.

....

....

....   *(3 marks)*

g)   Give **two** features of minimalist music that can be heard in this extract.

....

....   *(2 marks)*

6 Play this extract **three** times.

(Track 52)

a) Circle the **two** families of instruments that can be heard in the extract.

brass   strings   woodwind   keyboard   percussion

(1 mark)

b) Name **two** instruments that can be heard in the extract.

....

.... *(2 marks)*

c) What **four** features from the list below are found in this extract?
Circle your answers.

decorated melody	**canon**
fugue	**slides**
pitch bend	**swing rhythms**
polyrhythms	**major key**

(2 marks)

d) What word is used to describe the style of the melody played by the soloist?

.... *(1 mark)*

e) A drone is used in this extract.
Describe what a 'drone' is and how the drone is used in this piece.

....

....

.... *(3 marks)*

206

7 Play this extract **four** times.

(Track 53)

a) Name an instrument from the woodwind family that plays the melody at the
beginning of the extract.

.... *(1 mark)*

b) Circle **two** instruments that are heard later in the extract.

       bassoon **french horn** **tuba** **saxophone** **trombone** **euphonium** *(2 marks)*

c) What word describes the articulation used in the melody at the beginning
of the extract?

.... *(1 mark)*

d) What is the time signature of the music?

.... *(1 mark)*

e) i) Name the type of dance heard in this extract.

    .... *(1 mark)*

  ii) Suggest a composer for the music heard in this extract.

    .... *(1 mark)*

f) Give **two** reasons why this is a good piece of music to dance to.

....

.... *(2 marks)*

g) Circle the word that best describes the tonality of this extract.

atonal   **minor**   **major**   **pentatonic**   **chromatic**   *(1 mark)*

h) What dynamic markings are the most appropriate for this extract?
Tick the box next to your choice.

mf throughout   ☐

pp to *mp*   ☐

f to *p*   ☐

p throughout   ☐

mf to *f*   ☐   *(1 mark)*

208

8   Play this extract **three** times.

(Track 54)

a)   Name the family of instruments that is used in this extract.

....   *(1 mark)*

b)   How many beats are there in each bar?

....   *(1 mark)*

c)   Circle **two** melodic devices that are used.

imitation   sequences   repetition   augmentation   *(2 marks)*

d)   Complete the following sentence using one of the words given below.
     'The main melody is made up of ....'
     Underline your answer.

crotchets   dotted quavers   quavers   minims   *(1 mark)*

END OF TEST

Section One — Reading and Writing Music

Page 9 (Warm-up Questions)

1)

2) A sharp sign raises the pitch of the note (and other notes of the same pitch later in the bar) by one semitone.
A flat sign lowers the pitch of the note by one semitone.
A natural sign cancels out a flat sign or natural sign in the key signature or earlier on in the bar.

3) 𝟑/𝟐

4) Three beats

5) In simple time you count all the beats in a bar, but in compound time you only count the main beats / count every three beats.

6) Regular, irregular and free

Page 9 (Exam Question)

Track 1

a)

(1 mark for each correct note or correct interval between two adjacent notes, up to 8 marks)

b) *(1 mark)*

c) *(1 mark)*

d)

(up to 3 marks, one for each different feature identified)

Page 15 (Warm-up Questions)

1) ○ (semibreve)

2) ▬

3) Dotted crotchet, one and a half beats
Quaver, half a beat
Dotted minim, three beats

4) A tie joins two or more notes of the same pitch together. A slur joins two or more notes of different pitch together.

5) Presto, allegro, moderato, andante, largo

Pages 15-16 (Exam Question)

Track 2
a) dotted notes *(1 mark)*

b) allegro *(1 mark)*

c) forte *(1 mark)*

d) energico *(1 mark)*

Section Two — Keys, Scales and Chords

Page 25 (Practice Questions)

Track 10 a) Natural minor   b) melodic minor
c) whole tone   d) major

Track 11 Pentatonic (major isn't wrong, but pentatonic is more accurate)

Track 12 a) unison   b) perfect 5th   c) major 3rd
d) minor 3rd   e) major 7th   f) perfect 4th
g) minor 6th   h) augmented 4th/diminished 5th

Track 13 a) minor 2nd   b) major 3rd   c) perfect 4th
d) octave   e) major 6th   f) perfect 5th
g) minor 7th   h) major 2nd

Page 26 (Warm-up Questions)

1) Eight

2) They tell you what sharps or flats to play.

3) They are relative scales – they have the same notes/ same key signature.

4) Natural, harmonic and melodic

5) Major pentatonic

6) It includes every white and black note.

7) A harmonic interval.

8) Diminished 7th

Pages 26-27 (Exam Question)

Track 14

a) i) Four *(1 mark)*
    ii) Octave (or eighth) *(1 mark)*
    iii) Minor seventh *(1 mark)*
  b) C minor *(1 mark)*
  c) Loud then soft again *(1 mark)*

Page 34 (Practice Questions)

Track 17 a) major   b) minor   c) major
       d) augmented e) minor   f) diminished
       g) diminished h) minor

Track 18 a) root   b) 2nd   c) root
       d) 2nd   e) 1st   f) 2nd
       g) root   h) root

Pages 43-44 (Practice Questions)

Track 21 a) perfect   b) plagal   c) interrupted
       d) imperfect   e) interrupted   f) perfect
       g) imperfect   h) perfect

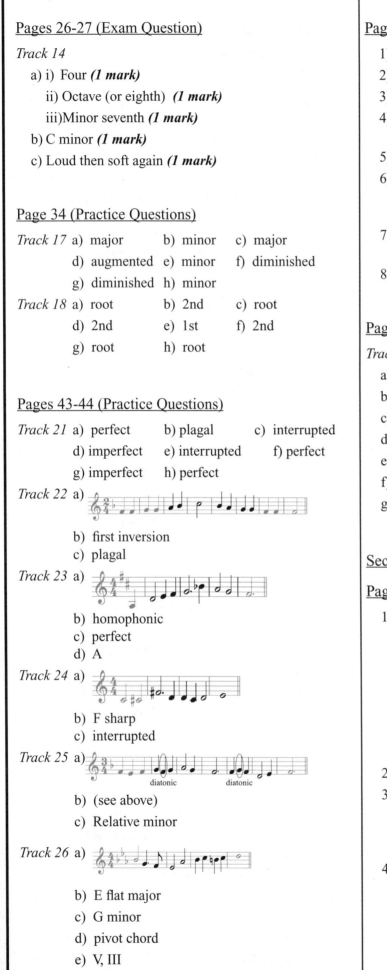

Track 22 a)

  b) first inversion
  c) plagal

Track 23 a)

  b) homophonic
  c) perfect
  d) A

Track 24 a)

  b) F sharp
  c) interrupted

Track 25 a)

       diatonic   diatonic

  b) (see above)
  c) Relative minor

Track 26 a)

  b) E flat major
  c) G minor
  d) pivot chord
  e) V, III

Page 45 (Warm-up Questions)

1) e.g. piano, guitar
2) I, IV and V or tonic, subdominant, dominant
3) First inversion
4) Block chords, rhythmic chords, broken / arpeggiated chords
5) Diatonic
6) Any three of the following: auxiliary notes, passing notes, appoggiaturas, suspensions, trills or other sensible answer.
7) In the middle of a piece, or at the end of any phrase except the last phrase.
8) Contrapuntal

Pages 45-46 (Exam Question)

Track 27

a) Piano *(1 mark)*
  b) Alberti bass / broken chords / arpeggios *(1 mark)*
  c) Imperfect *(1 mark)*
  d) G major *(1 mark)*
  e) Accidental *(1 mark)*
  f) Staccato *(1 mark)*
  g) Homophonic *(1 mark)*

Section Three — Structure and Form

Pages 55 (Warm-up Questions)

1) *Conjunct* — melodies move mainly by step. Notes are a major 2nd (a tone) apart.
   Disjunct — melodies have a lot of jumps. Notes are more than a major 2nd apart.
   Triadic — melodies made up of the three notes in a triad.
   Scalic — melody moves up and down the notes of a scale.
2) Exposition, Development and Recapitulation.
3) A repeated bass part, usually four to eight bars long that is played by the left hand on the piano or harpsichord, or by cello and double bass in an orchestra.
4) e.g. Jazz, rock and roll, R & B, Indian music.

Pages 55-56 (Exam Questions)

Track 28

a) i) G major *(1 mark)*

ii) Blue note *(1 mark)*

b) Call and response/question and answer *(1 mark)*

c)

(1 mark)

Track 29

a) Baroque period *(1 mark)*

b) Oboe, bassoon, violin, viola, harpsichord.
(1 mark for each instrument, up to 2 marks)

c) i)

(1 mark for each correct note or correct interval between two adjacent notes, up to 7 marks)

ii) Conjunct *(1 mark)*

d) Basso continuo *(1 mark)*

e) Bassoon / Harpsichord *(1 mark)*

Section Four — Instruments

Page 72 (Warm-up Questions)

1) E.g. slide — trombone
Single reed — clarinet or saxophone
Double reed — oboe or bassoon
Pizzicato — violin, viola, cello, double bass
Wooden bars — xylophone

2) *Tremolo* — trembling sound on string instrument (fast, long, light strokes with the bow). Guitars can also produce this type of sound.
Con sordino — 'with mute', mute placed on bridge of string instruments to make them sound further away. Brass instruments can also be muted.
Tenor — higher male voice.
Falsetto — someone with a lower voice singing extra-high to sound like a soprano.

3) A military band is a marching wind band, with woodwind, brass and percussion. A brass band has brass and percussion. A jazz band can include woodwind, brass, percussion and any other instruments too, and sounds quite different.

4) Piano trio — piano, violin, cello.
Clarinet quintet — clarinet, first violin, second violin, viola, cello.

5) MIDI — musical instrument digital interface
Sampler — record, process and play back samples of music
Remix — mixing together samples of pop or dance music to a fast drumbeat, often speeded up
Sequencer — computer program which records and replays many tracks of music together

6) Baroque

7) Acoustic guitar — e.g. played by strumming or plucking six or twelve strings.
Electric guitar — e.g. needs an amplifier and loudspeaker to be heard.
Bass guitar — e.g. has only four strings, is pitched lower than electric and acoustic guitar, needs amplification.

Pages 72-74 (Exam Question)

Tracks 30 and 31

a) Flute *(1 mark)*

b) Piano *(1 mark)*

c) Shape B *(1 mark)*

d) The left hand of the piano has chords, the right hand melody imitates the flute part. One follows the other around. / The melodies interweave in a two-part texture at a similar pitch. / The parts are contrapuntal.
(1 mark for each sensible comment up to a maximum of 2 marks)

e) Flute, clarinet *(1 mark for each)*

f) Strings *(1 mark)*

g) Chromatic *(1 mark)*

h) Shape C *(1 mark)*

i) Crescendo *(1 mark)*

212

Section Five — Western Classical Music

Page 94 (Warm-up Questions)

1) Clarinets, timpani
2) Music for soloists accompanied by an orchestra.
3) Three movements — first movement in sonata form (quick), second movement in ternary or variation form (slow), third movement in rondo, variation or sonata form (quick).
4) Exposition, Development and Recapitulation.
5) E.g. Mozart, Haydn.

Page 94-95 (Exam Question)

Track 32

a) (i) Turn *(1 mark)*
   (ii) Appoggiatura *(1 mark)*
b) Falling sequence *(2 marks)* *(Award 1 mark for 'sequence')*
c) Perfect cadence *(1 mark)*
d) 4/4 or C *(1 mark)*

e)

(1 mark for each correct note or correct interval between two adjacent notes, up to 8 marks)

f) Change of key / melody in the bass / alberti bass in left hand / repeated notes / repeat of turns and appoggiaturas / sequence / block chords in left hand / chromatic scales.
(2 marks, 1 for each valid point)

Section Six — Music in the 20th Century

Page 113 (Warm-up Questions)

1) Music that is not in any particular key.
2) The twelve chromatic notes of the octave are arranged in a particular order. This order (and rearrangements) form the basis of the structure of the piece.
3) E.g. Anton Webern / Alban Berg
4) Using repeated patterns called loops.

Page 113-114 (Exam Questions)

Track 33

a) Atonal *(1 mark)*
b) 1890-1950 *(1 mark)*
c) E.g. it has lots of dissonance / it is atonal / it has contrasting dynamics / it is always changing / there are no repeated musical ideas / it has melodic fragments rather than a melody *(1 mark for each suitable point, up to 4 marks)*

Track 34

d) Tonal *(1 mark)*
e) i) Tierce de Picardie *(1 mark)*
   ii) A piece in a minor key finishes with a major chord. A major third is used instead of a minor third in the last chord. *(1 mark for each valid point, up to 2 marks)*
f) *Track 33* — The texture switches between a polyphonic texture using a large orchestra and a thinner homophonic texture using a smaller range of instruments. This is typical of the expressionist period as the music is always changing and the texture is used to give a dramatic effect. *(1 mark for suitable description and 1 mark for a suitable explanation)*

   Track 34 — The texture is polyphonic/contrapuntal throughout the extract. The consistent texture is typical of the Baroque period, as there are no sudden changes.

   (1 mark for suitable description and 1 mark for a suitable explanation)

Page 119 (Warm-up Questions)

1) A musical is a stage production with songs, dialogue and dances.
2) Solo character song, duet, action song and chorus number.
3) There are 4 sections of 8 bars each. Sections 1, 2 and 4 use the main theme, and section 3 has a contrasting theme.

Page 119 (Exam Question)

Track 35

a) Clarinet *(1 mark)*
b) The trumpet is played with a mute *(1 mark)*. It makes the trumpet quieter and alters the tone *(1 mark)*.
c) Perfect fourth *(1 mark)*
d) Syncopation, cross rhythms *(1 mark for each correct answer, up to 2 marks)*

Section Seven — Popular Music

Page 127 (Warm-up Questions)

1)

2) Rhythms which avoid the strong beats of the bar.

3) It has African and European influences and came from the music of newly-freed slaves.

4) Any three of, e.g. trumpet, trombone, clarinet, piano, saxophone, drums, double bass.

5) A type of Jazz that can be danced to.

Page 127-128 (Exam Question)

Track 36

a) Jazz *(1 mark)*

b) Improvised *(1 mark)*

c) The beats are not split into equal halves. The first half of the beat is longer and the second half of the beat is shorter.
(1 mark for each valid point, up to 2 marks)

d) Trumpet *(1 mark)*

e) i) piano *(1 mark)*, drums *(1 mark)*

 ii) E.g. the piano is mainly playing in chords (homophonic). The drums are playing a repeated rhythmic pattern (ostinato).
(1 mark for each suitable point, up to 2 marks)

f) $\frac{6}{4}$ *(1 mark)*

g) The mood is relaxed/laid back. The dynamics never get too loud and range from quiet (*p*) to intermediate (*mf*). The pitch of the solo is mainly in the middle and lower registers so it does not sound strained. The tempo is moderate to give a laid back feel.
(1 mark for each valid point, up to 4 marks)

Page 133 (Warm-up Questions)

1) In the 1950s

2) Lead electric guitar, rhythm electric guitar, bass guitar, drum kit.

3) Chords made up of the tonic and the fifth.

4) Pop songs which tell stories.

5) E.g. Elton John, Bob Dylan, Sting, Kate Bush.

6) Singing with no instrumental backing.

7) In harmony, in unison, descant, call and response.

Page 133-134 (Exam Question)

Track 37

a) i)
(1 mark)

 ii) Drum kit *(1 mark)*

b) $\frac{12}{8}$ *(1 mark)*

c) 1990s

d) *Riffing* — decorating with personalised flourishes.
Vibrato — a quiver in pitch to give a richer tone.
Falsetto — men making their voices go really high.
Portamento — sliding from one note to the other.
(1 mark for name of vocal technique and 1 mark for correct description)

e) Harmony *(1 mark)*

f) Mostly minor *(1 mark)*

g) Any two musical reasons for liking / disliking the piece, e.g. I like the electronic effects used in the piece (e.g. delay) as they add interest to the vocals. *(1 mark for each suitable point, up to 2 marks)*

Section Eight — Dance Music

Page 149 (Warm-up Questions)

1) E.g. waltz, salsa.

2) Vienna

3) Any three of, e.g. three beats in a bar, fast tempo, oom-cha-cha rhythm, rhythm comes from accompanying chords, homophonic texture.

4) Clave

5) Son and jazz

6) Any three from, e.g. congas, timbales, bongos, maracas, a guiro, drum kit.

7) Any three from, e.g. slow rhythmic pace, syncopation, use of triplets, dotted rhythms.

Pages 149-150 (Exam Question)

Track 38

a) Salsa *(1 mark)*

b) Cuba *(1 mark)*

c) Drum kit, bongos, congas, guiro, maracas
(1 mark for each, up to a maximum of 3 marks)

d)

(1 mark)

e) Bass/electric bass/bass guitar *(1 mark)*

f) Break *(1 mark)*

g) Comping/playing rhythmic chords *(1 mark)*

h) Trumpet, trombone *(1 mark for each)*

i) Chords in harmony *(1 mark)*

j) Syncopated, cross-rhythms *(1 mark for each)*

Page 154 (Warm-up Questions)

1) European folk dancing

2) Any three from, e.g. violin (fiddle), Irish open-holed wooden flute, tin whistle, concertina or accordian, guitar, Uilleann pipes, bhodrán, spoons.

3) Reels, hornpipes, jigs.

4) Chaal

5) In the UK in the 1970s and 1980s.

6) Any two from, e.g. remixing, sampling, drum machines, scratching.

Pages 154-155 (Exam Question)

Track 39

a) i) Bhangra *(1 mark)*

ii) Bhangra rhythm, club dance sound, Indian and western instruments mixed with a dance beat.
(1 mark for each, up to a maximum of 2 marks)

b)

(1 mark)

c) Sitar *(1 mark)*

d) Drum kit, drum machine/sequencer, dhol, tabla
(1 mark for each, up to a maximum of 2 marks)

e) i) Electric guitar *(1 mark)*

ii) Minor to major *(1 mark)*

f) Bass guitar, keyboard, synthesiser *(1 mark for each, up to a maximum of 2 marks)*

Page 160 (Warm-up Questions)

1) Any two of, e.g. strong beat, catchy tunes, easy to dance to, easy to remember.

2) 4/4

3) Any three from, e.g. drum kits, drum machines, rhythm guitar, bass guitar, sequencers.

4) Strong rhythm and use of music technology

5) Any four of, e.g. techno, jungle, drum'n'bass, UK garage, trance, ambient

Pages 160-161 (Exam Question)

Tracks 40 and 41

a)

(1 mark)

b) Looping *(1 mark)*

c)

(1 mark)

d) Change of instrumentation / Adding instruments and taking them away *(1 mark)*

e) Dance *(1 mark)*

f) Drum kit, bass guitar, keyboard, sequencer, drum machine *(1 mark for each, up to a maximum of 3 marks)*

g) E.g. A has different number of beats per bar (4/4 not 3/4), A is electric while B is acoustic, B uses variation where A uses repetition, volume levels in A stay the same but vary in B *(1 mark for any sensible point, up to a maximum of 4 marks)*

Section Nine — World Music

Page 166 (Warm-up Questions)

1) Survived through oral tradition/people memorised them.

2) Any four of, e.g. pipe and tabor, fiddle, hurdy-gurdy, bagpipes, accordion, concertina.

3) Any three of, e.g. work songs, ballads, short songs, dance music.

4) a) Notes 1, 2, 3, 5 and 6 of the ordinary major scale.

   b) Notes 1, 3, 4, 5 and 7 of a natural minor scale.

Page 166 (Exam Question)

Track 42

a) Celtic folk music *(1 mark)*

b) The melody is the same in each of the verses. *(1 mark)*

c) compound time *(1 mark)*

d) pentatonic *(1 mark)*

e) i) pipes *(1 mark)*

   ii) Any two from, e.g. accordion, drums, bass, guitar. *(1 mark for each correct instrument, up to 2 marks)*

Page 181 (Warm-up Questions)

1) Djembe, dundun, donno, kagan.

2) Any two of, e.g. balafon, kora, mbira/thumb piano.

3) The leader of a group of drummers.

4) Mbube — a capella singing. Loud and powerful. Sung by all-male choirs and sometimes with a female lead singer.

   Isicathamiya — soft, gentle music. All-male groups. Four-part harmonies and call and response are used. Dance moves keep the singers in time.

5) Slendro and pelog

6) Balungan (in Java) or Pokok (in Bali)

Page 181-182 (Exam Questions)

Track 43

a) i) Africa *(1 mark)*

   ii) Any three of, e.g. cross-rhythms/polyrhythms, polyphony, repetition, call and response, heterophony, improvisation. *(1 mark for each correct point, up to three marks)*

b) Balafon *(1 mark)*

c) E.g. the music has a strong pulse. The music is polyrhythmic. The drums play an ostinato pattern. *(1 mark for each suitable point, up to two marks)*

d) unison *(1 mark)*

Track 44

a) Indonesia *(1 mark)*

b) Gongs mark time so the performers know where they are in the gongan. *(1 mark)*

c) Saron — a type of metallophone with a metal bar for each note of the octave.

   Gender — keys made of bronze over bamboo pipes.

   Bonang — two rows of gongs resting on cords across a wooden frame.

   Gambang — a Xylophone with wooden bars.

   Celempung — a plucked string instrument.

   Rebab — a two stringed fiddle.

   Suling — a bamboo wind instrument.

   Gong ageng/Kempul — Hanging metal gongs.

   Kenong/Ketuk — Gongs resting on a wooden box.

   Kendang gending/ketipung — drums.

   (1 mark for name and 1 mark for correct description, up to two marks)

d) four *(1 mark)*

e) The tune is repeated over and over again in a rhythmic cycle (called a gongan). *(1 mark)*

Section Ten — Descriptive Music

Page 191 (Warm-up Questions)

1) Music that describes something, tells a story or sets a scene.

2) The tritone can be used to create scary sounding music.

3) The main tune in a film that is often repeated throughout the film.

4) It is used to link different sections together. Repeated and transformed leitmotifs can reflect what's going on in the film. Repetition also creates tension and suspense.

5) They can be used to recreate the mood of an era or place.

Page 191-192 (Exam Questions)

Track 45

a) Violin *(1 mark)*

b) The accompanying string instruments play pizzicato to represent the sound of raindrops. *(1 mark)*

c)

(1 mark for each correct note or correct interval between two adjacent notes, up to 6 marks)

Track 46

a) Homophonic *(1 mark)*

b) Largo *(1 mark)*

c) E.g.

Instrumentation — A full orchestra is used for maximum impact. The brass section is used to accent notes. Lots of percussion is used. Cymbals are clashed to represent swords clashing.

Texture — Lots of parts are playing at the same time (polyphonic texture) to represent the complexity of a battle. Layers are built up to generate tension.

Rhythm — Syncopated accents are used for impact. The music is polyrhythmic to represent activity of battle. The ostinato in the string section sounds threatening.

Dynamics — A crescendo throughout the section increases the tension. Loud, harsh brass accents represent action in battle. All instruments in orchestra are playing *forte* to generate a heavy atmosphere of battle.

Tempo — There is a sudden increase in tempo at the start of this section. The music is driven forward by the accented notes. A quick march tempo reflects soldiers marching into battle.

(1 mark for each correct point. Allow up to two marks for each musical feature, up to 10 marks)

Page 194-208 — Practice Exam

1 *Track 47*

a) Jazz *(1 mark)*

b) Improvisation *(1 mark)*, chromatic notes *(1 mark)*

c) Introduction-A-A-B-A *(1 mark)*

d) E.g. introduction has chords in the left hand, right hand has high pitched downward chords/decorated melody.

First main section — left hand plays with decorated melody in the right hand above.

Contrasting section — the left hand has long loud main notes (a melody moving upward by step), while the right hand provides decoration.

(2 marks for each valid comment that refers to left and right hand, up to a maximum of 4 marks)

e) Major *(1 mark)*

2 *Track 48*

a)

(5 marks, one for each correct note. If all incorrect but note shape correct give 1 mark.)

b) Broken chords, vibrato, sequence, crescendo *(1 mark for each, up to a maximum of 4 marks.)*

c) Soprano *(1 mark)*

d) Aria *(1 mark)*

e) i) 1830-1900 *(1 mark)*

ii) Soaring melody, use of vibrato, wide leaps in vocal part *(1 mark for any relevant point)*

f) Harp *(1 mark)*

g) Andante *(1 mark)*

h) Strings *(1 mark)*

i) Opening harp solo. Repetitive rhythm. Vocal part has long held phrases. Rhythm very slow over the repeated quaver/continuous harp accompaniment. The string notes are also held. The texture builds up very gradually as each instrument/group of instruments/voice is added. Overall the texture is thin. *(1 mark for any relevant point, up to a maximum of 4 marks.)*

3 *Track 49*

a) Imitation *(1 mark)*

b) Trill *(1 mark)*

c) 4/4 *(1 mark)*

d)

(1 mark for each correct note, plus one for the tie, up to maximum of 7 marks)

e) i) A *(1 mark)* minor *(1 mark)*

ii) EITHER perfect *(2 marks)*; OR V *(1 mark)*, I *(1 mark)*; OR dominant *(1 mark)*, tonic *(1 mark)*; OR E major *(1 mark)*, A minor *(1 mark)*

f)

(1 mark for each correct pitch in the right sequence, up to a maximum of 8 marks. If there are more than eight notes, count the first eight only.)

4 *Track 50*

a) Orchestral *(1 mark)*

b) Bass drum / timpani *(1 mark)*

c) Syncopated, accented, loud, close harmony *(1 mark for each, up to a maximum of 2 marks)*

d) The first section uses voices, the second section uses no voices; the first section is slow and serious, the second section is fast and lively; the first section is in a minor key, the second section is in a major key; the first section uses dissonance but the second section doesn't. *(1 mark for each contrast identified, up to a maximum of 3 marks)*

e) i) Trombone / horn / violin / trumpet *(1 mark)*

ii) Key change from minor to major / modulation / tempo change *(1 mark)*

iii) Tambourine *(1 mark)*

f) i) Strings *(1 mark)*

ii) Bowed *(1 mark)*, plucked/pizzicato *(1 mark)*

5 *Track 51*

a) 3 *(1 mark)*

b) Finger picking, strumming chords *(2 marks)*

c) Syncopation *(1 mark)*

d) Ostinato/looping *(1 mark)*

e) Polyphonic *(1 mark)*

f) Accompaniment is moderately loud/*mezzo forte* at the start of the extract. *Diminuendo* in the accompaniment to piano before solo guitar starts. Solo guitar plays loud/*forte* strummed chords. *(1 mark for each correct comment, up to a maximum of 3 marks)*

g) Use of pre-recorded music/music technology. Looping. Note addition/additive melodies. Layering. Importance of rhythm over tune. Harmonies change slowly. Music has a hypnotic quality. *(1 mark for each suitable feature, up to a maximum of 2 marks)*

6 *Track 52*

a) Strings, percussion *(1 mark for both correct)*

b) Sitar, tambura, tabla, sarangi *(1 mark for each, up to a maximum of 2 marks)*

c) Decorated melody, slides, pitch bend, polyrhythm *(1 mark for up to three correct, 2 marks for all four correct)*

d) Improvised *(1 mark)*

e) A drone is a long, held on note. The drone is based on two notes from the raga. The drone is played all the way through the performance. *(3 marks)*

7 *Track 53*

a) Flute / clarinet *(1 mark)*

b) French horn / trombone / tuba *(1 mark for each, up to a maximum of 2 marks)*

c) Staccato *(1 mark)*

d) 3/4 *(1 mark)*

e) i) Waltz *(1 mark)*

   ii) Strauss *(1 mark)*

f) Steady/regular pulse, strong rhythm, emphasis on first beat of every bar, 4 bar/periodic phrasing *(1 mark for each suitable reason, up to a maximum of 2 marks)*

g) Major *(1 mark)*

h) *mf* to *f* *(1 mark)*

8 *Track 54*

a) Percussion/gamelan *(1 mark)*

b) 4 *(1 mark)*

c) Sequences, repetition *(2 marks)*

d) Quavers *(1 mark)*

Index and Glossary

Index and Glossary

bols Words that go with the drum beats in **bhangra** music. **153**

bonang family Instruments with two rows of gongs on a wooden frame, used in **gamelan** music. **179**

bouzouki A string instrument a bit like a mandolin. Played in **Celtic folk** music. **164-165**

Brahms 143

brass band Band with brass and percussion sections. **65**

brass instruments Metal instruments where the sound is produced by 'buzzing' the lips. **58, 65, 67, 70**

breakbeats Electronic music that has **syncopation** or **polyrhythms**. **137**

bridge Section in a piece of music used to link two different chunks together. **53, 93, 139, 151**

Britten, Benjamin 77

Broadway A famous theatre street in New York. **115**

broken chord Chord that's played as a series of notes. **33, 88, 130**

Buckley, Jeff 130

Burkina Faso A country in Western Africa and homeland of **Koko**. **176**

Bus Stop An **American line dance** popular in the 1970s. **151**

C

cadence Pair of chords used to finish off a phrase. **36-37**

cadenza Section of a **concerto** where the soloist can really show off. **52, 89, 97**

call and response A short melody (the call), followed by an answering phrase (the response). In **son**, the call made by the lead singer is called the sonero, and the response made by the chorus is called the **choro**. Call and response also features in **African music. 41, 49, 123, 132, 144, 173, 175-177**

calmato Play the music so it sounds very calm. **12**

candombe A style of music from Montevideo, Uruguay that influenced the **tango**. **147**

canon Where the same tune is played by two or more parts, each coming in separately and at regular intervals. The parts overlap. Also called a **round. 40, 86, 112**

Capercaillie 164-165

Carmina Burana **77**

céilí dances A type of Irish **social dance** for couples dancing in a square, line or circle. **152**

celempung A plucked string instrument a bit like a mini harp, used in **gamelan** music. **179**

Celtic folk music Western European **folk music** particularly popular in Scotland and Ireland. **164-165**

Cha Cha An American dance from the 1920s. **151**

chaal Eight-note rhythmic pattern used in **bhangra**. **153**

chaconne Ground bass style with a repeated chord pattern in the bass. **81**

chamber choir A small choir. **77**

chamber music Music written for small groups. It was originally played in people's houses. **66, 89**

chamber orchestra Orchestra with small string and percussion sections, and one or two of each wind and brass instrument. **67, 77**

Charleston An American dance from the 1920s. **151**

choir A group of singers. **64, 76-78**

Chopin 98-99

choral music Music written for **choirs**. **76-78, 84**

chorale A hymn. **84, 102**

chord progression Repeated pattern of related chords used in bass and rhythm parts, especially **ground bass**. **30**

chord symbols C, C+, Cm maj7 Symbols like these are shorthand for different chords. **29**

choro The chorus in **son** music. **144**

chorus Piece in an **opera**, **oratorio** or **cantata** sung by the chorus (**choir**). **84-85, 101**

chorus number A piece in a **musical** sung by the whole cast. Similar to a **chorus** in **opera**. **116**

chromatic notes Notes that don't belong to the main key of a melody. **93, 142**

chromatic scale 13-note scale containing all the notes (tones and semitones) within an octave. **21**

circle of fifths Madly complicated diagram showing how all the keys relate to each other. **20**

clarinet quintet Small group with clarinet, two violins, viola and a cello. **66**

classical <u>Either</u> any music that's not pop (or **jazz**, **folk**, **hip-hop**, R'n'B, etc.), <u>or</u> music composed in Europe from about 1750 to 1820. **79-84, 87-93**

clave rhythm The basic rhythm of a piece of **son** or **salsa** music around which the rest of the music has to fit. **144**

club dance music Electronically produced music. Has been played in clubs since the mid-1980s. **158-159**

coda A bit at the end of a piece that's different to the rest of it and finishes it off nicely. **53, 91, 93, 143**

col legno For string players — play the string with the back of the bow instead of bowing. **60**

complement The six semitones not used in a **hexachord**. **106**

compound time Time signature where each main beat can be split into three little ones. **7**

con arco Play with the bow. The opposite of *pizzicato*. **60**

con sordino Play with a **mute**. **60, 70**

concept album An album where all the tracks are linked by a theme. **129**

concerto Piece for an orchestra with a soloist, in three movements. **89-90**

concord Nice sound that you get when notes that fit together are played together at the same time. **28**

conjunct Where the **melody** is smooth — there aren't big jumps between the notes. **22, 48**

consonance Nice sound that you get when notes that fit together are played at the same time. Also called concordance. **28**

continuo A continuous bass part in **Baroque** music, often played on a **harpsichord** and cello. Also called a **basso continuo. 52, 79**

contralto Another name for an **alto**. **76**

contrapuntal = polyphonic Music with two or more tunes played at the same time and woven together. **39, 41**

Copland, Aaron 185

counter-tenors Male singers who sing within the female vocal range. **64, 76**

Index and Glossary

Index and Glossary

K

Kaoss A DJ program used to change **samples** in live performances. **136**

kempul A medium hanging gong used in **gamelan** music. **180**

kendang gending A large cone-shaped drum used in **gamelan** music. **180**

kenong and ketuk Gongs which rest horizontally on cords stretched across a wooden box, used in **gamelan** music. **180**

keteg One bar of **gamelan** music. **180**

ketipung A small cone-shaped drum used in **gamelan** music. **180**

key A set of notes all from the same **scale**. Most music sticks to one main key, though it might wander off (**modulate**) to other keys from time to time. **18, 20**

key signature Sharps or flats just before the **time signature**, to tell you what **key** the music's in. **5, 18, 20**

Klangfarbenmelodie A word meaning 'tone-colour-melody', made up by **Schoenberg**. It's a technique he used to break up melodies by passing them round different parts. **106**

Koko **176-177**

komal A note played slightly flat in some **ragas**. **168**

kora West African harp-like instrument. **174, 176**

L

Ladysmith Black Mambazo 175

Lanner, Joseph 143

largo 40-60 beats a minute. Broad and slow. **12**

layering **Minimalist** technique. Different length **loops** are played at the same time so they gradually go out of sync and then come back in again. **40, 109**

leading note Seventh note in a **minor** or **major scale**. **18**

leap A jump over notes that's bigger than a **tone**. **35**

legato Play smoothly. **13**

libretto The words of an **opera** or **oratorio**. **85, 101**

Lied A **Romantic** song for one singer and piano. The lyrics were often in German. **100, 102**

loop Section of music repeated over and over. Used in **minimalist** music and **club dance**. **40, 110, 135, 159**

low-pass filter Gets rid of background noise. **136**

M

Madison An American dance craze in the 1950s and 60s. It came before the **American line dance**. **151**

madrigal Song from the Renaissance times for five or six singers. **102**

major interval **Intervals** between the first note of a **major scale** and the second, third, sixth and seventh notes. **23**

major key **Key** using notes from a **major scale**. **18, 88**

major scale Series of eight notes. **Intervals** between them are: **tone**, tone, **semitone**, tone, tone, tone, semitone. **18**

major triad **Triad** with an **interval** of four **semitones** between the bottom note and middle note (a **major third**), and three **semitones** between the middle and top notes (a **minor third**). **29**

male voice choir A **choir** made up of two groups of **tenors** as well as **baritones** and **basses**. **64**

mambo A break between choruses in **salsa** music. **145-146**

marcato Play all the notes with **accents**. **14**

mass Piece of music sung as part of the Catholic church service. **76, 84, 102**

matras A set number of beats in a **tala**. **168**

mbira African instrument, played by twanging bent metal strips with your thumb. **174, 176**

Mbube A type of African **a capella** singing with high-pitched lead vocals. It's loud and powerful. **175**

mediant Third note in a **minor** or **major** scale. **18**

melismatic A single syllable of text is sung over a succession of notes. The opposite of **syllabic**. **76, 86**

melodic interval The difference between two notes played one after another in a tune. **22**

melodic minor scale 8-note **minor scale**. Like the **natural minor** but with the 6th and 7th notes raised a **semitone** going up and reverting back to the natural minor coming down. Used for composing melodies in **minor keys**. **19**

Messiaen 77

Messiah **76, 85-86**

metamorphosis **Minimalist** technique where you change one note of a tune each time it's repeated so eventually it's completely different. **109**

Metheny, Pat 111

metre Pattern made by the beats of a bar. Can be regular, irregular or free (totally random). **7, 141**

mezzo forte mf Fairly loud. **13**

mezzo piano mp Fairly quiet. **13**

mezzo-soprano voice A female voice that sings the top part of the **alto** range and the bottom part of the **soprano** range. **64, 76**

middle 8 Eight bars, in the middle of a song. Has different chords and/or tune to keep you interested. **53, 116, 132**

MIDI Stands for Musical Instrument Digital Interface — a way of connecting different electronic instruments. **68, 135-136**

milonga A style of music from Argentina and Uruguay that influenced the **tango**. **147**

minimalism A Western art music style, developed during the 1960s and 1970s, which tends to be very repetitive and sparse. It fuses ideas from different musical sources, e.g. **gamelan** and Indian **raga** music. **109-110**

minor interval Interval that's one **semitone** smaller than a **major interval** (i.e. 3 semitones). **23**

minor key A key that sounds sad. Uses notes from the minor scale. **19-20, 88**

minor scale Series of eight notes. **Intervals** between them are **tone**, **semitone**, tone, tone, semitone, tone, tone in a **natural minor** scale. **Melodic** and **harmonic minor scales** are slightly different. **19**

minor triad **Triad** with an **interval** of three **semitones** between the bottom note and middle note (minor third), and four **semitones** between the middle and top notes (major third). **29**

Index and Glossary

Index and Glossary

Index and Glossary

Acknowledgements

The publisher would like to thank the following copyright holders for permission to reproduce material:

Track 1 — *Caro Nome*, from *Rigoletto*, by Verdi, performed by the Slovak Philharmonic Orchestra, licensed courtesy of Naxos Rights International.

Track 2 — *Oboe Concerto No. 3 in G minor*, by Handel, performed by the City of London Sinfonia, licensed courtesy of Naxos Rights International.

Tracks 3-13 — Composed and performed by Sam Norman, © 2010 Coordination Group Publications Ltd.

Track 14 — *Sonata Pathetique*, by Beethoven, performed by Sam Norman, © 2010 Coordination Group Publications Ltd.

Tracks 15-26 — Composed and performed by Sam Norman, © 2010 Coordination Group Publications Ltd.

Track 27 — *Sonatina 3, Opus 36*, *un poco adagio*, by Clementi, performed by Sam Norman, © 2010 Coordination Group Publications Ltd.

Track 28 — *St Louis Blues #2*, by WC Handy, performed by Louis Armstrong, licensed courtesy of Naxos Rights International.

Track 29 — *Courante*, from *Suite No. 1 in C major, BWV 1066*, by J.S. Bach, performed by the Cologne Chamber Orchestra, licensed courtesy of Naxos Rights International.

Track 30 — *Le Merle Noir*, by Messiaen, performed by Patrick Gallois & Lydia Wong, licensed courtesy of Naxos Rights International.

Track 31 — *Flight of the Bumble Bee*, by Rimsky-Korsakov, performed by the CSR Symphony Orchestra, licensed courtesy of Naxos Rights International.

Track 32 — Rondo in D Major, by Mozart, performed by Balázs Szokolay, licensed courtesy of Naxos Rights International.

Track 33 — *Peripeteia* from *Five Pieces for Orchestra, Op. 16*, by Arnold Schoenberg, performed by the London Symphony Orchestra, licensed courtesy of Naxos Rights International.

Track 34 — Prelude No. 2 in C Minor, from the Well-Tempered Clavier, by J.S. Bach, performed by Jenö Jando, licensed courtesy of Naxos Rights International.

Track 35 — *Something's Coming*, from *West Side Story*, by Leonard Bernstein, original Broadway cast recording, © 2010 PRS for Music.

Track 36 — *All Blues*, from "Kind of Blue", performed by Miles Davis, © 2010 PRS for Music.

Track 37 — *Grace*, from "Grace", performed by Jeff Buckley, © 2010 PRS for Music.

Track 38 — *De Verdad*, by Ritmo Alegria © 2004 licensed courtesy of Union Square Music.

Track 39 — *Lok Boliyan*, by Surjit Singh & Pete Ware, performed by Anakhi, licensed courtesy of Naxos Rights International.

Track 40 — *Bass 'N' Buzz (56hz)* by Charly Says © 1991 Moving Shadow Ltd, reproduced by permission of Moving Shadow Ltd.

Track 41 — *Kaiser-Walzer, Op. 437 (Emperor Waltz)*, by Johann Strauss II, performed by the CSR Symphony Orchestra, licensed courtesy of Naxos Rights International.

Track 42 — *Skye Waulking Song*, from "Nàdurra", performed by Capercaillie, reproduced by permission of Survival Records Ltd.

Track 43 — "*Yiri*" performer Madou Kone, produced by Sunset-France, reproduced by permission of Sunset France.

Track 44 — "Srepegan" taken from the album "Gamelan from Central Java", courtesy of ARC Music Productions International Ltd.

Track 45 — *Winter: Largo* from *The Four Seasons*, by Vivaldi, performed by the Failoni Chamber Orchestra, licensed courtesy of Naxos Rights International.

Acknowledgements

Track 46   Suite from Gladiator, written by Hans Zimmer, performed by The City of Prague Philharmonic Orchestra, conducted by Nic Raine, published by Cherry Lane Music/Universal Music © 2002 Silva Screen Records Ltd.

Track 47   *Ain't Misbehavin'*, by Fats Waller, licensed courtesy of Naxos Rights International.

Track 48   *Ave Maria*, by J.S. Bach and Gounod, performed by Ingrid Kertesi & Camerata Budapest, licensed courtesy of Naxos Rights International.

Track 49   *Prelude No. 1 in C major*, from the *Well-Tempered Clavier*, by J.S. Bach, performed by Jenö Jando, licensed courtesy of Naxos Rights International.

Track 50   *The Battle on the Ice*, from *Alexander Nevsky*, by Prokofiev, performed by the Stanislavsky Chorus and the Russian State Symphony Orchestra, licensed courtesy of Naxos Rights International.

Track 51   *3rd Movement (Fast)* of *Electric Counterpoint*, from "Substring Bridge", by Steve Reich, performed by Mats Bergström, © 2010 PRS for Music.

Track 52   *Rag Des*, from "Rag Bagesri, Rag Des", performed by Budhaditya Mukherjee and Anindo Chatterjee, reproduced by permission of Nimbus Records / Wyastone Estate Ltd.

Track 53   *Rosen aus dem Suden: Waltz, Op. 388*, by Johann Strauss II, performed by CSR Symphony Orchestra, licensed courtesy of Naxos Rights International.

Track 54   "*Sampak (slendro nem)*" taken from the album "Gamelan from Central Java", courtesy of ARC Music Productions International Ltd.

Score p.55 and p.211   *St. Louis Blues* Words and Music by William C. Handy © 1914 Handy Brothers Music Co Inc, USA, Francis Day & Hunter Ltd, London W8 5SW. Reproduced by permission of International Music Publications Ltd. (a trading name of Faber Music Ltd). All Rights Reserved.

Score p.112   *Electric Counterpoint*, Steve Reich © Copyright Hendon Music, Inc. Reproduced by permission of Boosey & Hawkes Music Publishers Ltd.

Score p.118   *Something's Coming*, from *West Side Story*, Bernstein © Copyright 1959 by Amberson Holdings LLC and Stephen Sondheim. Copyright renewed, Leonard Bernstein Music Publishing Company LLC. Reproduced by permission of Boosey & Hawkes Music Publishers Ltd.

Score p.126   *All Blues*. Music by Miles Davis © Copyright 1959 Jazz Horn Music Corporation, USA Universal/MCA Music Limited. All Rights Reserved. International Copyright Secured. Used by permission of Music Sales Limited

Score p.133   *Grace*. Words & Music by Jeff Buckley & Gary Lucas © Copyright 1994 Sony/ATV Tunes LLC/El Viejito Music/Gary Lucas Music, USA. Sony/ATV Music Publishing (50%)/Universal/MCA Music Limited (50%) All Rights Reserved. International Copyright Secured. Used by permission of Music Sales Limited.

Score p.138   *Why Does My Heart Feel So Bad?* Words and Music by Richard Hall © 1999 The Little Idiot Music Warner/Chappell North America, London W6 8BS. Reproduced by permission of Faber Music Ltd. All Rights Reserved.

Score p.149 and p.214   De Verdad by Fayyaz Virjii © 2006 by Union Square Publishing.

Score p.160 and p.214   Reproduced by permission of Moving Shadow Ltd.

Score p.177   "*Yiri*" performer Madou Kone, published by Sunset-France, reproduced by permission of Sunset France.

Every effort has been made to locate copyright holders and obtain permission to reproduce copyright material. For material where it has been difficult to trace the originator of the work, we would be grateful for information. If any copyright holder would like us to make an amendment to the acknowledgements, please notify us and we will gladly update the book at the next reprint.

Make sure you're not missing out on another superb CGP revision book that might just save your life...

...order your **free** catalogue today.